FERRARO
MY STORY

FERRARO
MY STORY

Geraldine A. Ferraro
with *Linda Bird Francke*

BANTAM BOOKS

TORONTO • NEW YORK • LONDON • SYDNEY • AUCKLAND

FERRARO: MY STORY
A Bantam Book / November 1985

Library of Congress Cataloging in Publication Data

Ferraro, Geraldine.
    Ferraro, my story.

    Includes index.
    1. Ferraro, Geraldine. 2. Vice-Presidential
candidates—United States—Biography. 3. Legislators—
United States—Biography. 4. United States. Congress.
House—Biography. 5. Presidents—United States—
Election—1984. 6. United States—Politics and
government—1981–   . I. Francke, Linda Bird.
II. Title.
E840.8.F47A34   1985   973.927'092'4   85-47650
            ISBN 0-553-05110-5

Published simultaneously in the United States and Canada

PRINTED IN THE UNITED STATES OF AMERICA

FG   0 9 8 7 6 5 4 3 2

To Walter Mondale for his faith
and to John Zaccaro for his strength

CONTENTS

ACKNOWLEDGMENTS

As the events of the campaign took place, the highs and the lows, I promised myself I would share them with the people of America who made a new dream possible. I had no idea how terribly difficult the process would be. I never realized that writing a book would force me to relive the campaign over and over through interviews, first draft, and revision after revision. But the process was made easier by wonderful people who helped and encouraged me.

I am most grateful to Linda Bird Francke, a talented writer who spent countless hours talking to me, probing for feelings and details, and, finally, typing with a Queens accent. Because of her dedication to the book we were able to finish it. Left on my own, I'm not sure it would have been published in my lifetime!

Even in this project I turned to my mother for help. She pored through boxes and boxes of letters—literally thousands—some of which appear in the book. It was very tedious work, and as always she performed the job with love. Thanks, Mom.

I am grateful:
—To Nessa Rapoport, my editor, who always maintained her calm as I struggled with what could and should be said, whose patience and devotion to the task I admire immensely.
—To Madeline Albright, Barry Carter, Kay Casstevens, and Mary Ann Sullivan, for their assistance, one more time, in getting the issues right.

—To Bob Barnett, Mandy Grunwald, Victor Kovner, Tony Lapham, Steve Pollak, and Anne Wexler, the readers, whose judgment and advice I have valued in my career and whose judgment and advice I called upon in reading the manuscript.

—To Eleanor Lewis, who worked for months checking every detail to be sure that we were accurate.

—To Pat Flynn, who put up with it all, filling in whatever was needed to be done to meet the deadline.

—Thanks also to all those at Bantam who worked so hard on the book, especially Linda Grey. I knew we lucked out when she became publisher immediately after we signed the contract.

—To Esther Newberg, whose contribution was "above and beyond" that of a literary agent.

To John and our children, for their help and patience, and for letting me share our private moments with the reader.

There are so many others: Bella Abzug, Alison Acker, Charles Atkins, Michael Berman, Steve Engelberg, Irwin Ettinger, Judy Goldsmith, Addie Guttag, Joann Howes, Elaine Kaymarck, John Koegel, Demetra Lambros, Barbara Leahy, Arthur Liman, Joan McLean, John Reilly, and Frank Wright, who made my job easier.

Finally, I am grateful to the American people. This book would have not been written without you. It was your encouraging me for four memorable months in 1984, and your concern and interest since, that made this book a reality.

FERRARO
MY STORY

THE CONVENTION

"If we can do this, we can do anything."

—July 19, 1984, Moscone Center,
San Francisco, California.

IT STARTED ON SUCH A high. Even the weather in San Francisco seemed an endorsement, the wind whipping more American flags and red, white, and blue bunting than any patriot could imagine, the sun shining down on a peaceful city. The political demonstrations were, for the most part, tranquil nonevents. Those that were unruly were quickly broken up by the police.

For that alone I was thankful. When the Democratic National Committee had chosen San Francisco as the convention site, many members of the House of Representatives had been upset, especially the Southerners. For all its beauty, San Francisco does have a laissez-faire reputation and a highly visible share of crazies who would come out for the Convention. "What are you trying to do? Kill the Democratic Party?" the members had protested. But from the beginning, the Convention had gone without a hitch.

There were crowds everywhere, happy crowds, filling the hotel lobbies where the various state delegations and different constituencies were caucusing, clustering around the newspaper and political-souvenir vendors on every street corner. The button hawkers were cleaning up on the Reverend Jesse Jackson's Rainbow

Coalition buttons and on the competing Mondale/Ferraro and Hart/Ferraro buttons.

I watched the scene with a little envy through the windows of the bulletproof limousine as my motorcade sped from one political meeting to another. Suddenly I was no longer an independent member of the public but a major security risk. Suddenly I was no longer a member of Congress going about her business at her party's convention but a national celebrity. And it had all happened so fast.

"Who are those people waiting for? Who's coming in?" I had asked the first time my motorcade drew up behind the human walls of police holding back the crowds in front of my hotel.

"You," came the response.

"Me?"

"Yes, you."

There had been no time for me or any of my family to grasp the enormity of what was taking place. A week ago I had been a third-term congresswoman from Queens with aspirations for the Senate or a leadership role in the House. I was coming to the convention as the first woman chair of the Platform Committee, an honor in itself. I had taken great pride over the last six months in the formation and final drafting of this election year's Democratic National Platform, defining the positions and the principles on which every Democratic candidate for office, including our presidential nominee, Walter Mondale, would run in 1984 against Ronald Reagan. Drawing together the diverse factions in the Democratic party in support of a single platform has always been tricky, if not impossible. Our Platform could have been a disaster. It could have blown up in my face. But it didn't—another reason for thankfulness.

I had wanted my children to fly out to San Francisco for the big moment, my presentation of the Platform to the Convention floor on Tuesday evening, July 17. Now they were here for quite another reason. Tonight, July 19, 1984, I would become the first woman in United States history to accept a major party's nomination for the office of Vice President. Incredible.

For over a week now I had been adjusting to my new job description—and to my new convention schedule. Instead of meeting with the various state delegations and the press as Platform

Chair, I was now the vice-presidential nominee, making the rounds of Democratic fund-raisers with Fritz Mondale—to meetings with the Women's Caucus, the Hispanic Caucus, the Asian-American Caucus, and, on my own, the Southern governors.

The situation with the Southerners was especially sensitive. They didn't know me, after all. And it was very important to dispel my image in the conservative South as just another liberal from the Northeast. As a legislator in Congress, I told them over breakfast, I had been fighting hard for four years against Reagan's proposals on the budget and his ill-conceived and financially crippling defense policies. I did support a strong defense, I told them, but not a wasteful one. I also wanted them to know that I was just as strong against crime. As a prosecutor in the DA's office in Queens, I had put my share of criminals in jail.

I must have done all right. After our breakfast meeting, the governors were reported to have said to the press: "She'll sell down south because she's tough on law and order."

The emotional high of the week had been the Celebration of Women fund-raiser held at the San Francisco Opera House, followed by my first rally in my new role. Several thousand people jammed into a square a few blocks from the Moscone Center, surrounding us—literally—with unabashed enthusiasm. "Look behind you and wave," Fritz kept saying, because the crowds had pressed in from the rear as well. I had never felt such mass excitement. For the first time, I experienced what was to become a familiar campaign phenomenon: people reaching out of the crowd to touch me, even to grab hold of me and not let go. I remembered the Secret Service directive not to shake anyone's hand, because I could be pulled into the crowd.

"Just touch fingers and move on," they had told me.

"I can't do that," I had replied. "I can't stand people who give you those little finger squeezes instead of a firm handshake. That's not where I'm from."

"Well, you're going to have to learn," the Secret Service had said. Now I was.

The fervor in the Opera House before the rally had been overwhelming. Every woman activist from coast to coast seemed to be on that stage: Gloria Steinem, founder and editor of *Ms.* magazine; Senator Diane Watson of California; Madeleine Kunin, soon to be elected governor of Vermont; Betty Friedan, a founder of the National Organization for Women; Dorothy Height, president of the National Council of Negro Women; Lynn Cutler, vice-chair of the Democratic National Committee; former Congresswoman Bella Abzug; and virtually all the Democratic women in Congress. And that was just the beginning.

Talk about a celebration of women. You name her, she was there—black, white, Native American, Hispanic, Chinese—from the world of politics and business, from labor, from feminist groups, and from the media. It was the first time I had seen these women, many of whom were my friends, since I had been named by Fritz as his choice for Vice President. And when he and I walked in, the place absolutely exploded. History was being made. And every woman there was a part of it.

There were tears and cheers and chants and whistles until the decibel level got so high I worried about ear damage. The women in the Opera House were *kvelling,* that wonderful Yiddish word for emotion so deeply felt that it seems to come out of your pores. And on stage there were kisses and congratulations, most warming to me from five other vice-presidential possibilities— my colleagues in the House, Congresswomen Barbara Mikulski of Maryland, Pat Schroeder of Colorado, and Lindy Boggs of Louisiana; Mayor Dianne Feinstein of San Francisco; and Governor Martha Layne Collins of Kentucky. There were hugs, too, from my other congressional colleagues, Barbara Kennelly of Connecticut, Mary Rose Oakar and Marcy Kaptur of Ohio, Barbara Boxer and Sala Burton of California. I couldn't help but think as I stood in the spotlight of this celebration that the choice might have been Dianne Feinstein or somebody else; that I might have been standing beside her now, applauding. But this was my moment, and I was going to enjoy it. At the same time I felt an enormous responsibility to all these women. No matter what I did, I was doing it for everybody.

My years in Congress had taught me the value of friendship among women. Today there's a lot of emphasis on moving ahead at any cost, but I had had the benefit of working with such fantastic people as Barbara Mikulski and Barbara Kennelly, women who go to bat for each other and join forces to get things done.

All my working life I've believed in minorities helping minorities, and in women helping women. I always tried to share what expertise I've gained with the people who were coming up behind me and spent a lot of time with other women, giving them tips I had picked up along the way. I'm a competitive person, but I have never understood people's competitiveness at the expense of their colleagues. We're all in it together, and I think in many instances we hold ourselves back from participating—and winning—by the fear of being surpassed.

Maybe it's because I never had sisters, but it was a privilege to be able to work with such good friends. Mikulski and Kennelly in particular won when I won, hurt when I hurt. I rooted for them. They backed me one hundred percent. I had so much confidence in these women—and felt so honored by their public confidence in me now.

Convention week flew by, packed with meetings, rehearsals, and speeches. Suddenly, it was the afternoon of Thursday, July 19. At the Moscone Center, my nomination process was going very smoothly—and very quickly. Traditionally, the potential party nominee does not appear at the convention hall until his—or, now for the first time, her—name is put before the Convention delegates, followed by the seconding speeches and the introduction of the candidate. While I took what I thought would be a leisurely bath—my surefire way of relaxing—my family and staff watched the nominating speeches on the four TV sets in our hotel suite, each set on a different channel so that everyone could see all the coverage at once.

I had asked several of my friends who were also elected officials or high-profile members of the Democratic Party to participate in my nomination. Each honored different constituencies and would reach out to key Democratic supporters. While I soaked in the tub, Barbara Kennelly put my name in nomination. Originally I had wanted Congressman Peter Rodino, chairman of the Judiciary Committee and Democratic congressman from New Jersey, to do the honor and Barbara to second me. As a child of immigrants, I was very proud of being the first Italian-American to run for national office, and I wanted to highlight the opportunity America had given me by having the dean of the Italian-American Caucus in the House nominate me. But Peter hadn't planned to come to the Convention and couldn't leave New Jersey at the last minute, so I had asked Barbara to nominate me instead.

She had readily agreed, understanding as only another politician can. And her presence was just right. Barbara's key position pointed to the role of women in politics, which I obviously felt was very important.

Barbara Roberts Mason, a black educator who had worked with me on the Platform Committee, came next as one of my seconders, and Toney Anaya, governor of New Mexico, a Hispanic, followed. I wanted to point out not only by words but concretely that my campaign was one in which all Americans had a stake.

I was supposed to leave my hotel during the calling of the roll of states, which should have taken a sufficient amount of time to get me to the convention center. But suddenly my family was yelling, "It's going very fast." In came a phone call from the Moscone Center announcing that my nomination was going to be by acclamation and on the first ballot, eliminating the time it would have taken if other vice-presidential possibilities had been placed in nomination from the floor. That was certainly a good omen. And it got me out of the bathtub fast. I threw on my clothes, brushed my hair quickly, decided I could check my makeup at the convention hall, and we were out the door. Hastily we piled into the cars in our motorcade to go the few blocks to the center while the nominating process was winding down and the roll call of the states began.

The vote was going fast, very fast. Normally, the states, all fifty of them plus the U.S. territories, are called in alphabetical order to vote for their choice of candidate. But this was not a normal nomination. The majority of delegates to the Convention had already decided that a woman on the Democratic ticket could be the weapon that just might unseat Ronald Reagan. A united party is always a more formidable party. And besides, this was an historic moment. Nobody wanted to challenge the making of history.

In the spirit of the evening, Arkansas, the fourth state in the roll call, passed to my home state of New York. The chairman of the New York delegation, my old friend Bill Hennessy, then moved to have my nomination acclaimed from the floor. The moment was electric, I was told later by friends who were there.

"Madame Chairman," Hennessy began, "the great state of New York, proud home of Geraldine Ferraro, on this historic occasion casts all 283 votes for her nomination and moves that she be nominated by the Democratic Party for the office of Vice President of the United States by acclamation."

Then Martha Layne Collins, the Convention Chair, announced, "The motion has been made. Do I hear a second"—a chorus of seconds interrupted her—"that the rules be suspended and Gerry Ferraro be nominated by acclamation? All in favor please indicate by saying aye."

"AYE!" the nearly four thousand delegates chorused as one—and everyone else in the hall for that matter. "AYE! AYE! AYE!"

I was the Democratic Party's vice-presidential nominee. And pandemonium erupted.

I could hear the roar of the demonstration taking place on the convention floor before we even got inside the Moscone Center. But this was still not the time for me to go out and accept the nomination. There was another piece of political business to transact. On stage now was House Majority Leader Jim Wright, whose role was to present me to the Convention. Why Jim Wright? He was—and is—a top member of the leadership of the House of Representatives and a good friend of mine from Texas, as well as someone whose oratory I admire. I knew his introduction would be fabulous.

And yet I was impatient as I watched Jim on the closed-circuit television set in the center's "holding room," the peculiar appellation given to the private waiting areas where speakers cool their heels before going on stage. This one was the first in a seemingly endless number of holding rooms, a descriptive phrase used throughout the campaign that always made me laugh. "Who's the lucky one we're holding tonight?" I'd kid.

The holding rooms would always drive me crazy because I hate to wait, but it was particularly bad that first night. The point was to get on with it, to get out there in front of the Convention and deliver the acceptance speech I had been writing in fits and starts for the last week. It was the most important speech I would ever make and I wanted it to express my thoughts perfectly. I ran through it again in the holding room, gave my mother a quick call so that she could wish me luck, and then, to pass the time, I checked the makeup I had slapped on hastily at the hotel and the safety pins in my dress so that it wouldn't open under the scrutiny of the television cameras. I also double-checked to make sure I hadn't put on a half slip out of habit.

I had learned the slip lesson the hard way during a parade in New York. Naturally I had waved to the onlookers, and just as naturally my dress had come up along with my arms, leaving behind my slip. In the delicate way of the press, a Chicago television crew had focused its cameras on my hemline, but luckily I realized before they interviewed me that I had been caught.

"What is unusual about campaigning as a woman?" the loaded question came.

And I was ready. "Well, there are things that happen," I said casually. "For instance, if you're walking along in a parade and you raise your arm and your slip shows, people might be critical of you. No guy has a problem like that."

Male candidates have it easy. All they have to worry about is which striped tie they're going to wear with which dark suit. Before the first presidential debate in Louisville, Kentucky, Walter Mondale evidently ran through some forty ties before one was declared the most presidential looking. My problem as a woman was how to look vice-presidential. Actually my staff had much more of a problem with the issue than I did. Short-sleeve dresses are a no-no, they would protest when I set out in one in the heat of summer to deliver a speech. Forget it, I would reply. I would look far sillier roasting in long sleeves in bathing-suit weather.

"You should wear only suits" was another campaign dress theme I ignored, except for the vice-presidential debate. Why dress like an imitation man? I never wore slacks in public, of course. It could have been considered offensive in the more conservative areas of the country. But that's where I drew the line. I was a woman, I had worn dresses and skirts all my life, and I wasn't about to change now. Besides, there was no dress code for a female vice-presidential candidate, so I was writing it. Two things were important: comfort and quiet good taste.

But the first clothing controversy had already come up. For the acceptance speech I was about to deliver, I had chosen to wear a white dress I thought looked dynamite on TV when I had given the Marymount Fifth Avenue High School graduation address just a few weeks earlier. What I didn't know—but my staff did—was that Joan Mondale was also planning to wear white, a new suit she had bought just for the occasion. My staff didn't want Joan to think I was preempting her choice. That was one concern. The other involved their conviction that the wife of the presidential candidate and the vice-presidential nominee should not wear the same color. I had wondered why they seemed so relieved when a boutique highly recommended by Congresswoman Barbara Boxer sent over some dresses for me to try on. (I couldn't go out, so they nicely came in.) But none of the choices was right for the acceptance speech, so to my staff's increasing dismay I decided to go with my white dress.

I didn't find out about the color conflict until my daughters Donna and Laura, along with Pam Fleischaker, a long-time friend and first director of the Women's Campaign Fund, were dispatched to the department stores at the last minute to look for more alternatives. I thought the flap was ridiculous, like the mother of the bride getting to pick out the color of her dress first, the mother of the groom second. But this wasn't a wedding. It was a political convention, and more than anything I wanted to feel comfortable in what I was wearing. If I don't feel at ease, I tend to flush, get distracted, and hurry through what I'm doing so I can get out of the limelight as quickly as possible. This was hardly the moment for those impulses, so when none of the six dresses Donna, Laura, and Pam brought back worked either, I called a halt to the fuss. I wore the white dress I had bought on Orchard Street in New York, Joan wore her new white suit, and nobody cared—least of all Joan Mondale.

In the holding room, I glanced over my speech for the last time. I felt secure about it, having given it its final test that afternoon on my old friend and Queens district office manager Pat Flynn. From 1974 to 1978, Pat had been one of the secretaries in the district attorney's office and had stuck with me ever since, joining my exhausting and nasty first congressional campaign in 1978, and then sharing six years of the day-to-day business in the Ninth District. Having been through so much together, we were each other's toughest audience. And also softest.

"Now we'll know if the speech is any good," I said to the three speechwriters who were helping me. "If Patsy cries, we've got it."

So Pat came into the room, sat down, listened to the speech

for the first time, and started to cry. "I'm sorry," she sniffed. "I can't help it."

I turned to the speechwriters. "We've got it," I said.

Delivering the speech from a TelePrompTer instead of written copy had also lost much of its terror for me. Before this evening, I had used a TelePrompTer only a few times—and the last time had been disastrous. A New York political-consulting firm, D. H. Sawyer & Associates, had offered the month before the Convention to help me with the art of reading a speech candidly and casually from a TelePrompTer for my upcoming platform presentation, which would be nationally televised.

I needed the help. Instead of my head moving naturally from one TelePrompTer to the other (which Reagan does like a pro), I darted my eyes frantically back and forth, giving the impression someone was chasing me.

"Slow down," Scott Miller, one of the Sawyer associates, had advised me then—and again today. Mondale's staff had set up a practice TelePrompTer in one of the hotel rooms, and after Fritz had run through his speech on it, I ran through mine. Miraculously, it looked as if I had been using a TelePrompTer all my life. But still, Scott cautioned me to speak even more slowly, worried that the audience wouldn't understand my rapid Queens speech.

"Remember, you're going to be speaking to millions of people," he said.

"You don't have to remind me," I protested.

"Congresswoman Ferraro, time to go," said Peter Kyros at the holding-room door, a Washington lawyer and Mondale aide who had been assigned at the beginning to help me. I took a deep breath and turned to my husband, John. While I felt remarkably calm, John was a bundle of nerves. After all, I had a job to do, to go out and accept the nomination and then to address the Convention. What he had to do was stand around and worry while everyone watched. He wasn't thinking, "Good God, she's making history." He was anxious on a personal level. Here was his wife of twenty-four years and the mother of his children going out there in front of a convention hall filled with thousands of people, in front of a television audience of fifty million people, a far cry from my constituency in Queens. What if I messed up? "We're going out there and we're going to do it," I said to him, trying to calm him down. It didn't work.

The eloquence stakes were very high that week in San Francisco. Mario Cuomo's keynote address had been terrific, and I had looked closely at how relaxed he had seemed while delivering it. I wanted to appear as comfortable as he had. I'd missed Gary Hart's speech because I was busy working, but I caught ninety percent of Jesse Jackson's. While his speech was long, Jackson was spellbinding. There was no way, however, I could duplicate his delivery. I'm not capable of that kind of oratory. It's not me.

Later, watching Ted Kennedy introduce Fritz Mondale illustrated again just how great the pressure was. Though Kennedy is the ultimate professional, whose 1980 Convention speech would go down in history as oratory at its best, from behind, where I was sitting, I could see that his body was actually rippling with tension. This was hardball time. No getting around it. And here was my chance to show that women could be just as familiar with the vehicles of media power as men were, maybe even more so. After all, as a congresswoman I had been giving speeches for six years. Before that, I had spent four years in court arguing criminal cases. It wasn't public speaking that was new to me. But standing up in front of the entire country as the first woman to accept the vice-presidential nomination—that was new. And so was having all three networks plus cable focused on my every word and expression.

Finally, we were getting close to my moment on stage. While Jim Wright came to the end of his introduction, John and I were moved to the side of the platform behind a vice-presidential escort made up of members of Congress and Democratic Party officials and friends, such as Senator Pat Moynihan from New York. Standing by the stage I listened to Jim say that I was an example of "womanhood at its very best." I was delighted by his comment. But as he spoke, I felt that in the last few days I hadn't been able to live up to his praise—although not for lack of trying.

For example, Pat Moynihan and his wife had planned a big reception for me Sunday night in San Francisco for the work I had done as Platform Chair. Since the whole New York State delegation—all my friends—had been invited, it was one of the events I was really looking forward to. But three days before the reception I had gotten the vice-presidential nod in Minnesota along with the directive from the Mondale campaign that I wasn't to return to San Francisco or make any public appearances without Fritz. Overnight I had stopped being me and had become a member of the Democratic ticket.

For the first time I had to face the fact that I would be reined in, that I was no longer the free agent I had been in Congress, and that for the next four months, at least, I wouldn't be speaking only for myself but as part of a national campaign. Having to miss Pat Moynihan's reception by canceling at the last minute was my first taste of my new role; it would take some getting used to. There was talk of sending my children in my place, but not only did the Mondale staff feel uneasy about my kids facing the public alone just one week into my candidacy, but they also didn't want anyone, including the Zaccaro children, to upstage Fritz's and my arrival in San Francisco the next day. And as their mother I was also a little concerned for them. They had never spoken publicly before. Could they handle the press? Could they handle crowds? Was I putting too much pressure on them?

The staff asked Pat Moynihan if an appearance by the Mondale children, who by this time were political pros, would do instead. Fine. But still I believe strongly that if you make a commitment, you keep it. And there I was, having to break one.

And then at last it was time for me. As I started toward the podium, the roar began to swell from the Convention floor. "Gerr-eee. Gerr-eee." I'd heard the chant a couple of times before during convention week, but not from ten thousand voices at once. I couldn't believe it. The band broke into the medley of music my staff had suggested, "New York, New York," "The Lady Is a Champ," and Archie Bunker's theme music from *All in the Family*, set in my district. What a moment. I shot the thumbs-up sign to John. And I was on.

Speak slowly and don't trip. Don't trip and speak s-l-o-w-l-y. Loftier thoughts should probably have been going through my head as I walked the last few feet to the podium. After all, this was a moment women had been dreaming of and working toward for generations. Now it was actually happening, and happening not only to me but through me. Yet I wasn't thinking about the extraordinary symbolic significance of this event. I had faced that before deciding to accept the vice-presidential nomination, recognizing the responsibilities of the office and all its implications. What seemed far more important now was to remember not to trip on or off the elevated platform that would raise my five-foot-four-inch frame high enough over the podium to be seen from the convention floor and to s-l-o-w-l-y introduce myself to the entire country. Just in case the TelePrompTers failed, I carried a copy of my speech and my glasses with me.

In the end, you can't worry about these things. You just get out there and do. But perhaps I had talked myself into feeling too comfortable. All I wanted was to deliver my speech well, to communicate to those millions of Americans my ability to help Walter Mondale lead our nation into a more secure and just future—and not to make a mistake. So what happened? I made a whopper, saying in the course of my remarks that I, the daughter of an Italian immigrant, had been chosen to run for President, instead of Vice President, of this great land. Luckily I didn't notice my slipup at the time and kept right on going. Since Fritz didn't get upset about it later, I didn't either.

We'd had a run-through the night before in the then empty convention hall while the cleaning staff swept up. Brady Williamson, a Madison, Wisconsin, attorney and long-time Mondale aide, guided me through every step of the process. I don't like surprises and I wanted to make sure I knew everything about the layout, including the positions of the cameras that were shooting the speakers from the front and the back that week, and tomorrow would be focusing on me—and my feet. Carefully we had regulated the height of the platform so that I would be able to read the TelePrompTers without my glasses. (At forty-eight, I was entitled to fall apart piece by piece.) I had also checked the exact place on the stage where the Mondale family (on my right) and my own (on my left) would join together at the evening's end.

"WFM remains on right side of rostrum and applauds Ferraro as she comes on stage from left. They shake hands at rostrum and the two candidates wave together at rostrum with outstretched arms. *No joined hands held aloft—now or at any time during demonstrations*," the internal memo had read. That suited me just fine. Fritz said he didn't like armpit shots, and besides, I look ridiculous stretching up to hold hands with someone taller.

The run-through had not been without some laughs. Ronnie Eldridge, director of the New York State Division for Women, and her husband, columnist Jimmy Breslin, along with old friends of John's and mine from Queens, had followed us over in a staff van, which somehow got separated from our motorcade (a mystery in itself since the distance to the hotel was shorter than the length of the motorcade). A cop had suddenly materialized beside the van, telling the driver to pull over. He wouldn't, until the policeman's hand went to his gun. "If you don't pull over, I'll put one into your head," the policeman threatened. Everyone was a bit edgy, but that did it, sending the men, those profiles in courage, diving under the seats, and leaving their wives sitting up there alone to take the bullet.

For all the laughs that night, however, looking out over the vast space which I, along with millions of others, had seen only on TV that week had made me feel very small. Now I would be the focus, and for the first time I felt apprehensive. I took in the acres of empty seats, the miles of red, white, and blue bunting, the gigantic closed-circuit TV monitors now blank, the temporary network newsrooms built on stilts. When I accepted the nomination of my Party to be the vice-presidential candidate, my life would be forever changed. Was I really up to it? Did I really want to do this? Yes, I decided. Yes. And the moment passed.

"Gerr-eee. Gerr-eee." The noise from the convention floor rolled up and over the podium until I could almost feel it. Enthusiastic demonstrations have always been the stuff of political conventions, of course, those orchestrated extravaganzas of support and party optimism. But this display was unbelievable, even to an old political hand like me. I was so happy that my husband and our three children, Donna, twenty-two, Laura, eighteen, and John, Jr., twenty, were all here on the platform to share this moment with me. "Gerr-eee. Gerr-eee." I wished that my mother weren't so terrified of flying, so that she could have been there, too, but I knew she was watching the Convention in her apartment in Queens along with an NBC-TV film crew picked by Barbara Leahy, a staffer in my congressional office, to represent the major networks—and my mother-in-law; my brother, Carl; his wife, Teresa; my nephews Alexander and Gerard (their brother Chris was at the Merchant Marine Academy); my aunts; and the entire district office, at least those who were still in Queens tending congressional duties; and neighbors and friends!

They weren't the only ones who weren't alongside me. I searched the platform for Tip O'Neill, the Speaker of the House, but I didn't see him. I had wanted Tip to be part of this night, to introduce me to the Convention or at least join my family on the platform. But he had declined. "I'm the reflection of the old politics according to a lot of these people, and you're the future" was his answer to my pleas. "I don't want to hurt you in any way."

Politically, if not emotionally, I understood. Tip had been in Congress for thirty-two years, elected first during the Eisenhower years and then becoming Speaker of the House in 1977 during the Carter Administration. Along the way, in the mind of the public, he had been associated with the domestic spending and social-welfare programs of Lyndon Johnson's Great Society; in the 1982 elections he had even been the butt of a Republican commercial, mockingly identifying him as an "old-line liberal." That image didn't sit too well. Tip knew it and was concerned.

But politics only goes so far, and I wanted to thank Tip personally for all he had done for me in Congress. From the minute of my arrival in Washington, he had been so helpful. There he was, a legend in the Democratic Party, having served with seven different presidents, and yet always finding time for a new congresswoman from Queens. I would go to him for advice—and he always gave it freely, along with his support and natural warmth. In the six years we had worked together, we had become very close. My father had died when I was eight, and I thought of Tip as part of my family.

I wouldn't have been standing at that podium if it weren't for Tip, if it weren't for a lot of people who believed the time for a woman had come. And every one of them must have been there. It seemed as if the roar from the Convention floor would never end, first dying down a little and then rising again while the band played on. There was no way I could begin my address, so I decided to relax and try to take in the scene.

What a sight. I couldn't make it out too clearly without my glasses but certain homemade signs stood out, like Guam Loves Gerry, El Tiempo Es Ahora ("the time is now"), and one huge cardboard poem: The Republicans May Think They're Hot. But We Have Gerry and They Do Not. An amazing number of children were in the crowd, even little babies, and I worried about them in the crush. Later I was told that many delegates had brought their daughters and even their granddaughters onto the convention floor the night of my nomination to bear witness to this moment in American history.

The theme music for the Convention was Kool and the Gang's "Celebration," and tonight nothing could have been more appropriate. The words said it all: "It's time for everyone to come together, everyone around the world. Come on. Let's celebrate." In the Moscone Center, no one needed any urging. I couldn't resist shaking a little hip myself up on the podium while the delegates danced with their fellow delegates, danced alone in the aisles, and waved American flags, banners, signs, and their state standards in time with the music. Snaking in and out of it all was the Hawaiian delegation in a conga line, wearing huge straw hats.

There seemed to be a sea of women on the floor. Some of the male delegates had given up their floor passes to female friends and alternate delegates. This night belonged to women, and emotions were running high. Many were hugging each other, laughing and crying at the same time. In a lovely touch, a lot of women had taken advantage of San Francisco's overflowing flower markets and brought bouquets of fresh flowers to a political event that traditionally was better known for its clouds of cigar smoke.

"I love it," I said to myself, forgetting that the microphone in front of me was sending out my words all over the world. But I meant what I said. I felt so lucky to be the one standing in for millions and millions of American women. Would I let them down? I certainly hoped not.

"My name is Geraldine Ferraro." Pandemonium again, but soon I discovered that when I started to speak the audience quieted down to listen, and when they applauded, it automatically slowed down my way of speaking. We were joined in a sort of dance; I was as fascinated by their reactions as they were interested in what I had to say. From Martin Luther King I took the quote: "Occasionally in life there are moments which cannot be completely explained by words. Their meaning can only be articulated by the inaudible language of the heart." His sentiment was perfect. There were no words for me to adequately explain what I was feeling now.

For hundreds of years America had held out a promise to those who reached her shores: if you were willing to work hard and live by what you believed, you could earn your share of this country's great blessings. That the daughter of Dominick, himself an immigrant, and Antonetta Ferraro, a first-generation Italian-American, who believed in America with all their hearts, was standing before her people now on this remarkable day was proof that the promise was still alive.

My parents' journey had not been without sacrifice. After my father's totally unexpected death, young, of a heart attack, my mother was left alone at the age of thirty-nine to support my brother and me. She never talked about her problems. And neither did I. She was a proud person. My mother was dedicated to being independent, to doing what was right for her kids, and she wouldn't ask anyone for anything.

Soon after my father's death we sold our house in Newburgh, New York, and moved to a tiny apartment in the South Bronx, the run-down neighborhood of garages where *Fort Apache* was filmed. From that dead-end place my mother sent me away to school, urging me on, never letting me quit.

"Don't forget your name," she would tell me. "*Fèrro* means iron. You can bend it, but you can't break it. Go on."

I wanted to pay public tribute to my mother, to give her recognition for all she had done for me. That was why I had kept her name professionally after I got married, to honor her. She had fought for our future against so many odds after my father was gone.

I had been special to him because I was the baby, the only girl after four boys, and because I had brought my mother back to life. My older brother's twin had died when he was six days old. My second brother, Gerard, had been killed in my mother's arms at the age of three in a car accident. She'd had a late miscarriage in between the boys. "I only have children to put them in the cemetery," she used to say. At the family doctor's urging, she had become pregnant again to take her out of her depression. But her sons' deaths had left a terrifying imprint, and she delivered me at home in sheets sprayed with Lysol because she was afraid if she left my brother Carl to go to the hospital, something would happen to him.

I remembered the day my father died with the perfect recall of a child whose life was utterly transformed. We'd all had supper and then he had gone out with some friends. The next morning I walked into my parents' bedroom, I saw a doctor there, my father opened his eyes and looked at me. And he died. "Daddy's gone to heaven," my mother said, leading me out of the room. He was waked in the house, and for the next ten years whenever I walked by a florist or smelled flowers anywhere, the aroma would envelop me and bring the whole scene back.

He had never told anyone he had a heart condition. It was only later when my mother went through his things that she found various pills from his doctor. I resented that as a child. I resented that he hadn't taken better care of himself, that he hadn't let us know so that we could have taken care of him. And I felt guilty. He used to give me piggyback rides up the stairs to my bedroom, even when I was eight. For a while I thought that maybe I had caused his heart attack, and after his death, I got very sick with anemia. The doctors said I had internalized my grief.

My father's death changed my life forever. I found out how quickly what you have can be taken away. From that moment on, I had to fight for whatever I wanted, to work and study my own way out of the South Bronx and take my mother with me. For every plan I made, I made sure I had an alternative to fall back on. I had learned that the hard way—and so had my mother.

"What are you going to knock yourself out for, sending her to college," one of my uncles had said to my mother at my high school graduation. "She's pretty. She'll get married."

"Forget it," my mother told him. "She's going to have an education."

My mother taught me by word and example how important it was—for men *and* women—to be self-sufficient. When as a young girl I begged her to show me how to crochet beads onto dresses, which was how she supported us, she deliberately gave me the hardest bead to try because she knew I'd fail—I did—and be forced to realize how much an education mattered.

And so through college I held two or three jobs at times. Afterward I kept going, putting myself through law school at night by teaching grade school during the day. Then for fourteen years I stayed home, raising my three children. I went back into the work force as an assistant district attorney in Queens, so that I could stay close to my family, and, after that, went on to Congresswoman.

I owed my mother so much, not only for her material support but for the values she had instilled in me: hard work, perseverance, resourcefulness, and a family that comes through for each other. These were the strengths I brought to my candidacy, and so I said, "Tonight, the daughter of a woman whose highest goal was a future for her children talks to our nation's oldest party about a future for us all."

I wanted to point out that although nine hundred people live in Mondale's hometown of Elmore, Minnesota, whereas in Queens there are two thousand people on some blocks, we all have the same values, the same hopes for our children.

There was one myth I wanted to dispel, and that was the accusation that the Democratic Party was ruled by special interests. Anyone who grew up in hard times knows that the Democrats were the ones who came through for working Americans. We still are. I don't believe in getting something for nothing. I don't think anyone is born entitled. I had gone to school with kids who had far more than I could dream of, and I knew that if you don't have, then you work—and work hard—for what you want. But those who have more shouldn't be paying less for the privilege. "It isn't right that every year the share of taxes paid by individual citizens is going up while the share paid by large corporations is getting smaller and smaller," I said.

A lot of the rules about what was decent and fair were being broken by the Reagan Administration, and I wanted to speak out, strongly. I knew how afraid senior citizens were that their hardwon security might be taken away. "Social Security is a contract between the last generation and the next, and the rules say you don't break contracts," I told this audience. Any society that cannot respect its past by granting those who built it financial security faces moral bankruptcy in the future.

In the dawn of a new technological age, when we needed educated young people more than ever, the Republicans wanted to savage student loans, cut support that would broaden educational opportunities, and grant tax exemptions to segregated schools. "You fit the classic definition of a cynic," I said, ostensibly to the Administration but aiming at Reagan himself. "You know the price of everything but the value of nothing."

Being the mother of a son of draft age, I made clear my anguish over our present confrontational policies in Central America, the Middle East, and other tense areas. "Let no one doubt we will defend America's security and the cause of freedom around the world," I said. "But we want a President who tells us what America is fighting *for* . . . not just what we are fighting against. We want a President who will defend human rights, not just where it is convenient but wherever freedom is at risk, from Afghanistan to Chile, from Poland to South Africa."

One of my deepest worries was the present Administration's dangerous indifference toward nuclear-arms control. At that point, Reagan was the first president since Herbert Hoover not even to talk to the Russians about arms control. I wanted the country to know that, unlike the Republicans, we would make a verifiable nuclear freeze our highest priority. "We want a President who will keep America strong, but use that strength to keep America, and the world, at peace," I said. "A nuclear freeze is not a slogan: it is a tool for survival in the nuclear age. If we leave our children nothing else, let us leave them this earth as we found it—whole and green and full of life." And who should that President be? "I know in my heart Walter Mondale will be that President," I said.

I thought back to 1980, when I had watched my President, Jimmy Carter, concede to Ronald Reagan. Carter had been dedicated to stopping the arms race, to preventing the spread of nuclear weapons to countries that didn't already have them. Reagan seemed just as dedicated to adding new and even deadlier nuclear weapons to our arsenal. After the 1980 election I had resolved that I would do everything possible to get this misguided and dated man out of office.

In the course of the Platform hearings, more than one young person had said to me: "We're young, but we have no idea whether we're going to have kids. It doesn't seem fair to bring children into an unsafe world." What a very sad way for young people to feel. And what an insecure world the present Administration was creating for them. "It isn't right," I said this night in San Francisco, "that young couples question whether to bring children into a world of fifty thousand nuclear warheads."

I spoke directly to women, to let them know I shared their concerns firsthand, and that finally we could have a voice in the highest ranks of government. "If you play by the rules," I said, "you deserve a fair day's pay for a fair day's work." It is outrageous in this day and age that women are still making only fifty-nine cents on the dollar for the same work as a man; that by the year 2000, if current trends play out, nearly all the poor in this country will be women and children; that we still haven't been guaranteed equal status under the Constitution by passage of the Equal Rights Amendment. And the floor broke into its biggest outburst of the evening. "E-R-A! E-R-A!"

I did not take these women's issues lightly. For the last six years I had represented not only my own congressional district in Queens but the women of our country as well. I, along with many of my female colleagues in Congress, regularly received mail from women in every state, detailing the frustrations and inequities relating to their gender. Under such an inescapable weight, we ended up feeling like congresswomen-at-large for the women of America. Now, if Fritz and I were elected, we would really be able to do something. "By choosing an American woman to run for our nation's second-highest office, you send a powerful signal to all Americans," I said to the Convention. "There are no doors we cannot unlock. We will place no limits on achievement. If we can do this, we can do *anything*."

Before the speech, I had told my children I didn't want to see any tears, that they couldn't break down in the emotion of the moment because the television cameras would be on them. This was not an easy assignment for children coming from an Italian-American family. And sure enough, it turned out to be too much. I ended my remarks by declaring the obligation I felt very deeply as a public official to pass on a better country to our children than the one we had inherited. Of course such a sentiment addressed my own children in one generation and my mother in another. So in closing I spoke directly to them: "To my daughters, Donna and Laura, and my son John, Jr., I say: My mother did not break faith with me . . . and I will not break faith with you. To all the children of America, I say: The generation before ours kept faith with us, and like them, we will pass on to you a stronger, more just America."

That did it. Laura evidently turned to her older sister Donna to see tears in her eyes. "Donna, you can't cry," she said, remembering my admonishment. But two seconds later Donna looked over to see Laura begin to blubber, and they both went over the edge. So much for emotional self-control. But then, though all three of my children had seen me at work when they had summer jobs in Washington—Donna twice as an intern, the two younger children as congressional pages—they had never expected their mother to become a vice-presidential nominee.

Now they rushed toward me on the podium, my son John wrapping his arms around me. "Oh, Mom," he kept saying. "Oh, Mom." It was all pretty mind-blowing for them, having been dumped in the middle of this fantastic happening with no warning at all. It had been less than a week since John, Jr., had heard the announcement of my selection on a car radio in Hawaii, where he had a summer job working as a deckhand on the S.S. *Constitution*. Since we had been unable to reach him, the news was a real surprise. And he felt a little funny about the idea of sharing it with his friends. They didn't know his mom was a member of Congress or his dad a successful businessman. All they knew was that he was one of the guys, who came from New York and liked to surf. So John waited until he got back to the ship before calling home. The shock still hadn't worn off. Even during my acceptance speech my candidacy hadn't seemed real to him, he told me later, until he had looked up at one of the convention center's television monitors and seen his mom on TV. Only then did it begin to sink in.

I've always considered my kids quick studies, but this was a whole new territory. And they reacted on stage like veterans. While the cheers and the whistles and the foot stomping went on and on, we stood together on the podium, all of us waving back at the crowd. If the scene felt unreal to my family, it felt almost as unreal to me. Only having them there grounded me.

"Gerr-eee. Gerr-eee." No one on the Convention floor wanted to let go of this moment. I felt proud and exhilarated, relieved that my speech was over, eager now to get on with the hard work that lay ahead. Unseating Reagan would be the steepest of uphill battles, maybe even impossible. But there was such a spirit in the convention hall that night, such euphoria right through Fritz's acceptance speech to Jennifer Holliday's stirring rendition of "The Battle Hymn of the Republic," which moved all the delegates to join hands and sing along with her, that anything seemed possible. Tonight San Francisco, tomorrow the country, November the White House. All the pieces were there, and there was no way that amazing energy shaking the rafters wasn't going to propel us to victory.

What a high that night was. As I looked out over the convention floor, I saw the faces of America: farmers, factory workers, young professionals, the elderly, business executives, blacks, whites, Hispanics, Native Americans, Asian-Americans, and women—so many women. No one wanted to leave. Even my normally more sobersided peers and colleagues were caught up in the celebration, from city mayors to delegation whips, from governors to union leaders, from Party officials to members of government from the smallest towns and on the highest federal level.

Did I think we could win the election? Sure did. The Democratic Party had already bucked the odds by selecting a woman as the vice-presidential candidate. We were leaving the Convention unified, the bitterness of the presidential primaries buried by the candidates themselves—Gary Hart, Jesse Jackson, John Glenn, Alan Cranston, Fritz Hollings, Reuben Askew, and George McGovern— all of whom now joined hands on the podium. The Democratic Party had never seemed more together.

There wasn't a cloud on my horizon as we left the Moscone Center to share a bottle of celebratory champagne with Joan and Fritz Mondale. The *New York Post* had already taken off after John, running a story during the convention about a tenant who wasn't his tenant claiming she had to take her baby to bed to keep it warm. John had no connection to the building and no idea who she was. But some nastiness is always expected in politics, and I dismissed these opening salvos.

What I didn't know then was the personal agony that lay ahead, an agony that at times would seem almost unbearable. More than once in the next four months as the euphoria faded and the highs were equaled by the lows, I would ask myself not only what John and I had done to deserve this, but how we had gotten to this point in the first place.

SELECTION
PROCESS:
THE IMPOSSIBLE
DREAM

"They're never going to choose a woman."

—*National Women's Political Caucus,*
San Antonio, Texas, July 1983.

I NEVER REALLY THOUGHT
I would be the vice-presidential nominee. Even as I left New
York on July 10, 1984, to go to the Democratic Convention in
San Francisco, I didn't think the slot would end up going to a
woman. No way. The idea was terrific, of course. But I am, if
nothing else, a pragmatic politician. As the time for the bottom
line approached, I was sure the male political structure, personi-
fied by the inner circle surrounding Walter Mondale, would go
for a man, probably Gary Hart. And I had said so.

Spirits had been high at the biennial meeting of the National
Women's Political Caucus in San Antonio, Texas, in July 1983.
For the first time, men had come to women to court their vote.
One by one the Democratic presidential candidates—Mondale,
Hart, Glenn, Cranston, and Hollings—made their case to the two
thousand politically active women assembled there. (Jesse Jackson
had yet to declare his candidacy and Reuben Askew had declined
the NWPC's invitation, perhaps because of his antichoice position on abortion, which he knew was most important to the
feminist community.)

They were all good candidates, an amazing array of talent.
And they all supported the women's agenda: prochoice, pro-ERA,

24

pro-pay equity; antiwasteful defense spending and the current federal policies accelerating the feminization of poverty. It felt nice to be wooed. In other years the candidates had merely sent their position papers to the NWPC. This time they had finally come themselves, and the women felt somewhat vindicated. "We've got the issues, we've got the gender gap on our side, and at long last the men are going to pay attention to us," I told *Time* magazine at the time.

But the real buzz at the convention centered on the political strategy women were going to use in the upcoming presidential election. For months a loose coalition of women's activists such as Gloria Steinem, Bella Abzug, former (and elected again in July 1985) NOW (National Organization for Women) president Ellie Smeal, committed feminist Frances Lear, and others had been kicking around the idea of running a woman for the Presidency. But time was running out, there wasn't a suitable candidate, and at this meeting the delegates had shifted their sights to the Vice Presidency. Out of all these impassioned voices, I was the only doomsayer.

"There is no way any presidential candidate is going to choose a woman as a running mate unless he's fifteen points behind in the polls," I had said to a closed meeting of the increasingly displeased members of the Democratic Caucus there. "I just don't see these guys doing it, and it's guys who run these campaigns." If the candidate is so far behind that there's really no chance of winning, I went on, then and only then he might decide, why not? And even at that, it was still a long shot. "They're never going to choose a woman because they think it's the right thing to do," I concluded.

The reaction had been immediate. "That's a terrible thing to say," Millie Jeffrey spoke up, a feisty feminist in her seventies and long-time labor activist. "They will pick a woman," she insisted, pointing to the newly identified vote that women in this country were ready to channel. Brooklyn District Attorney Liz Holtzman agreed. "The gender gap exists," Holtzman called out. "If we can register enough women we can make a difference then we can insist they choose a woman for the Vice Presidency."

Though I wanted to believe them, I just couldn't. The increasing numbers of elected women officials were not being ignored, but they still did not constitute enough of a power base to

gain equal status with the good old boys. It would take registering many, many new women voters and having many more
women who agreed with us on the issues take an active role in
politics to challenge the status quo.

But I was bucking a strong emotional tide and, not surprisingly, my remarks left a lot of ruffled feathers. As I left the
caucus meeting, Lynn Cutler, vice-chair of the Democratic National Committee, chided me.

"You have plenty of people angry at you," she said. "You
shouldn't put down the idea of a woman Vice President."

But I wasn't putting down the idea, I told her. I was just
facing reality. "They're not going to pick a woman unless they
are way behind."

It wasn't the first time my bluntness had gotten me in
trouble—and certainly would not be the last. Still, on this issue
anyway, I took Lynn's advice. If the women honestly believed
they could get a woman on the ticket, great. Go for it. But it
seemed like pie in the political sky to me.

Now, on July 11, 1984, almost exactly a year later, I was
about to eat my words. After an extraordinary sequence of political events, I was waiting in my hotel suite at the Democratic
Convention in San Francisco for the vice-presidential phone call
from Fritz Mondale, either asking me to be his running mate—or
explaining to me why I was not the one he had selected. I still
wasn't sure what he was going to say, but all the signs were
suddenly pointing to go.

The momentum of the last twenty-four hours had been unprecedented. Just a few hours before I was due to leave New
York for the convention in San Francisco, one of Mondale's top
aides, Michael Berman, had flown in to do a vice-presidential
check on the Ferraro-Zaccaro finances. His last-minute visit had
caught me by surprise. Either the Mondale campaign was taking
the candidacy of a woman seriously or they were determined to
give that impression so that they wouldn't be criticized later when
they ended up with a man. Berman's visit was also inconvenient.
I had made an appointment to get my hair cut en route to the
airport, and nothing short of a presidential decree was going to
make me miss it. As the first woman chair of the Platform Committee I'd be the object of press attention throughout the conven-

tion week and would be presenting the Platform itself on prime-time television. I wanted to look good. My hair had gotten too long, and because of the rush of platform and congressional business I hadn't had time to deal with it.

Luckily Berman had been flexible, if incredulous, when I asked him during our phone conversation the previous night if his visit would have to preempt my hair appointment. Evidently vice-presidential candidates are not supposed to think about their hair. "Is this person for real?" Berman had phoned back to Mondale headquarters after my query. They must have said yes because he agreed to fly in at seven-thirty a.m. (He didn't tell us from where, so that we wouldn't know what other vice-presidential candidate he had been checking out. It was too early for the Washington shuttle, so I decided he must have come from Philadelphia and Mayor Wilson Goode. Wrong. I found out later it was Boston and Governor Michael Dukakis.) In any event, Berman finally arrived at our house in Forest Hills, New York, having gotten lost in our local labyrinth of roads. I made him an English muffin and coffee and tried not to dwell on the incongruity of serving breakfast at this discussion.

"Your candidacy is a real possibility now," Berman said, sitting with John and me at the kitchen table. "We're down to the finalists. Is there anything in your backgrounds we should know?"

I had to take his interest seriously. No one who looked that wiped out was just playing political games. And so we thought carefully. There was the matter of the loans my campaign committee had taken from my family in 1978, loans I had paid back when the Federal Election Commission (FEC) deemed them improper, I told him.

"We know all about that," Berman said.

My husband's in real estate, I went on, and we'd had some slumlord smears emanating from the same campaign.

"We know about that, too," Berman said.

Obviously, the Mondale staff had done its homework, and I was impressed. Maybe this was for real.

Berman had a long questionnaire with him, and we ticked off the answers as he went down it: Had either of us had relationships with other people? No. Did we have any physical or mental health problems in the family? No. Had we ever been arrested, sued, or charged with a crime? No. And he warned us about the scrutiny, both personal and financial, that we would be subjected to. We weren't concerned at all.

"Could we see your tax returns?" Berman asked. I had no problem with that. My background was already a matter of public record. But John was more reluctant. "Are you going to release them?" he asked Berman, not wanting the world to know his private business.

"No," Berman assured him. "They are just for us to see."

"Fine," John said. "I just don't want them released."

"Would you have any problems releasing a financial statement?" Berman asked John.

"No, none at all," John said.

And Berman was satisfied. After all, why shouldn't he be? There was no law then, nor has there ever been, that requires either a vice-presidential candidate or a spouse to release his or her tax returns. In fact, John was doing even more, by agreeing to release a financial statement.

I had to leave then, and gave my sleeping daughter Laura a kiss good-bye before going off, finally, to the hairdresser. Berman's next stop was with Jack Selger, our family accountant of forty years, to complete the questionnaire. If I was to become the nominee, I would have to file a form with the FEC reporting my income and holdings in several categories, and unless I claimed an exemption (an idea that John and I would have discarded even if it had not been ruled out by our understanding with Berman to release John's financial data), also reporting similar information as to John and our dependent children. But in this check with Selger, Berman's primary interest was to determine if John and I had paid our fair share of taxes. While he was en route to our accountant's office, John called Jack to ask his cooperation in showing Berman his tax returns and whatever else he wanted to see. John would join Berman there later, along with another Mondale lawyer, Tony Essaye.

Immediately I put aside all thoughts of the Vice Presidency. I couldn't afford to be distracted by anything so uncertain as I faced my platform responsibilities at the Convention. My schedule was to start that very night in San Francisco with a dinner for me hosted by a successful agribusinessman, Bill Armanino, who was also a Mondale fund-raiser. After my years in Congress, I had set my sights on the Senate as an alternate career goal to House leadership, and Armanino had invited several dozen potential campaign contributors to drinks on his yacht followed by dinner. I never got to finish my meal.

"John Reilly wants to see you privately tonight," Mondale staff member Peter Kyros had phoned to tell me as soon as I had arrived in San Francisco that Tuesday afternoon. John Reilly? Mondale's senior adviser, in charge of the vice-presidential selection process? Berman in the morning on one coast, Reilly at night on the other? Over cocktails I confided my conflict to Armanino, giving the excuse to the others that I had last-minute work on the Platform. We rearranged the agenda so that I spoke immediately on sitting down to dinner. Hurriedly I answered a few of their questions and then rushed back to my hotel room for the meeting at nine-thirty p.m.

Suddenly, there was John Reilly standing in my suite, looking even more intense than his morning counterpart. This was getting very heady. As I ordered us both coffee from room service, again I wondered whether the Mondale staff was playing a tremendous endgame with the women so as to lock in their support for the election.

"How'd it go with John today?" I asked, looking for a clue. "Things went very well," Reilly said. No clue. But it soon developed that while Berman in the morning had been interested in our finances, Reilly was more interested in my role in the upcoming campaign as the possible vice-presidential candidate. Did I realize if I got the nomination that I'd have to give up my congressional seat? Yes, I said without hesitation. The Vice Presidency would enable me to make a difference on a larger scale. Did I understand the scrutiny that would be focused on me and my family as well? Yes, I did. I was, nonetheless, concerned about thrusting the people around me into a limelight they hadn't asked for. We had all been through it when I had first run for Congress, but this would be rougher. The spotlight on a vice-presidential candidate had to be more intense. Yet the facts hadn't changed, I said. I'd had nothing to hide in 1978 and had nothing to hide now.

Reilly went on to detail the demands on me if I were to be the candidate, what I would be expected to do as Mondale's running mate. But none of that was news to me. As an elected official, I was well accustomed to the extraordinary strains of political campaigns, albeit on a local rather than national scale. This campaign would just be more—much more—of the same. Did I have any personal problems that should be taken into Mondale's consideration? Reilly asked me. Anything about the kids vis-à-vis drugs, alcohol, school? No, I answered firmly. And once again I went through the FEC ruling, which he already knew all about. Reilly then said, "Fritz will get back to you tomorrow."

But that wasn't quite good enough for me. I wanted time to think through the consequences of this possibility. Most important, I wanted to talk to my husband before I talked to Fritz. If Mondale were to ask me to be his running mate, my whole family would be involved, especially John. Our life together would be disrupted, changed, maybe forever. I knew where I had been heading in Congress and felt comfortable about it. Now an extraordinary element had been introduced, and I wanted to be sure when I talked to Fritz the next day that my answer would take John's feelings into account as well. It was too late to call him now, two-thirty a.m., New York time; I asked Reilly to call me the next day before Fritz did. That would guarantee me the time to square away with John whatever response I would have for whatever Fritz had to say. And Reilly agreed.

It was a sobering moment. For months my name had been bandied about as a vice-presidential possibility, but until this moment it had never seemed a probability. John and I had discussed it, of course, but more in the vein of our own amazement that I, along with the other women being considered, was attracting such national attention. Now, suddenly, everything was moving.

And with such high drama. Reilly's "secret" trip to San Francisco from North Oaks was turning out to be no secret at all. The intrigue of the vice-presidential selection process that had been so delighting the press was nearing the payoff, and the media were determined not to miss the tiniest beat. Throughout the entire time Reilly and I had been talking in the suite the phone had never stopped ringing. CBS, it turned out, had been tipped off in Minnesota to Reilly's sudden visit to San Francisco, though the network did not know whom he had come to see. Reilly had walked off the plane to find himself bathed in TV lights.

"Are you here to see Feinstein?" the CBS correspondent had asked him, not an unreasonable question since she was the mayor of San Francisco.

"No," came the reply.

"Are you here to see Ferraro?" the correspondent persisted. That was smart, inasmuch as I had arrived in San Francisco only that afternoon, almost a week before the convention officially convened.

"Yes, and that's all I have to say," said Reilly.

That was more than enough. My hotel was listed in the convention program, and CBS never stopped calling during our entire meeting—from the airport, from their offices at the convention center, from the house phones in the hotel lobby. Hotel security would not allow any camera crews up to our floor, so at least we were spared that pressure. We finally had to ask the hotel switchboard to hold the phone calls. But there was nothing we could do about the house phones. "No comment," one of my staff answered CBS each time.

But Reilly was trapped. How to get out of the hotel without having CBS mob him?

"I guess I'll just have to spend the night here," Reilly quipped.

"Not on your life." I laughed.

Finally, with the help of hotel security, he did get out down a back elevator and walked with Michael Cardozo (a Mondale lawyer I would meet the next night) and Peter Kyros back to Mondale headquarters at the Meridien Hotel.

That threw the press off. They do not expect their targets simply to stroll down the street. When CBS did pick up the scent, Reilly jumped into a cab to go back to the airport.

"Was that John Reilly?" the reporter asked Cardozo and Kyros, but they played dumb.

Knowing for sure something was brewing, the reporter jumped into his van to chase Reilly.

"Lose that car," Reilly snapped to his driver.

And he must have, because Reilly made it back unscathed to Minnesota, arriving to report on our conversation to Mondale at six a.m.

While Reilly flew back to Minnesota, I lay awake, weighing

the prospect that was staring me in the face. There had been a lot of conjecture, of course, about Mondale going with a woman Vice President. If he was going to choose a woman, the field had been narrowed down to me and Dianne Feinstein. But would he? Or was it just a good publicity stunt? In this lackluster election year, the press had leapt on the idea. There had been camera crews staked out around our house in Queens for weeks now. *Time* magazine had run Feinstein and me on the cover in early June, and Barbara Walters had queried me about the Vice Presidency on *20/20*.

I had found the media attention very flattering, though a distraction at times. But there was no point in not availing ourselves of the free exposure to promote the Democratic Platform and to make our points against Reagan. At the same time, all the attention was placing me in the public eye. It was amazing that through all the vice-presidential intrigue I had never considered my potential candidacy a serious probability. Now I had to.

Lying there in the dark that night, I ran through Reilly's checklist of what would be expected of me if the Vice Presidency were to come my way. Did I have the stamina to get through the actual campaign? Yes. I had proved that to myself during the sixteen-hour days I had put in for my congressional races and my three terms in Congress. I knew I could take it if the campaign got dirty, too. There had been smears during my first campaign. I had also been criticized for the fact that I sent my children to private instead of public schools. "Are there any parents here who don't want more for their children than they had?" I would challenge my audiences, silencing the accusers.

I would not have been who I was without the kind of education I had. I feel very, very strongly that education is important, not only for individuals to achieve what they want for themselves, but also for our nation, because we're not going to be able to compete in ten or fifteen or twenty years if we're so shortsighted that we don't address the problems of educating our young. That's one of the reasons I always pushed for loans and grants—to make available the best that money can buy, whether private money or government money, for anyone who wants to become more than he or she is.

In Congress I would get letters from people saying to me, "I worked my way through; let them do it." I believe in hard work too, but as for suffering for its own sake, who needs it? I don't think unnecessary suffering builds character at all. It doesn't make you a better person, it makes you a bitter person, and anyone who walks around claiming it's good for you is kidding himself and trying to kid the nation.

I knew my candidacy would be controversial, but I was used to that. My prochoice stand on abortion had always drawn hecklers, and my standing as a good Catholic had been publicly questioned. I was used to that. Even my relationship with my husband had been attacked in 1978. A detective friend of mine, Joe Scavo, from the DA's office had called during dinner one night to ask if John was there and if everything was all right. When I said yes but why, he said the talk on the street was that John had left me because I was having an affair with a man—or a woman! Those rumors didn't last very long, but politics can be an ugly game, and in a national election the stakes get higher while the tactics get lower.

And this was the Vice Presidency. Government was my profession, and I knew just how tough the job was going to be if we were elected, the enormity of the responsibility, the work involved. I wouldn't have even considered accepting the nomination if I had thought my role would be ceremonial. I wanted to be productive. But first we had to get elected. Could I fulfill the vice-presidential nominee's job of representing the presidential candidate, of supporting him and promoting his policies? Yes again. In the six years I had known Fritz Mondale, I had come to admire him greatly as an intelligent, thoughtful man, capable of outstanding leadership. And we both had the same vision for the country.

But still, I was relatively inexperienced. Could I move with assurance into the second-highest elected office in the nation? And again, my checklist came up positive. I would bring with me the ability to work with the members of Congress, a critical asset in turning presidential policies into law. I had traveled to Central America, the Middle East, and the Far East. I could serve as the representative of the United States in foreign countries. I wasn't an expert, but I could become one. I also felt at ease in the vital area of defense. Like Fritz, I wanted a safe, strong America. Unlike Ronald Reagan, we could differentiate between sensible spending and squandering. Yes, I decided. Though I was still "only" a member of Congress, the extraordinary and varied experience I'd had in those six years made me confident I could uphold the responsibilities of the office of Vice President.

What I didn't know, I could learn. I knew myself. There wasn't anything I couldn't do—and do well—if I put my mind to it. I wasn't going to master pro basketball, of course. I did have some problems there. But I trusted that I had the ability, if I wanted, to learn a job and to see it through. That has been the story of my life, from the first day I walked into a classroom almost thirty years ago to see all those kids' eyes fixed on me, right through the four and a half years I spent in the district attorney's office and my years in Congress. "How are you ever going to do it?" I had wondered every time I launched myself on a new course. But I found out. You work hard, you prepare, you give it your all, and within a short time you're on top of it.

The toughest transition had been the jump in 1974 from being a full-time mother to working full-time in the district attorney's office. Fourteen years had flown by since I had graduated from law school—fourteen years of staying at home and raising my kids. Although I had gone into John's office occasionally to do some real-estate work, and although my bio lists the years from 1960 to 1974 as a time when I engaged in the general practice of law, it's a good thing I didn't have to support myself on what I earned.

A whole new criminal code had been written in the interim. What was I going to do? Take the new statute with me on vacation with the kids and plunge in, studying all the new laws and legal terms—that's what. As long as I have the time to prepare, to learn the details of whatever project I'm working on, I feel confident. I'm a big list maker and I drive my family crazy, checking off every detail one by one, whether it's the intricacies of the law or of a dinner party.

Preparation is one thing. Doing the job is another. And I'm always anxious to get going, to move on it, even when it doesn't seem easy. After going through the first five bulging file folders on upcoming cases in the DA's office, I had worried aloud to Tim Flaherty. He was to become one of my best friends, helping out on my congressional campaigns and working as my executive assistant for a couple of years in my district office. So often during this campaign, when the world seemed to be crashing around our heads, Tim would stop by our home to give John and me his legal advice and his friendship.

"How do you keep all the witnesses straight, the defendants, the histories of each case?" I had asked then.

"Don't worry," Tim had replied. "You'll learn."

Talk about details. There were hundreds of them. I lost five pounds from anxiety the first month I was there, but after a while I was handling forty cases at a time. Your mind just expands to incorporate what it has to know.

In 1977 I was appointed a bureau chief. The reponsibility of my bureau was to handle all the sex crimes in the county, all the referrals from family court on child abuse, all the violent crimes against senior citizens, as well as to implement the recent battered spouse legislation.

The victims were women, children, and the elderly—the most vulnerable people in our society. And the purpose of the bureau was to get them through the courts as painlessly as possible. Under the old system, each case had been presented at various proceedings by a different assistant, and each time the victim had had to relive the horror of the experience in retelling the story.

Now one assistant stayed with the case through criminal court and grand jury to the supreme court. This was a humane innovation, and the bureau became a model in the city.

Because I was the chief, I felt a responsibility to every victim who came in. I would speak to the assistants handling the various cases about each one, and if it was a particular problem—a young child, a traumatized senior—I would handle the case myself.

The result was that every abused kid became mine, every sexually abused young woman was my daughter or me, every frightened senior, my mother. I knew it was wrong. I shouldn't have personalized the cases, but I couldn't help it. These people had been through so much.

One winter evening Mario and Matilda Cuomo were giving me a lift from a function. I was describing the anguish of my job and the frustration of seeing what I saw every day. I told Mario I was thinking of leaving and perhaps running for office. Mario said, "What about Congress?" I told him I hadn't thought about it. But when I got home, I did.

I wanted to contribute more. I had had enough of reacting to problems by punishing without solving. I wanted to do what I could to make this life a little bit easier for all of us who face problems not of our own choosing. I am not now and was not then a bleeding-heart liberal; I knew better than most how ineffective rehabilitation usually is. I knew criminals aren't in jail long enough, but I also knew that the majority go back to crime once they're out, no matter what their sentence. The defendants I had come across were mostly from poor families, were usually unemployed, with a low literacy level that kept them unemployed, and lived in the jungle of high-crime neighborhoods.

We had to change those neighborhoods. If we invested in Head Start programs, health care, adequate nutrition, and parenting courses, education, and job-training, programs we could break the cycle of poverty—and eventually of crime—in this country for many. It's cost effective, and it's the right thing to do.

Working with victims of crime, I saw firsthand that there were real limitations to how much the current laws could help people with fewer resources or power: the elderly, poor mothers and their children, the undereducated. I wanted to make a difference in the most direct way I could, to create opportunities instead of neglect. It was my neighborhood, and these people were my neighbors, and so in 1978 I ran for Congress in the Ninth District of Queens, New York.

Although I was running against three people with more political experience than I—in the primary a city councilman and a district leader, and in the general election my opponent Al DelliBovi, an assemblyman—I had a different kind of experience to offer. DelliBovi was right wing to the extreme, and against everything I cared about for my city and my country. His vote in Congress could never represent me.

When I won the election, I knew from the beginning what I wanted for the people of Queens: a congressional office that functioned as a storefront, where people could feel free to walk in off the street any time and find someone to help them. In fact, I insisted that the entrance have no steps at all, not only for the symbolism but for the practical use of the handicapped and the elderly, who I hoped would come to us, some for the first time. I even vetoed blinds on the windows, so that people walking by would see us working—for them. I wanted to capture the feeling that is the best of the American spirit: informality and a helping hand.

Immediately I hired four devoted caseworkers, the kind of people who really cared. More than once, when a constituent couldn't make it into the office, we'd go to the home.

We went to them in other ways as well, with a mobile office parked three days a week all over the district, and a caseworker whose job it was to encourage drop-ins.

During congressional recess I would schedule three or four town meetings at home. Slowly the turnout grew as people spread the word. I didn't talk; I listened, and then tried to act on what I heard.

With an elderly mother and mother-in-law so much part of my life, I had a special sensitivity to the fears of older people. I knew how much my mother had struggled alone for a measure of security, and how frightening it must be at the end of a productive life to worry about such fundamentals as food and a roof overhead. These people, who had contributed their working lives, did not deserve to be ignored now. Among other things each year they feared that they would not get the annual cost-of-living adjustment (COLA) to their Social Security check. When I visited senior citizen centers in my district, I'd say: "Don't you worry. It's my job down there to worry for you."

The office was humming. The top of my congressional newsletter said, "We're Here to Help," and when all the phones were ringing at once, my staff used to joke that they knew each time they picked up the receiver they would hear, "You said you were here to help. Well, I have a problem . . ." But that's what we wanted.

Looking back, I remembered how when I was first elected in 1978 I knew less about the inside of Congress than my daughter Donna, who had spent a week on the Hill that summer in a

program called A Presidential Classroom for Young Americans.
It is a week of total immersion in the workings of Capitol
Hill. The young people get to meet their representatives, visit
with Administration officials, and attend committee hearings
and sessions of the House and Senate. Later I would often be
asked to address the students in the program, but in 1978 I
needed help.

As soon as I arrived in Washington I went into total congressional immersion myself, attending every breakfast meeting given
by the Library of Congress on a wide range of subjects, and
joining numerous congressional caucuses to gain expertise on a
whole range of issues. My right arm must have stretched two
inches lugging around my briefcase stuffed with reading material
from the Library's Congressional Research Service on everything
from the latest on nuclear arms to political unrest in the Philippines. I've never been one to pretend to know more than I do,
and I made sure to hire real pros for my staff, who were knowledgeable both about the issues and about the way Congress worked.
In short order I was as comfortable in Congress as I was with my
constituency in Queens and as familiar with the issues as any of
my peers were.

But we weren't talking about Congress now. The subject
was the vice-presidency. And the Vice President is only a heartbeat away from being President, a sort of President-in-waiting.
Reagan, after all, had been shot and wounded, and I had to face
the possibility that something might happen to Walter Mondale.
He understood that. And so did I. When I had flown out to
North Oaks, Minnesota, on July 2 for my vice-presidential interview, Fritz had told me he would insist that his Vice President
always be included in the daily presidential briefings, both foreign
and domestic. "Quite frankly," Fritz had said, "if something were
to happen to me I would want my Vice President to be able to
move right in and take over, not like Harry Truman, who was
left in the dark and suddenly had to fill in for Roosevelt." Jimmy
Carter had felt the same way, which was one reason I had such
confidence in Fritz. He had had a firsthand view of the job.

Now I had to face another question—was I prepared to be
President, the sort of President I would want to lead the country?
If, God forbid, Walter Mondale were to die on inauguration day,

then I certainly would be in a tough situation. But if I had six months to absorb all the details . . . ? I felt confident that I could lead the country.

I knew where I came from and trusted that legacy. I had years of experience working with legislation as a lawyer and as a congresswoman. Equally important to my mind was my experience in working with people. My life and the life of my parents had exemplified so much of the hopes and dreams that unite all Americans—and I believed that my background gave me a gut feeling about what America stands for and where we should be heading.

This is not to say the concept of my suddenly becoming President didn't make me feel slightly intimidated. But it did not overwhelm me. No one can even consider accepting the vice-presidential nomination without coming to grips with the possibility of becoming the President. If you feel you can do one, then you have to feel ready to do the other.

There were the alternatives to consider as well. What if Fritz told me tomorrow that I wasn't going to be his running mate, that he had chosen someone else instead? Then I'd go right on doing what I'd been planning to do: work as hard as I could for the Democratic ticket, stand for reelection in my congressional district, and evaluate my chances of moving further into the House leadership or, alternatively, winning the New York Senate seat in 1986.

It would be tough, of course, to have the vice-presidential nomination go to another woman. I'm human. Dianne Feinstein had been visited by another top Mondale aide, Jim Johnson, on July 5 in San Francisco. Even now, although I didn't know it at the time, Michael Cardozo and Peter Kyros had spent the next two days with Feinstein and her husband, Richard Blum, an investment banker also involved in real estate. But I knew if Dianne were to be the chosen one, I could handle it. The pieces were in place if Mondale offered me the job. And if he didn't, that was all right.

Waiting for Fritz's phone call the next day, I went to sleep, musing over the remarkable turn of events that had put me in this position. It was, after all, only a year since I had insisted there was no way a woman would be on the presidential ticket. It wasn't even such a long time since the slogan of the National Women's Political Caucus had been "Make Policy—Not Coffee," and Christmas aprons had sported such mild protests as "For This I Went to College?" and "A Woman's Place Is in the House— and the Senate." What had happened so quickly in the interim to catapult women into such political prominence?

SHOWDOWN AT GENDER GAP

*"Do you think it's appropriate to promote
yourself as a woman?"*

—question from a male member of Congress during
campaign for Budget Committee, December 1982.

Ｓ O MUCH HAD CHANGED.
When I arrived in Congress in 1979 I had joined the Congresswomen's Caucus. But there were too few women in the House
and Senate—only eleven Democrats and six Republicans—to sway
any votes among the 435 members. Legislation on women's issues languished in several committees. There was only one woman
in the House leadership, and only a few women served on the
prestigious committees such as Budget or Ways and Means (none
of them Democrats). Lindy Boggs was on Appropriations, but
we remained a sprinkling of females in a male bastion, without the numbers to be a force.

Like many institutions, Congress was stuck in its old, and
all-male, ways. It had taken women like Bella Abzug to break
through the first lines of defense. Even after her tenure in the
House, Bella had continued to argue as a member of President Carter's National Advisory Council on Women that the environment, the budget, and the arms race were women's issues. Bella
was always an organizer, a fighter for women and their concerns.

Without women like her, my female colleagues and I would
still be fighting to get in, instead of concentrating on the work at
hand. Bella had made it far easier for us, even down to taking a

swim in the congressional swimming pool. When she was in Congress, the men had first refused to let her take a dip, claiming it infringed on the delights of their swimming in the nude. Bella had made short shrift of that, and the pool had gone coed. On more than one occasion I thought of her with gratitude as I swam laps in that pool.

I wanted to be part of what was going on in the House, to be an effective, not passive, member of Congress representing my district and my state. And I wanted to do women proud. All new members of Congress are assigned to committees, assignments that are retained for the most part throughout their careers. Mine were the Public Works Committee, the Post Office and Civil Service Committee, and the Select Committee on Aging. I wanted to learn the ropes in Congress—and to learn them fast. At one of the first hearings of the Public Works Committee, the subject was the retrofitting of engines to meet noise standards. I sat there listening to the male members asking questions during the testimony, and every one of them sounded like an expert.

"Is it in their genes that they know all this stuff about decibel levels?" I asked my staff. No, my staff told me. These guys had been sitting through hearings on this same subject for years. "Do me a favor," I said. "Get me the transcripts from the past hearings so I don't walk in there and look dumb." From then on, before any committee meeting I read whatever testimony there was ahead of time so that at least I could ask intelligent questions. It happens that some of the issues that matter most in my district came under Public Works. Congress is where you fight for the basics—and New York City needed them. I pressed for federal funds to repair city streets and subways and to rebuild the Queensboro Bridge; a great city can work and grow only if its infrastructure isn't falling apart.

Crime was an obvious worry in my district. When there was a move to save money by cutting the number of customs inspectors at Kennedy Airport, I argued the result would be an increase in drug smuggling and saved four hundred jobs—and, I hope, made a minor dent in a major problem. I also got more money for the New York City police.

As a parent I cared about bequeathing a liveable world to my children, and so I fought to protect New York's water supply and to stop nuclear waste shipments through Queens. My constituents were not going to be anonymous to their government if I could do anything about it. It was my job to make sure that some of the money they sent to Washington came home to their own neighborhood.

I had run on the slogan, "Finally . . . a tough Democrat," but I didn't realize until I got to Washington how true that slogan was.

You had to be tough to be a female member of Congress. Because there were so few of us, still only twenty-four in House and Senate in 1983, we were very visible and therefore ripe targets for criticism. There were traps everywhere, even on the most insignificant details, and I made sure I fell into as few of them as possible. When I first went down to Washington I overheard a male member say about a new female member: "She walked off the floor of the House and couldn't even find her way to the ladies' room." No one was ever going to be able to say that about me, I decided. So before I walked out of any door, I mentally walked to wherever I was going, mapping out my exact route. Silly, right? And totally inconsequential. But you have to look as if you know where you're going—and nothing is worse than looking as if you don't.

I felt terribly frustrated by what seemed to be the male indifference to women's issues, especially the economic predicament confronting women of all ages—single or married, homemakers or women who also worked outside the home. Though women represented forty-three percent of the work force, the "feminization of poverty" was growing. For most, their paychecks were essential to support either themselves or their families. Fully two-thirds of the women in the work force were single, widowed, divorced, or married to men who earned less than fifteen thousand dollars a year. In my district alone, there were 25,667 households headed by women—more than twelve percent of all households. In this country 2.8 million women over the age of sixty-five lived in poverty, almost three times the number of men.

Not only were women paid just over half what men were paid, but the jobs many women held usually provided few of the essential benefits for economic security, such as health insurance and pension plans. Pensions—or lack of pensions—for women was a critical problem. My office in Queens heard regularly from my constituents, many of whom were elderly, whose stories about their loss of income after the death of their husbands were heart wrenching. Younger women who had taken time off during pregnancy or to raise their young children had also been denied any pension benefits. Other women had lost their financial security after a divorce or the premature deaths of their husbands. One woman whose husband had worked for a major corporation for twenty-four years didn't receive a penny of his pension, because he had died of cancer at fifty instead of fifty-five.

These terrible predicaments were not theoretical to me. "Single head of household" was not an IRS phrase; it was my mother, going without meat (not because of health concerns but because she couldn't afford it) so her kids could go to good schools. We had been lucky to have the support of an extended family. My mother's sister, Aunt Jenny, had lived across the street, and my cousin Millie was nearby, so there was always someplace for us to go when we were home—and a lot of love. What about women who had fewer resources?

"Displaced homemaker" was another meaningful term. Going back into the work force after years of child-raising wasn't easy, even with a lot of backup, which I certainly had thanks to John's hard work for our family. I did well, but I was shocked to discover that the male bureau chiefs in the district attorney's office were making significantly more money than I, for doing similar work. When I asked why, I was told, "You don't need the money, Gerry, you've got a husband." If you're wondering what the statistic about women earning fifty-nine cents on the dollar means, that attitude is part of the reason why.

Women reentering the work force face psychological hurdles as well—on the part of others. When I began to work full-time as a lawyer, people assumed that because I was older and because my cousin Nick Ferraro was the district attorney at that time, I was a stupid relative who was going to goof off and not do her job. I felt the strain of proving myself then, and so understand from the inside what it's like—the fear that your skills have rusted, that you can't compete.

In 1981 I introduced a bill to make private pensions fairer and to recognize marriage as an economic partnership. It permitted all workers to start participating in pension plans at age twenty-one instead of twenty-five, broadened eligibility requirements, and guaranted access to benefits and continued participation during job absences such as maternity leave. This provision gave women who take leave from their jobs for child-rearing the same rights as men who leave for military service. Another bill I introduced would have given a two-year tax credit to employers who hired displaced homemakers—women forced back into the workplace because they had divorced or because their husbands had died. But the bills went nowhere.

I was not alone in my frustration. My female colleagues had bills of their own. For example, Pat Schroeder of Colorado had one on civil-service pension equity that was also gathering dust. Another of Pat's bills, to help former military spouses receive retirement and survivor benefits, did become law. Other colleagues' bills on day care, alimony and child support, and nondiscrimination in insurance languished in committees. We had to get them moving.

So in March 1983, we again introduced our bills, this time as one major piece of legislation—the Women's Economic Equity Act—with significant improvements in the separate bills that were its components. The package included my two previous bills on private-pension equity and on tax credits for employers of homemakers forced back into the workplace, and a third to provide Individual Retirement Accounts (IRAs) for homemakers. Other provisions called for tax relief for single heads of households, whose incomes were usually low and family expenses high; civil-service pension reform to aid wives and widows in receiving their spouses' retirement benefits; tax credits for child- and elderly-dependent care and funds for community child-care information and referral services; nondiscrimination in insurance; elimination of federal rules and regulations that hampered women in business; and a fairer system of child-support enforcement, recognizing that both parents have a financial responsibility for their child's welfare.

We knew our package would not pass in its entirety, but its many parts would attract publicity and make it easier to pass at least some of them. Though the Republicans were the majority in the Senate, they knew about the gender-gap vote, too, and knew they had to reach out to women. And so we worked with members of the Senate to introduce the package in that body at the same time.

As a result, legislation spearheaded by Barbara Mikulski to require insurance companies to base premiums and benefits on factors other than sex was debated fully in committee. Although we lost, the debate was nevertheless a first step toward greater public awareness of the inequity of current insurance practices.

On other fronts we were more immediately successful. Barbara Mikulski was able to create a child-care information and referral services program. A modified version of Pat Schroeder's civil-service pension reform proposal gained approval during the final weeks of that Congress. Barbara Kennelly's bill to insure the availability of child-support enforcement assistance to all families who request it became law on August 16, 1984. And a week later so did my private pension reform legislation, following a herculean effort by my friend Bill Clay, chairman of the House Education and Labor Subcommittee on Labor-Management Relations, who had hurried my bill to the floor so that it could pass while I was still a member of Congress. President Reagan signed my pension-equity bill into law on August 23.

But let no one think winning came easily. My pension-equity legislation had been signed three and a half years after I introduced it, a time loss that somewhat muted my gratification. It would be muted even further when Republican commercials during the presidential campaigns would give credit to their members of Congress for all of our initiatives!

Not all the women in Congress worked as a team, of course. And more than once I got the Republican women annoyed at me. Under President Carter, the women who joined the Congresswomen's Caucus—Democrats and Republicans—had spoken in one voice on women's issues, regardless of party affiliations. We had to be united to be effective because our caucus rules called for the unanimous consent of all the members before any policy statement could be issued. And mostly we did agree.

After Reagan's election, however, many Republican women didn't bother to join the caucus at all, and some of those who did voted along straight party lines. So much for unanimous consent. But then, it's always easier to stay on the right side of your party,

and several of the Republican women suddenly forgot their gender to align themselves with Reagan's popularity—and his de-
structive and heartless budget proposals that hurt the very
constituency we in the caucus were supposed to be guarding. I
was angry with many of the Republican women, especially Margaret (Peggy) Heckler, who, as cochair of the caucus, vetoed
whatever criticism the caucus leveled at her President's policies.

Several of us were dismayed. The Congresswomen's Caucus
had become powerless. We needed numbers to effect change, and
the solution was simple. In 1981, we opened the caucus to men,
inviting those whose stand on the issues was the same as ours to
join us. The caucus was renamed the Congressional Caucus for
Women's Issues, and over a hundred and twenty-five qualified
men eventually joined, making the new caucus the biggest single
group and one of the most influential in the House. You don't
have to a be a woman to dislike discrimination. Most men do,
too.

In fact, by 1981 the balance of sexual power was shifting.
The gender gap began to show itself, and both male and female
members of Congress started using it as leverage. I was always
fascinated by the internal political process in Congress, the lobbying for favorite legislation, the trade-offs, the jockeying for plum
committee assignments. You had to learn to play the game in
order to be effective. With the 1982 elections looming, we women
members of Congress were suddenly in great demand as our male
colleagues asked us to campaign for them in their home districts.
I was happy to oblige—in exchange for backup on legislation. I
went out to Orange County, California, for Jerry Patterson to
speak with him at a women's event. I campaigned in Connecticut
for Bill Ratchford, in Oklahoma for Michael Synar, and in South
Dakota for Tom Daschle. In return I got their support for my bill
on Flexitime, a bill that allowed federal employees to fill their
required forty-hour work weeks with various alternate schedules
to better accommodate the needs of their families. When Congress passed the bill in July 1982, I was delighted.

But still many of the Republican women persisted in supporting Reagan's budget proposals, and in 1982 I found myself in
the ironic position of stumping for men against women. In Massachusetts I went all out for Congressman Barney Frank against
Congresswoman Margaret Heckler, both of whom were incumbents

running for the same seat because of redistricting. Their differences, however, were more than biological. The Reagan budget was a woman's issue. By that I mean that though the budget hurt all middle-income and poor Americans, the cuts fell disproportionately on programs that affected women: eighty-eight percent of the recipients of Aid For Dependent Children were women, as were sixty-nine percent of those getting subsidized housing, and sixty-one percent of those on Medicaid.

Peggy had voted for the budget. Barney had voted against it. It was that simple. I even made a television commercial for Barney, saying he cared more about the issues concerning women in this country than Peggy did. I did the same, though not as intensely, in the New Jersey Senate race between Democrat Frank Lautenberg and Republican Millicent Fenwick, who was a colleague in Congress. Millicent's record was better than Peggy's, but still she had voted for most of the Reagan policies that hurt women. I couldn't forgive that—and thankfully, neither could the voters.

But the Republican women, it turned out, couldn't forgive me. During the lame-duck session of Congress after the 1982 elections, the sparks flew one night in the Members Dining Room. I was having dinner, as I often did, with my Democratic colleagues Barbara Mikulski, Barbara Kennelly, Mary Rose Oakar, Lindy Boggs, and Pat Schroeder. Twelve feet away at another table was Millicent Fenwick. And she let me have it.

"What you did to Peggy Heckler was a disgrace," Millicent called out loudly, never mentioning my involvement in her own race.

I didn't want to make a public scene, so I got up and went over to her table. "I'm sorry you feel that way," I said quietly to Millicent. "But I feel strongly about this President and his policies. I thought Peggy was wrong and I had every intention of speaking out about it."

Millicent bristled. "We'll do that against you someday," she threatened.

That seemed fair enough. "I would expect you to if you didn't agree with me," I said and went back to my table.

It was a good exchange. Millicent is very much a lady but extremely frank. And so am I.

I believed—and believe—strongly in the Democratic Party,

in its principles and ideals. No one will ever be able to persuade me that the Republicans have more compassion, more sense of fair play, more commitment to rewarding an honest day's work.

But if the Democrats were to get Reagan out of office in 1984, we needed to smooth out our differences and develop a comprehensive agenda. To that end, I accepted as many party appointments as came my way, serving on the Committee for Party Effectiveness chaired by the late Gillis Long of Louisiana from 1981 to 1984; the Commission on Presidential Nominations chaired by Governor James Hunt of North Carolina in 1981 and 1982; and, as Secretary of the Democratic Caucus, served as House liaison to the National Party Conference in June 1982.

These assignments were not glamorous ones, but the work was essential to unify and strengthen the Democratic Party. For the Committee for Party Effectiveness, I headed the task force on women, which drafted a comprehensive Democratic position paper covering every women's economic issue from pensions to the budget to child care. Reagan's anti-women policies were becoming a hot political topic. Our roundup of the disproportionate economic beating women were taking in the Reagan economy gave the Democratic candidates running for office in 1982 much of the ammunition they would need to court the gender-gap vote.

We did the same, though on a much broader scale, for the Democratic Party task force reports that came out of our Party's mid-term conference in June 1982. We had to. Out of all the panels set up to draft the Democratic Party's position on a range of issues from the environment to defense, there was to be no panel on women's issues. A panel on women, Democratic National Committee Chairman Chuck Manatt told me, would necessitate panels for other minorities, such as the blacks and gays. I thought that was shortsighted: the gender-gap vote could make all the difference in the presidential elections of 1984. And besides, we weren't a minority!

Instead, my colleagues and I made sure that the task force reports would include the unique impact of each issue on women. We drafted the additional language, tried to be represented on as many panels as possible, and—where that proved unrealistic—dispatched someone to incorporate our specific points into the reports. And we were successful. In what became known as the

Women's Agenda, every Democratic position paper published in the subsequent report included the concerns of women.

The bigger challenge would come from my appointment to the Hunt Commission in 1981, a seventy-member commission set up after our loss in 1980 to review our presidential delegate selection rules. Reform was critical. In the last decade, grass roots Party members had replaced elected officials as delegates to the nominating convention. In 1980, the Democratic Convention had been a disaster, the delegates splintering into factions while Ted Kennedy challenged Jimmy Carter for the nomination right up to the very bitter end. While the country watched on national television, the Convention had been torn apart by Democrats fighting Democrats, with the Kennedy challenge erupting into twenty-three Kennedy-supported minority planks fought out on the convention floor. The Convention—and the Democratic Party—was a shambles.

We couldn't allow it to happen again. Elected officials had to be brought back as delegates into the convention process. We needed professional legislators who were used to working with different constituencies, who had experience in implementing legislation, who would be involved in the development of the 1984 Democratic Platform and would therefore back it. But how to reintroduce elected officials as delegates, most of whom were white males, without alienating our grass roots constituencies, without upsetting the hard-fought-for "equal division" rules for women and affirmative action for minorities, which had been mandated after the 1976 Convention.

We created a new category of convention delegates called "add-ons" or "super-delegates," elected officials who would come to the convention uncommitted to any delegate. And for the next five months I would meet with all the various factions in the party to strike a compromise between just how many super-delegates there would be, and how the division would break down along minority and gender lines. Everybody had his—or her—interest to defend.

Though Mondale hadn't declared his candidacy, he was planning to run. He wanted as many super-delegates as possible to come to the convention from Congress, the Senate, and other elected offices. The number John Reilly, who was representing Fritz, put into the negotiations was thirty percent. These were people who knew Fritz, who had worked with him when he was a Senator and Vice President, and whose support he felt he could count on.

He was right. As it turned out, Fritz went to the Convention with 166 out of the 200 super-delegates eventually chosen from the House and Senate.

Kennedy was also in the running at the time, but he was against any super-delegates, as he didn't want to give Mondale that number of built-in supporters. Tip O'Neill, on the other hand, wanted at least two-thirds of the Democrats in Congress to be included as super-delegates, a number I thought too high. I was worried about a rerun of the 1980 Convention experience, where many of the delegates from Congress did not appear, and made for a poor showing of support. Meanwhile minorities and women were protesting loudly that the addition of super-delegates would diminish the strength they'd just won. Given the underrepresentation of women and minorities among the ranks of elected officials, equal division—and therefore equal representation—would be impossible.

I refused to give up. And at the final meeting of the Hunt Commission at the Shoreham Hotel in Washington in March 1982, I sold what became known as the "Ferraro Plan." The super-delegates would constitute fourteen percent of the total delegate count. Up to three-fifths of the House and Senate members would be attending the Convention in that category. Equal division for women and affirmative action for minorities was endorsed but not mandated among the super-delegates, although every effort would be made to attain it. And it would still be required of every state delegation. The job was done.

The *Washington Post* called my solution "a personal victory for a little-known member of the House." But I didn't care if I was known or not. What mattered was that we were on our way back to being a united, strong party. Ferraro "is a bridge between the new and old politics and between the feminists and the organization Democrats," my colleague on the compromise, Mark Siegel, said to the *Washington Post*. "And she's tough enough to take them all on." I liked that bit.

After my reelection in 1982, I set my sights on a seat on the powerful House Budget Committee, which sets the target of funding for every program that comes before Congress and frames the debate on spending priorities for each proposal. Budget would be not only an important position but an educational one, a challenging addition to Public Works and Aging. Members of the Budget Committee commanded the attention of a wide range of constituencies, since Budget deals with every issue before Congress. The committee heard testimony from such people as David Stockman, then director of the Office of Management and Budget, Secretary of Defense Caspar Weinberger and the Joint Chiefs of Staff, advocating such matters as a higher allocation of funding for defense, to Marian Wright Edelman, head of the Children's Defense Fund, talking about hunger in America because of our distorted defense budget priorities. It was here that I would be able to speak up on behalf of the people in my district and state on issues such as housing and transportation—and, I hoped, put a strong and Democratic imprint on what would be a fair allocation of resources to the citizens of this country.

My chances of getting elected to Budget, however, were slim. There were already two Democratic members from New York on the committee, and no other state had more than two. In fact, with fifteen members on the committee altogether, most states didn't have any representatives at all. But so what? I'd faced odds like that all my life. I used the fact that there was no Democratic woman member on the committee as an argument for my bid. The nominations for Democratic seats on all the House committees are made by the Steering and Policy Committee. As Secretary of the Democratic Caucus I was automatically a member of that committee and so had a slight edge in gathering votes.

But eight Democratic members wanted the four openings on Budget. So I campaigned for the seat the way the guys did. I swapped votes with other Steering and Policy members who wanted me to vote for them or their candidates' appointments to various committees. I lobbied other Democratic members, because Budget committee assignments must be voted on by the full Democratic Caucus. I pointed out that I had paid my dues on the Commission on Presidential Nominations and at the National Party Conference, and that women deserved to be represented in the highest echelons of Congress.

"Do you think it's appropriate to promote yourself as a woman?" one member asked me.

"It's just as appropriate as male members asking me to campaign for them in their districts *because* I am a woman," I replied.

The campaigning was fun. I've always loved a fair fight. What I didn't anticipate was the totally unexpected offer that was about to come my way.

"Gerry, I'd like to have lunch with you," came the call in December 1982 from John Reilly, Mondale's alter ego and top political adviser. I was surprised. I had worked with Reilly on the Hunt Commission—he was one of the members for Mondale— but I didn't know him well.

"Gerry, you know Fritz and I think very highly of you, as do many others," Reilly said over dessert in the Members Dining Room. "He's getting organized to run now and we'd like you to be national chair of his campaign."

I was momentarily speechless, a rare condition for me. Here was another door opening, another opportunity coming my way. But this time I resisted.

I really wanted Budget. I had been working and traveling nonstop for candidates in the mid-term election for months. I had just stood for reelection in my district (winning, with seventy-three percent of the vote). And I had to think of my family. With all the traveling I'd have to do as national chair for Mondale, I would hardly be home at all. Besides, with the election two years away, it seemed too early to make a commitment, not only to a candidate but to such demands on my time.

"Let me think about it and get back to you," I said to Reilly, who was pressing me.

"We really want you," he said.

I called my husband John, who reinforced my reluctance. "Think about it," he said. "You're probably going to get Budget. You've just been reelected. This job's going to involve a lot of traveling, and I really would like you home." I wanted to be home, too. I missed my family. For all the challenge of my congressional work and the energy I put into it, I was lonely in Washington and looked forward to returning to Queens on weekends.

When I had first gone down to Washington in 1979 I had

rented a one-room efficiency apartment near the Hill and furnished the living room–bedroom with two trundle beds. When
John and the kids came down, I figured, we could turn the apartment into wall-to-wall beds for the night. But after several attempts to sleep through the night on the sporadic visits John
made to Washington, he had given up. "I'm just not used to
sleeping with a refrigerator in the bedroom," he finally confessed.
"You're absolutely right." I laughed, because I wasn't sleeping
well either. It was the cheap kind of refrigerator that thumped on
and off all night long, practically shaking the apartment. And
promptly at seven every morning, church bells that could be
heard all over Capitol Hill pealed right outside my window.

When another apartment became available, I moved to a
bigger place with a separate bedroom, which I furnished from a
discount store in North Carolina. My mother-in-law made cur-
tains and dust ruffles for the bed out of matching sheets, the kids
donated some posters they'd gotten sick of in their dorm rooms,
and I brought down a stereo they had outgrown. It was a slightly
quieter apartment, but in the four years of Reagan's stay in the
White House, John was there only twice. With a Republican
President, our invitations had just about ceased. And besides,
while my professional life, for three days a week anyway, was in
Washington, John's was in New York. Our two older children
were away at college, but Laura was still living at home. For
twelve years John had been a one-man car pool, driving the kids
to school every day in Manhattan on his way to work. And he
still was.

If it weren't for John, I could never, ever have accomplished
what I did. He was always the Rock of Gibraltar for me and
countless people and causes who turned to him over the years. I
never saw him say no to anyone who needed help—and this
without taking credit or needing the spotlight.

In spite of all my obligations, he never complained. Not only
that, but when I was making the political rounds in Queens, he
would come with me from place to place, night after night, without a word. At one point I was so exhausted that I said to him, "I
just can't go tonight." That should have been music to his ears,
but John always had my priorities straight. John certainly didn't
need to go, but he said, "Come on, Gerry. You've got to do it,"
he urged me. "Let's go." And we went.

Men in public life have always had that kind of quiet support from their wives. But in the new world of two-career couples, not all husbands have the security and self-confidence to back their wives all the way. John did. He never let me down, or the kids. He was our foundation, and the kids and I adored him.

It was a family worth coming home to, and I tried to keep to a strict schedule, heading down to Washington on Tuesday morning for the votes that were usually recorded midweek, then heading back to New York late Thursday to work in Queens. When the kids had a school function, I added another round trip. Often John and I would be the only two-parent team at whatever recital or French play was being presented, even though we barely understood a word. But it was important to me, very important, to be there for my children and not let my job interfere.

Sometimes things got crazy. John and I shared the swings around colleges with John, Jr., taking him to visit twelve colleges the summer before his senior year. Other times, I overcompensated. When it was Laura's turn for the college tour, I flew back through ten time zones from a congressional visit to Japan to chauffeur her around. Between the sixth and seventh colleges I momentarily dozed off at the wheel. Laura screamed. I jerked awake as the car hit the shoulder of the road. After that, I took a friend along to share the driving.

The kids often came down to Washington during their summer vacations. All of them worked at some point on the Hill, which was a lot of fun for me. One day when I was chairing the session, Laura, who was working as a summer congressional page, came onto the floor. I didn't know she was there until another page delivered a note from her: "Lookin' good," it read. John, Jr. probably had the best summer, when one of the Hill softball teams discovered his skill with a bat. He came home only to sleep, but that was all right. I loved the company.

I never entertained in the apartment. That's what you did at home, and our home was in New York. There wasn't even any food in the refrigerator you could actually eat except for some orange juice, maybe a frozen dinner or two, and a bottle of wine. Normally I worked late in my office, until ten or so, or went out to grab a hamburger with my colleagues, and then returned to the apartment to watch the eleven p.m. news before bed. What was there for me to go home to unless my husband and children were there? An empty apartment. And I hated being alone.

I'd had enough of that as a child. I was well taken care of and had friends at the boarding school I was sent to, but it wasn't the same. I never showed anyone how lonely I felt. I did what I had to do and I got through it. But the memories remained, and even as an adult I didn't like being away from home and my family.

In Congress, I buried myself in work. On any given day, there were several committee hearings going on and legislation being debated on the floor. There were also constituents and legislators to meet, my own committee work to do, volumes of mail to answer, and votes to record. When I had first gone down to Washington, I worried about how each vote I cast would be accepted back home. I was from a conservative district in Queens, and often my conscience conflicted with my obligation to be sensitive to those I represented. My support for the gay-rights bill, for example, might have been upsetting to my constituents, but to me gay-rights is a matter of civil rights. So I worked out a compromise with myself. When I was asked to cosponsor the gay-rights bill, I declined, not wanting to enflame my constituents. But had it come to a vote, I would have supported it as a matter of conscience. It was important for me to vote for what I thought was right, despite political risks, but there was no need to be provocative about it.

Like other members of Congress, I received numerous speaking requests. I accepted as many of them as I could. One of my favorites was A Presidential Classroom for Young Americans, the high school program my daughter Donna had attended, which was designed to show students the processes of government first-hand. Sometimes these meetings, held on the floor of the House before the House went into session, became lessons in sexism as well.

At one, I opened the floor to questions. Immediately the lines in front of the microphones were filled with boys. Since there wasn't time to hear all the questions, I moved up two girls so that they would have a chance, too. As I was walking out later, one of the young women came up to me and said, "You must not believe in the ERA, because if you do you didn't treat the boys fairly."

I shook my head. "Until men and women treat each other fairly because it's the *right* thing to do, you're going to have to force them to treat each other fairly," I said.

"But that's discrimination," the young woman protested.

"No, it's not," I said firmly. "That's affirmative action."

We were seeing the results of inbred discrimination ourselves in Congress. For all that my female colleagues and I had achieved, we still had to do more, work harder, and produce more to be judged the same as men. The double standard continued to exist not only for us but for women in any profession to which women were new. In the very male and highly competitive world of politics, however, the stakes were very high.

There was power involved, money, influence, winners—and losers. Women were not supposed to be able to play in such a high-stakes arena, let alone succeed. A board game my staff gave me for Christmas one year summed up the double standard in politics. One square read: "You're twice as qualified as your opponent. You've worked twice as hard. The two of you are now dead even. Move to his square." And move I did, regardless of the double effort it took. How else were women ever going to make a difference?

Women's voices were essential in government, and not because they were necessarily better than men or more caring or more effective. Rather, women added another dimension to the political process—one that was crucial. Instead of engaging in confrontation, women were more apt to negotiate, I learned from reading Carol Gilligan's book, *In a Different Voice*. Instead of looking at short-term solutions to problems, women were more apt to think in terms of generations to come. Instead of thinking in win-lose terms, women were more apt to consider the gray areas in between.

Just as minority members of Congress were sensitive to the issues affecting all minorities, or as those members who were veterans reflected the concerns of other veterans, women in Congress were sensitive to women's concerns. Tom Daschle of South Dakota had served in Vietnam, for example, and in Congress he led the fight to compensate others who had served there for their exposure to Agent Orange. Out of his own experience, Tom was highly aware of a problem others may have neglected, and so he tried to do something about it. Most of the women in Congress acted the same way.

Did I feel my presence in Congress made a difference? Definitely. Did I feel it was worth the sacrifice I had chosen to make in my family life? Yes again. Still, I did everything I could to minimize the separation. I spoke to my kids almost every day on the phone, and to my husband sometimes twice a day. And he was always such a comfort. When I am sometimes hotheaded and impulsive, John is patient and steady. During the twenty-five years we have been married, I have learned to value his support and his often very different perspective on decisions. He has never let me down, and I listened very carefully to his views on the offer I had just received from Walter Mondale to chair his presidential campaign. John and I had agreed that the timing wasn't right for either of us.

"I just wanted to make sure that's how you felt," I said to him over the phone.

John had given me personal advice. Now I went to Tip O'Neill for political advice. And he, too, advised me against signing up so early with Mondale. "You're going to have to give yourself totally to that campaign," he said as we sat on the empty Republican side of the House during a meeting of the Democratic Caucus. "National politics is very tough and so are the Mondale people. The only important thing to them is their candidate. If something goes wrong, they'll have you to blame. And there will be a long time for something to go wrong."

I would remember his prophetic words two years later. But now I took his advice. "Stall them," Tip suggested. "Say you can't make a decision like this now, that it's too early to see what the future holds." So I did.

I've never told anyone else about Mondale's offer. At the time I didn't want it to look as if I had turned Fritz down. And I didn't want whoever ended up as national chair (it was shared by Barbara Mikulski and New York's Charlie Rangel) to know that I had been asked first. My decision would have made great press had it been leaked: "Congresswoman Says No to Top Mondale Campaign Slot." But that wasn't me.

Instead I took the Mondale offer as a great compliment, relieved to get my career back on the track that I, and not others, had set. And I got the seat on Budget. But even stranger things were beginning to happen. Soon after I had lunch with Reilly, nearly two years before the presidential election, Gary Hart called me to have breakfast. He, too, had yet to declare his candidacy, but we all knew he was going to run. What did Hart want?

Our breakfast, back in the Members Dining Room again, was very relaxed, the talk mostly about the upcoming campaigns. Afterward my staff grilled me on our conversation. Did Hart say he was going to run? No. Did he ask you for your support? No.

But what he had asked me had stopped me cold. "What do you think of the idea of a woman as the vice-presidential candidate?" Hart had dropped his question casually at the end of the meal. Outwardly I didn't blink an eye, but inside I was shocked that the idea had even occurred to a potential presidential candidate.

WOMAN POWER

*"As Democrats, we are convinced that four more
years of Republican rule would be disastrous for women."*

—*presidential candidate's letter,
April 27, 1983.*

T HOUGH THE FINAL AN-
nouncement of a woman as the vice-presidential nominee seemed
almost apocalyptic, politically it made sense. No politician, especially a presidential candidate, makes such a choice without running the numbers, without weighing the regional pull a running
mate can bring in, without identifying the candidate's national—
and natural—constituency, who will be not only potential campaign contributors but deliver votes as well. And by 1984, the
writing on the political wall spelled out this dramatic new
possibility.

The potential power of the women's vote had been growing
steadily since the 1980 elections, when Reagan had drawn fifty-
six percent of the male vote but only forty-seven percent of the
vote from women. That spread of over six points in a national
election had happened only once before—when Eisenhower had
run against Stevenson. Equally important in 1980, for the first
time in history, more women had voted than had men. Overnight, it seemed, pollsters discovered a new voting bloc that voted
not only in greater numbers than men but differently from them.
And the gender gap was recognized.

The gender-gap theory picked up momentum in 1982, when

exit polls showed that more women voted for Democratic candidates than Republican, by a seventeen-point margin, and that more women had voted for a Democrat than had men in thirty-three of forty-four U.S. Senate and gubernatorial races. Indeed, three gubernatorial races were decided by the women's vote: James Blanchard by 6.8 percent in Michigan, Mark White by 7.6 percent in Texas, and Mario Cuomo by 3.2 percent in New York.

Not only were women emerging as a potential voting force, they were also running for office themselves. In 1971, Congress (House and Senate) had 15 women members, state legislatures had 362, and seven cities with populations of over 30,000 had women mayors. By 1983, the numbers had risen to 24 women in Congress, 992 in state legislatures, and 76 serving as their cities' mayors. In Florida alone, where NOW had actively recruited women candidates, the numbers of women in both legislative chambers had more than doubled. Not an overwhelming increase, to be sure, but a steady one.

Women's issues were also being pinpointed as separate from those of men. The disparities between the sexes were outrageous: in terms of financial equity—or inequity—a female college graduate could expect to earn in a lifetime the same amount as a man who had not finished eighth grade; and the female unemployment rate, at 10.3 percent, was the highest since the end of World War II.

Women's attitudes on the issues were also found to be different from men's, especially toward social policies, environmental concerns, and matters of war and peace. A 1982 Harris survey found that fifty-nine percent of women when asked how concerned they were about nuclear war replied "very," whereas only forty-eight percent of the men said the same. Women's disappointment in the Reagan Administration continued to grow. In a June 1983 *New York Times*/CBS News poll, a revealing spread of twenty-one percent separated Republican men's approval of Reagan's performance from that of Republican women.

The potential power of the women's vote was beginning to make the Republicans nervous. Soon after Reagan's election in 1980, a White House memo cautioned that the gender gap "could prove dangerous for Republicans in 1984." Reagan's staff took the polls seriously and worked to improve, if not overcome, his record with women. Shortly thereafter, in 1981, Sandra Day

O'Connor became the first woman appointed to the Supreme Court. And in 1983 Elizabeth Dole and Margaret Heckler joined the male members of the Reagan cabinet as Secretary of Transportation and Secretary of Health and Human Services respectively.

Not all the members of the Reagan Administration were so shrewd, however, and Republican policies continued to enrage women. Programs were being cut back or eliminated, ketchup was being substituted for vegetables in school lunches, the President was blaming trees for pollution, and Interior Secretary James Watt was describing the members of his coal commission as "a black, a woman, two Jews, and a cripple." Unbelievable. But there was more. When unemployment reached twelve percent during the recession, Reagan attributed part of the problem to the numbers of women in the labor force, ignoring—or maybe not even knowing—that many women were the sole support of their families. And moans instead of applause greeted the President when he offered the fifteen hundred delegates to the National Federation of Business and Professional Women's (BPW) Clubs what he took to be a compliment: "I happen to be one man who believes if it wasn't for women, us men would still be walking around in skin suits, carrying clubs."

Republican women, including the predominantly Republican members of the BPW, began to defect. Kathy Wilson, the Republican chair of the National Women's Political Caucus, even publicly called on Reagan to withdraw as a candidate for reelection. "Mr. Reagan, one term is enough," said Wilson. "As a matter of fact, it is entirely too much."

The women were quick to press their long-awaited political advantage. If the candidates wanted the women's vote, they were going to have to earn it. Coalitions of politically active women formed to determine who among the Democratic presidential candidates would best represent their concerns in the upcoming battle against Reagan. In April 1983, one of these groups, the Women's Presidential Project, sent an eleven-point questionnaire to each of the candidates, asking his position on every major women's issue, from employment to the military budget.

No fewer than one hundred and seventy women activists from forty-five states signed the statement, a diverse group that included Mary Tyler Moore and Shirley MacLaine, Coretta Scott

King and Shirley Chisholm, Sharon Percy Rockefeller and Gloria Steinem, and several of my colleagues, Barbara Mikulski, Barbara Boxer, Barbara Kennelly, Cardiss Collins, Katie Hall, and Pat Schroeder.

But I did not feel comfortable adding my signature as well. I agreed with them totally on the issues, of course. My problem was with their strategy. The questionnaire had gone on to imply that if the candidates did not immediately commit themselves to supporting the women's agenda, women might abandon the Democratic Party. "Whether women turn out, turn off, or turn elsewhere in the political spectrum depends on the choices and programs offered us," the presidential-candidate statement read. ". . . Otherwise, women may stay home on Election Day or be very selective in deciding where to direct our political energies."

Even the implication of withholding votes didn't seem right to me. I did not want any of the candidates to think for one minute that I would sit on the sidelines and not work for the Democratic ticket if the candidate wasn't one hundred percent with me on the issues. Obviously I wanted someone who shared my values to be chosen as the candidate, but I would have campaigned for any Democratic candidate who would run against Ronald Reagan. Even an imperfect candidate would be better than Reagan—that's how strongly I felt. So I didn't sign that letter.

Instead, a week later, I sent a letter to the candidates, signed by eight other female colleagues in Congress. I wrote that no Democratic presidential candidate could hope to win in 1984 without addressing issues of concern to women. What I wanted to do was move beyond confrontational politics toward strategies that would unite and win. "We are here to needle you, to remind you, to provide you with information, to work with you to address the pressing issues confronting the female majority of our population—confronting all of us," I wrote. "As Democrats, we are convinced that four more years of Republican rule would be disastrous for women."

Because members of Congress were now guaranteed delegate spots at the Convention, the candidates actively sought our support. I chose to remain neutral. But the candidates wouldn't take neutrality for an answer. A full eighteen months before the election, they were already pressuring the members of Congress for their individual support. I had to duck all of them, remaining a one-person nonaligned nation. (Later I found out that had I given any endorsement, I would not have been eligible for the position of Platform Chair.)

Certain candidates were less attractive than others, of course. Reuben Askew was on the wrong side of the abortion issue, which would have made it hard for me to campaign for him. And though Jesse Jackson had not yet declared, I would have had difficulty with his candidacy. I didn't agree with his views on recognition of an independent Palestinian state—and neither did the Democratic Party.

Fritz Hollings was acceptable to me as a candidate. He had a good sense of humor and was probably the best speaker of the lot. More important, he was talking seriously about how to deal with the budget deficit. Alan Cranston was also appealing. Long before it became a matter of popular discussion, Cranston was talking about the importance of stopping the insane arms race. He expressed the concerns of every caring individual in this country on how we deal with the Soviet Union, based on his own extensive discussions with senior-ranking members of the Soviet military.

Gary Hart was also acceptable. Though he too had yet to declare, we all knew he was going to run. And I liked him. I had participated in a weekend meeting he had organized in South Carolina in January 1983 on international trade policy and had found him to be insightful and very much in control of the meeting. In his debates he had articulated the basic principles and ideals of the Democratic Party, but he had done so in a refreshing way that appealed to the young people of the nation. In fact, he had written a book in 1983, *A New Democracy,* which was his search for a vision that would preserve the Party's commitment to social concerns without the old dependence on big government and regulation. His ideas had a lot of appeal to those who were looking for a way to translate the values of the past into a program that was workable. And of course there was George McGovern, who had run in 1972 and whose views I respected.

I felt the most comfortable with Mondale, and if I had had to declare my support, I probably would have gone with him then. I had known him longest. And though all the candidates were addressing the issues that concerned me, he alone had experience in the White House. He could step right into the Presidency.

Mondale had even been prepared to discuss the revolutionary possibility of a woman vice-presidential candidate in July 1983 at the National Women's Political Caucus, I found out later from one of his advisers, Carol Tucker Foreman. The night before he was to be questioned by the NWPC's delegates panel, his staff had told him to expect a question on whether he would consider a woman as a running mate. "Of course I would," he had decided to respond. "I'm going to take the most qualified person to be my running mate." If there were a follow-up question asking Mondale just what "persons" he considered qualified, Carol had suggested that he name a few women, one of whom was former Congresswoman Barbara Jordan. But Mondale had quashed that idea immediately, not wanting anyone to think he had already made up a list.

Overnight, however, he had obviously thought about it a great deal. "I'm going to say that there are women sitting on this stage who are qualified. By mentioning people who are sitting right behind me I won't run into the problem of 'you've made a list,' " he said to Carol in the elevator on his way to the meeting. "You know: 'I've worked with Eleanor Holmes Norton. I've worked with Patsy Mink. I know they're qualified.' "

But Mondale, it turned out, had been more prepared to go the whole mile on the concept of a woman Vice President than were the women themselves. Though he was all set to prove his sincerity by actually mentioning names of women he considered qualified to be Vice President during his presidential review, the question never came up. It was too bold, the NWPC delegates had decided, to press Mondale on just which women he had in mind for the job. They preferred to rest with his already epic promise simply to consider a woman as a running mate. And so they lowered their sights and asked him whether he planned to appoint women to his cabinet in the more powerful roles of Secretary of Defense or of State rather than to the posts of Health and Human Services and Transportation currently held by the Republican women.

At least Mondale got the chance to give the answer he had prepared for the tougher question: "Yes, there are qualified women sitting right here on the stage." And he named them.

Beyond Mondale's obvious appeal as a candidate for women, his gut reaction to the issues and his views were very similar to mine, whether it was Central America, our relationship with the Soviet Union, the environment, or the necessity of reducing the budget deficit. And I liked him personally as well, having worked with him as Deputy National Chair for the Carter-Mondale reelection campaign in 1980. I thought he would be a strong candidate to take on Ronald Reagan.

But who did I think would ultimately win the Democratic nomination? John Glenn. He seemed at the time to have everything going for him: he was a moderate, was strong on social and women's issues, came from the Midwest, had some celebrity as an astronaut, and could pull crowds. In 1982, Bob Torricelli, running for Congress in New Jersey, had asked John Glenn to campaign for him in his district. A reception was organized for Labor Day—a terrible time for any political event because nearly everybody is on the beach. Knowing this, Bob had rented a small place, expecting to sell maybe two hundred tickets. But a huge crowd had turned up instead, paid the full price, and then hung around outside just to see Glenn. The people loved him.

I was looking forward to meeting Glenn myself. In the ongoing parade of presidential candidates, all six who had announced (no Jackson or McGovern yet) were scheduled to appear before the Democratic Caucus in the House of Representatives starting in July 1983. The candidates had drawn slots for the scheduling, and on July 13, the first two went to Mondale and Glenn. The meetings were closed to the press, to provide a more informal question-and-answer period so that the uncommitted members of the caucus could evaluate their potential candidates.

When, as secretary of the caucus, I had had coffee with Glenn before the meeting, he continued to live up to my expectations as the probable candidate. There was only one problem I wanted him to clear up. Later, in the Cannon House Caucus Room, I took the microphone to ask him to explain his Senate vote supporting Reagan's tax- and budget-slashing proposals, cutting services to the poor, to children, to students, to women, and to the elderly.

"If you are the candidate for the Democratic party, how can I go back to the same areas where I campaigned against women candidates in 1982 who voted as you did and justify supporting you and not them?" I asked Glenn.

"What do you mean?" Glenn asked.

"You voted for the President's budget," I reminded him.

A pause. "Specifically what are you saying?" Glenn finally said, looking more flustered by the moment.

I repeated my question, this time referring to the budget as Gramm-Latta, which it had been called in the House.

"I'll get back to you on that," Glenn said to me on his way out the door.

But the damage had been done. "If he can't answer this question here, how is he going to deal with the whole thing in the presidential race?" read a note slipped to me by Congressman Dan Glickman of Kansas.

And, of course, someone leaked Glenn's performance to the press: "Glenn Said to Fumble Budget Issue in Caucus" was the headline on the story the *New York Times* ran the next day.

I felt terrible. Glenn could have solved the whole problem simply by saying: "I voted for all kinds of amendments to correct the package, an opportunity we had in the Senate but which you didn't in the House." That would have satisfied me and other members of Congress as well. Then I could have gone out to campaign for him with a clear conscience, explaining that Glenn had tried, that he had voted for every single amendment that would have made a difference for women and the poor, but when the amendments hadn't passed, he had gone with the package as a minority member in the Senate.

My question had had an effect I had never expected, but Glenn did fumble it. It was a very embarrassing moment for both of us. And when Fritz Mondale followed Glenn in front of the caucus, he stopped on his way into the room and quipped, "Do me a favor and don't ask me any questions, Gerry."

In and out of Congress, women were continuing to play an increasingly large role in the selection and election of the Democratic presidential candidates. At the NOW national conference in October 1983, once more the Democratic candidates—Mondale, Glenn, Hollings, Cranston, Hart (Askew was not present), and now McGovern—faced a panel of women. And once more the women's agenda was put to each one of them. This time all the questions were asked: How would you feel about choosing a woman as a running mate? What is your stand on women's issues? How visible would these issues be in your campaign? What roles could women expect to play?

With about a quarter of a million members nationally, NOW was an influential power base no candidate could choose to ignore. Against the spectre of four more years of Ronald Reagan, Walter Mondale was becoming the favorite son. Two months after its fall conference, the previously nonpartisan NOW would endorse him for the Presidency, the first presidential endorsement the seventeen-year-old organization had ever made.

The endorsement was startling enough in itself. But at the October conference, Judy Goldsmith, then president of NOW, had called for an even more startling move. No longer would the dreams of a woman Vice President be confined to the hope chests of women activists. It was time to take that dream public.

"There are those who have said that the country is not yet ready for a woman Vice President, a seriously questionable assumption," Judy said. "What, we ask, are we waiting for? Women are ready now; the time for a woman vice-presidential candidate is 1984." With one sentence, the call for a woman vice-presidential candidate had become a matter of public record.

Not missing a beat, Mary Stanley, the Republican Task Force chair of the NWPC from California, had privately printed up a bunch of women–for–Vice-President buttons to give the concept some political razzmatazz. And they started popping up at the NOW conference: Mikulski for VP, Schroeder for VP, Boggs for VP, Feinstein for VP, Griffiths for VP, and me—with my name spelled "Farraro" instead of "Ferraro." Shows how well known I was at the time.

I thought the whole idea was great and bought a complete set of the buttons to show my future grandchildren. But I didn't take it as seriously as many of the other women did, even when women did well in the November 1983 elections. Both Kathy Whitmire and Dianne Feinstein were reelected as the mayors, of Houston and San Francisco, respectively. And Martha Layne Collins was voted in as the first woman governor of Kentucky. Quick to pick up the trend, influential labor leader Victor Gotbaum urged the leading candidate, Mondale, to go with a woman. At the same time my name started cropping up as a dark horse vice-presidential possibility in the New York *Daily News* and the *New York Times*.

But that's just what I considered myself—a dark horse. These were my hometown papers, after all. The other vice-presidential possibilities were probably getting as much play in their local papers. The press had been having fun with the woman vice-presidential theme for some time. "Madame Vice President" was the title of one of the first articles, running in August 1983 in *The Washingtonian* magazine.

A groundswell for a woman on the ticket was beginning to build, delighting the pollsters who now had something new to test on the public. Gallup, Harris, *New York Times*/CBS, even political analyst David Garth started testing the voters' waters. And the responses buoyed the women's hopes while startling old-time pols. Would a woman on the ticket (A) not affect your vote, (B) make you more likely to support the ticket, (C) make you less likely? the pollsters asked. And the answers to all the polls were remarkably consistent. The biggest chunk, in the good old American way, said that a woman on the ticket would make no difference at all. But there were always more who said they would feel positively about such a ticket than negatively. "Both parties should give serious consideration to naming a woman as their vice-presidential candidate," the Garth Analysis had found. ". . . The party that first taps the potential support for a female national candidate could reap important dividends, especially in a close election."

Politics is a game of numbers. The numbers are in the votes. As many as nine million more women than men were expected to vote in the 1984 presidential election. The gender-gap weapon was growing.

WHY ME?

"You will win big in '84."

—*fortune cookie, November 1983.*

O UT OF ALL THE VICE-presidential possibilities, why did the nomination come home to Queens?

My first clue came on July 19, 1983—exactly a year before I accepted the nomination in San Francisco—when I received an unexpected letter from Tom Foglietta, member of Congress from Philadelphia. It read, in part: "Although the 1984 presidential election is more than fifteen months away, the attention of the American people is already focused on the Democratic Party. . . . [Since] the vice-presidency has become, increasingly, a position of significant responsibility, . . . I believe we must move beyond the current practice of waiting until the national convention to seriously discuss candidates for the second-highest office of our nation. . . . Your presence on the ticket would provide the party and the country with [a candidate] who can speak to the majority of the population in a way that no other major party candidate has ever been able to do before."

I was flattered by Tom's consideration, but I dismissed the idea.

Even though "The time is right—the time is now" had become the familiar rallying cry of those promoting a woman on the ticket, I thought it would never happen.

My next clue came in November 1983, when my administrative assistant, Eleanor Lewis, asked me to have dinner with a small group of women I had come to know in Washington. They wanted to discuss my political future with me, Eleanor said. What a compliment. In the highly competitive world of politics, anyone taking an interest in anyone else's career is more than welcome. It was the form of their interest that was surprising.

"You will win big in '84," read the prophecy inside my fortune cookie that night over our order-in Chinese meal in an apartment on Connecticut Avenue. The other fortune cookies were just as loaded: "You will meet a man in San Francisco and travel with him," read one, referring to the upcoming Democratic Convention eight months away. Still another carried the message: "You will move into a big gray house on a hill," meaning the Naval Observatory, where the Vice President lives.. What had been going on behind my back?

A lot, it turned out. While I had been going about my own business, this group of five politically active women had meticulously been going through the records and backgrounds of every possible woman vice-presidential candidate—and decided I was the surest shot. One by one they had knocked out my congressional colleagues: Mary Rose Oakar from Ohio and Lindy Boggs from Louisiana because they were both antichoice; Pat Schroeder of Colorado because she came from the middle of the country, as did both Mondale and Hart; Barbara Kennelly of Connecticut because she was in her first term; and Barbara Mikulski of Maryland because—I don't know why. Mikulski, who stands just under five feet tall, later became fond of saying that I got the nomination because of five inches.

Looking outside Congress, the group had ruled out Martha Layne Collins, governor of Kentucky, because she was a newcomer, while San Francisco mayor Dianne Feinstein, they felt, had less foreign policy experience than I and no national exposure. They had arrived at their choice of me, I found out later, by tacking descriptive clauses onto our names. My clauses evidently had nothing overtly problematic: "Ferraro: Italian-American; three-term congresswoman; married and the mother of three; friend of labor, the elderly, and women; respected by House leadership; East Coast blue collar; conservative ethnic constituency." I could have been anyone's colleague, sister, or daughter, they reasoned. By those criteria, I was in their eyes the most acceptable woman vice-presidential candidate.

This group of five women, who called themselves "Team A," probably had as much to do with my nomination as any single group. And I never knew the half of it. Ranging from Joan McLean, a staffer of the House Committee on Banking, to Joanne Howes, the executive director of the bipartisan Women's Vote Project, the core group also included Nanette Falkenberg, executive director of the National Abortion Rights Action League; Millie Jeffrey, labor activist; and my own senior staff member, Eleanor Lewis. Later their number would grow to seven, absorbing "Team B": Joanne Symons, political director of the American Nurses Association, and Ranny Cooper, the executive director of Ted Kennedy's Fund for a Democratic Majority.

The story of this small group of women has never been told.

They had twin goals, Team A said to me that first night over our Chinese dinner. The first was to create the strongest possible ticket to defeat Ronald Reagan. That sat fine with me. The second was to become my personal political-advocacy group in return for my cooperation in advancing the concept of a female Vice President. That sat fine with me, too. Then they threw in the hook. There was no point in advancing the concept if there weren't a viable candidate. Would I stay open to the idea of becoming the actual nominee if the concept caught fire?

I was both flabbergasted and flattered. After all, in many instances these women knew more about what was going on in Washington than I did. They were plugged into the feminist network far more than I was and were well connected to numerous political organizations around the country. They were friends. They were savvy. They were brilliant political tacticians. And they believed that if Reagan could be beaten at all, it would happen only with a woman on the Democratic ticket. Was I willing to be the hypothetical woman?

I had to think fast. There was no doubt that my being considered for the vice-presidency was very appealing. It could help all women in politics, which mattered a lot to me after my own experiences. For all the ground we had gained, we still had much farther to go. If we saw this idea through, we could always use it after the election as a bargaining chip for cabinet posts or other positions high in the government. And the possibility of a woman Vice President would lend excitement to the Democratic campaign.

On the other hand, the actuality of getting the vice-presidential nomination continued to seem very farfetched to me and out of reach. But I had learned my lesson at the National Women's Political Caucus four months before, and this time I kept those thoughts to myself. I was not about to throw cold water on these women, who were offering their remarkable talent, energy, and very valuable support.

Of course I was willing, I told them, putting my vice-presidential "fortune" in my wallet to keep as a souvenir. But the idea still seemed off the wall to me. "I can't believe what we just talked about," I confided to Eleanor on our way home. "Am I the only woman in Washington who doesn't think a woman can get the vice-presidential nomination?"

Looking back, I can now see that the idea did make sense. Reagan had a commanding lead. There was a growing consensus that the Democrats could not hope to win with politics as usual. And the polls were beginning to show that a woman on the Democratic ticket really might make a difference.

Activist women's groups had already started to implement their strategy. Phase 1, Team A told me, was to convince the male-dominated media to take the concept of a woman Vice President seriously, to legitimize it for the public. That was turning out to be remarkably easy. Writers such as Jane O'Reilly at *Time* magazine and *Washington Post* columnist Judy Mann had begun to advance the idea in print, with no opposition from their editors. "They thought it was a nice story in a slow political year," Jane said. "They loved the idea of a woman candidate but were totally baffled when the concept turned out to be a real woman."

Phase 1 also involved gaining the support of influential public officials for the concept. And judging from just one week in September 1983, that was proving easier than expected. On September 23, Gary Hart had told a meeting of the Americans for Democratic Action that the women's vote would be the key to the 1984 elections. Addressing the same group the next day, Walter Mondale went even further, stating publicly that he wanted to "bring women into positions of power like they've never been before." In judging the criteria for a vice-presidential candidate, Mondale continued, "you cannot limit your search to white males."

The concept gained even more momentum the very next day at a meeting of two hundred Democratic women from across the country sponsored by the Democratic National Committee. There both Lieutenant Governor Marlene Johnson of Minnesota and Lieutenant Governor Martha Griffiths of Michigan, as well as DNC vice-chair Lynn Cutler, urged the Democratic Party to actively promote the idea of a woman Vice President. The day after that, Ted Kennedy drew cheers from the same group when he declared it was time for the Democratic Party to consider running a woman candidate for President or Vice President. "It is fair to ask why the other democracies are so far ahead of us in this respect," he said, "and to wonder when America will join India, Israel, Britain, and other nations that have chosen a woman for the highest office in the land."

The momentum for a woman vice-presidential candidate was picking up. But some were a little slower than others to catch on. "There will be no woman or black on the ticket this year," Democratic party chairman Chuck Manatt announced confidently. "Hopefully there will be by the turn of the century." Three months later I was to say the same thing at the National Women's Political Caucus. And we were both on the wrong wavelength.

Such views notwithstanding, phase 1 of the vice-presidential project was well on its way.

Now it was time for phase 2, which involved the advancement of specific names for the VP slot. Bella Abzug had already canvassed me and my colleagues Barbara Mikulski and Pat Schroeder, as well as former Congresswoman Barbara Jordan, to see if we would consent to have our names mentioned as possibilities. The answer was a yes from all of us—but with caution from me, anyway. I can't speak for the other women, but I felt it would be politically dangerous for me to be seen as running for the Vice Presidency.

In the first place, one doesn't run for Vice President. In the second place, it would have jeopardized my standing in my congressional district, which elected me to represent them. Third, the nominee, especially if the revolutionary choice went to a woman, would have to be a consensus candidate, supported by many diverse groups in the Democratic Party—Convention delegates, state chairs, labor, and minority groups, as well as women's groups. And fourth, such an extraordinary choice would far better be brought about in the traditional way. It was important that whoever ended up as the Democratic presidential candidate be seen as making his own choice of running mate with the least amount of pressure.

But phase 2 seemed to be gaining a life of its own as well. In a surprise move in October 1983, a full eight months before the Wisconsin state Democratic Party Convention in June, Matt Flynn, the Wisconsin state party chair, had spoken to a group of Democrats in Madison and endorsed me for Vice President, which I did not know at the time.

I had never even met Matt Flynn, but it turns out that he'd been very moved by a statement I'd made on the senseless violence in Northern Ireland. A twelve-year-old girl had just been killed in Ulster by a plastic bullet fired by the British army, and I had spoken out against such violence on the floor of the House.

To keep this momentum for the Vice Presidency going, Team A was developing its strategy. The concept of a woman candidate would have to be advanced from an emotional or exciting possibility to a substantive one, they concluded. For me to be the choice, I would need national press to become better known. I would also need the backing of the Democratic hierarchy. The perfect vehicle, they decided, would be the upcoming Democratic National Convention in July. And so, while I was getting on with my life, contemplating a possible Senate run in 1986 and determined to work for the ticket in 1984, Team A was working on how to increase my visibility.

The three possible roles for me to play at the Convention were the next subject of discussion. First was Convention Chair, to run the proceedings and be highly visible throughout the whole week (a role to be outstandingly performed by Martha Layne Collins).

A second possibility was Platform Chair, responsible for putting together the national agenda on which all Democratic candidates would run. No woman had ever been named Chair of the Platform Committee, and in 1980 the Platform had been such a source of contention that the Party had become bitterly divided. So the risks in assuming that role were high. On the other hand, it would enable me to acquire substantive knowledge that I could not gain any other way.

The safest role was the third, that of Rules Chair, acting as both mediator and judge of any challenges brought by the candidates. (This would prove to be an important spot during the Convention, when both Hart and Jackson challenged the allocation of delegates.) But Rules Chair was the least appealing to me. I had actively participated in the Party's rewriting of the delegate-selection rules as a member of the Hunt Commission and was looking forward to a different role in the 1984 Convention.

Weighing the three, I was undecided between Convention Chair, which I felt was more visible, and Platform Chair: though a long shot, it had clout and would give me the opportunity to shape the direction of the Party for the future. Together Team A and I made up a list of my preferences to give to Chuck Manatt. In spite of the risks, Team A wanted me to go for Platform, but I was still unsure. As much as I was excited by the challenge, I knew how explosive the job could be. But who knew what role I'd get, if any? I decided I might just as well go for it. Since you usually don't get what you ask for in politics, we decided to try first for Convention Chair, second for Platform, and third for Rules.

Without telling me anything about it, Team A set their strategy for Platform in motion. They recruited many sources to start dropping my name to Manatt as a solid candidate for Platform Chair. These sources, including the DNC's own Lynn Cutler, emphasized my record not only with women but with other Democratic constituencies as well. My approval rating in Congress ranged from ninety-five to one hundred percent from labor, one hundred percent from the American Federation of Teachers, and one hundred percent from the elderly for my work on the Select Committee on the Aging. A minicampaign was under way.

In December I invited Manatt to lunch in the Members Dining Room in the House, wanting to deliver my list of Convention preferences to him firsthand. The Christmas recess was coming up, and I was getting ready to leave Washington. In early January I would be off on a fact-finding trip to Central America, and the Convention appointments would probably be made while I was away. Our lunch created quite a bit of interest. A parade of people began to drop by the table to say hello to Manatt, cocking quizzical eyebrows in my direction. The members of Congress, both male and female, are highly competitive people, and anything out of the ordinary does not go unnoticed. What did my having lunch with Manatt mean? I told Manatt quietly—and with all honesty—how much I wanted to be involved in the upcoming elections, to contribute to the Democratic efforts to remove Ronald Reagan from office. How did I want to be involved? he asked. Either as Chair of the Convention, Platform Chair, or Rules Chair, I responded, being careful to put Platform Chair second.

I wasn't thinking about the Vice Presidency. Always the realist, I was thinking about what a breakthrough my role as Platform Chair would be for women and that it would put me in a more substantive, visible position to campaign effectively against Reagan. Always the dreamers, or so I thought, Team A had their eyes set on the vice-presidential nomination and the experience I would gain as Platform Chair. And so the stage was set.

On domestic issues and my ability to work with the different Democratic constituencies, I felt I was a strong candidate for Platform Chair. What weakness I had was in the area of foreign policy. I knew it. Team A knew it. And now, so did the public. In one of my dumber moves I had fingered myself in an interview with *Passages* author Gail Sheehy for the *East Side Express* in October.

"I can't write a total puff piece about you," she had said. "Tell me a weakness."

"Foreign policy," I promptly offered.

And there it was in print, under a picture of me lugging my own suitcases as usual in my shuttling back and forth to Washington, with the headline: "Will this Queens housewife be the next Vice President?" I knew as much about foreign policy as most members of Congress, and probably knew more than some. But I didn't think I knew enough. And once more my candor had gotten the best of me.

But it was true. I didn't feel right unless I knew as much as possible about the issues we were voting on in Congress, every detail, every nuance. And so, in order to learn more about the places that were the subjects of current debate in the House, I decided to do some more traveling.

*   *   *

Now, soon after my lunch with Chuck Manatt, I was setting
out on a congressional trip to Central America with two of my
colleagues in the House, Barbara Kennelly of Connecticut and
Teddy Weiss of New York. The Reagan Administration had asked
Congress to approve a huge increase in military and economic aid
to nations in the region—$8.9 billion over the next five years. I
needed more information to decide whether this would be a wise
expenditure of our tax dollars, whether that money would be
well spent, and what relief it would bring, if any, to the cycle of
poverty, warfare, and despair there.

Our ten-day trip to El Salvador, Nicaragua, Honduras, and
Costa Rica in January 1984 was grueling, starting with meetings
early in the morning and continuing into the night. We met with
forty-seven different groups in the four countries, including representatives from both the leftist guerrillas and the rightist government in El Salvador; the Contras, the Sandinistas, and the
Maryknoll nuns in Nicaragua; political and business leaders in
Honduras; and the Miskito Indians and a group of former
Sandinistas called the ARDE in Costa Rica. The trip helped
convince me that the United States could not achieve a military
solution in Central America without involving our own armed
forces, a disastrous outcome. Once more, because of my seeing
firsthand what was going on in Central America and talking to
representatives on all sides of the conflicts, I felt any vote I would
cast when I got home would be more informed and intelligent.

But the ten-day congressional trip turned out to be a nine-
day trip for me. By the time we got to Costa Rica, a stop that
was also scheduled for R and R after an exhausting trip, I was
sick. The embassy in Honduras had given me an antibiotic, which
helped, but I should have taken a lesson from the seventy-year-
old former president of Costa Rica at lunch, who had been ill and
couldn't eat at all. Instead I politely downed my bowl of spicy
fish broth, and two hours later, I knew I was in trouble.

By one-thirty in the morning the pain in my stomach was as
severe as the labor pains I'd had having my first child. I thought
my appendix had burst and feared that I was bleeding internally. I
sweated it out until five a.m., not wanting to wake anybody up,
and then called the home of our control officer to ask him to get
me back to the U.S. fast. If I was going to die, I wanted to die in

my own bed. And twelve hellish hours later, complete with a sold-out commercial flight, a customs stop, a plane change in Miami, and Teddy Weiss's nursing me all the way, I made it.

My doctor wanted to put me in the hospital, but I refused. My own bed looked too good to me. Four days after I got back from Central America more dead than alive, the phone rang. It was Chuck Manatt. I had gotten Platform Chair. He had run my name past the presidential candidates, Manatt told me, and been given the go-ahead. He had reviewed my record in Congress and my work on the national level, campaigning for Democratic candidates and working for the Party. He had also recognized the fact that appointing a woman to such a high-level position in the Democratic Party would further invite the gender-gap vote. Manatt was pleased. And so was I.

Team A's strategy was right on track. These women saw my appointment as an important step toward their goal of the Vice Presidency. I saw my role as Platform Chair as an opportunity to create the Democratic Party's best offense against Reagan. We were not at cross purposes but parallel ones. Now, unbeknownst to me, the team started dropping my name in discussions about the Vice Presidency in political circles.

For the next six months I worked nonstop on the Platform. I had called and written each of the candidates at the time of my selection, assuring them of my intention to work with them in a spirit of cooperation so that we could draft a document our party could run on and win with in November. Unstated was my determination to keep the lid on the various factions of the Democratic Party. Every bit of political skill I possessed would be necessary to navigate the Platform Committee through a stormy, multicandidate presidential-nomination race. Could I pull it off? I sure hoped so.

The Platform senior staff would be all-important. With seven candidates still in the running for the presidential nomination, all would have a vested interest in the Platform. The potential for conflict would be enormous, each candidate wanting to make sure the Platform staff wasn't favoring one candidate's wishes over another's.

With all this in mind I chose Susan Estrich, a Harvard law professor, as my executive director. I wanted a woman in a top spot on Platform to further women's political credibility, and Susan's qualifications were almost perfect. She had worked on Platform issues for Ted Kennedy in 1980 and had been brilliant in orchestrating all the minority fights at the Convention to challenge Carter.

My only hesitation was her active support for Walter Mondale— and his for her—for the job on Platform. I didn't want any of the other candidates to feel her appointment would give Mondale an edge in the Platform process. Her loyalty had to be to me. "No one is to get the impression that you're working for Mondale," I warned Susan. And no one ever did.

The number-two spot, deputy director, went to Charles Atkins, a lawyer who had served in the Carter White House and was then working for Senator David Boren of Oklahoma as his legislative counsel. Charles was not only important symbolically as a black male, but was also very sharp, extremely nice, and effective with politicians.

I signed on Jan Kalicki as our foreign policy adviser, a position he had filled for Ted Kennedy for eight years. Several of the other candidates had supported Jan for executive director, largely, I think, because of Susan's identification with Mondale. But Jan's slot on the senior staff would show my commitment to bring unity to the Platform process at the outset and send a clear signal to all the candidates of my intentions to be fair. Jan, who volunteered his services, was very smart, knew the Hill, and came highly recommended by Jack English, one of Kennedy's top aides. And Kennedy had not walked away from the possibility of running himself at that point.

As we developed the strategy for producing the Platform, I insisted that if the staff met with one candidate they should immediately arrange to meet with every one of the other candidates as well. And at the beginning that meant meeting separately with Askew, Cranston, Glenn, Hart, Hollings, Jackson, McGovern, and Mondale. It would have been simpler, of course, to meet with the candidates as a group, but politics doesn't work that way.

Our goal was to have the Platform be thematic in its content rather than advocating specific legislation. Acid rain, for example, is a complex issue that encompasses sharply divergent regional interests. Coal-producing and coal-burning industrial states have a different view of what the details of an acid rain control program should be than do the New England states that suffer from the effects of acid rain. To bog down the Platform process into legislation-specific details would create unnecessary conflict. But the Platform would still be very clear about the need to take action to control acid rain.

A thematic Platform would also prevent the Republicans from attaching blown-up dollar values to a specific program and then using it as ammunition. We had to resist the pressure to detail our jobs programs in the Platform, for example, to avoid stating the number of jobs a Democratic victory would create. Although our Party is known as the party of jobs, we could not afford to let the Republicans stick their favorite "big spender" label on us.

We also didn't want to make promises on which we couldn't deliver. Many labor organizations, for example, were lobbying heavily for pending legislation, such as the Domestic Content bill, to be included in the Platform. The bill, which would have required fixed levels of American labor and parts in foreign cars sold in this country, was a highly emotional issue. But there was concern from Gary Hart and other Democrats that such legislation would violate international-trade laws. So instead of mentioning the bill by name or listing any of its details, we compromised by drafting language encouraging foreign producers of cars to make them here. All Democrats could agree on that.

Agreement, after our recent history, was essential. And as winter moved into spring, the presidential primaries were certainly not helping the Democratic Party. I wasn't happy with all the bickering going on between the candidates, whether it was between John Glenn and Gary Hart or between whomever. Mondale was having the most trouble with Hart. Hart kept accusing Mondale of being ruled by special interests, a charge Hart hung around Fritz's neck that Fritz never could get rid of. The backbiting was so exasperating because it was giving ammunition to the Republicans instead of showing the Democrats as a cohesive party. Every time I saw the candidates debate on television I'd wince, thinking of the fractious picture the Democrats were presenting. Keeping the Platform general rather than specific wouldn't harm any of the candidates and would actually help Mondale, who did not want to be seen as caving in to any outside pressures.

A more general Platform was also important to me as a member of Congress. I did not want to include anything in the Platform that the other Democratic members couldn't live with. I didn't want a single member of Congress to turn away from the Platform or the Convention thinking it was designed for the fringe.

Setting down the principles and goals we hoped the country would live by for the next four years was not an insignificant undertaking. We wanted input from the public on the Platform as well. On March 27 we held an organizational meeting of the 184-member committee, after which public hearings were scheduled on different themes all over the country—the first, on foreign policy, for April 9 in New York. Over the next two months, others were to be held on human resources, in Birmingham, Alabama; on agriculture, in Springfield, Illinois; on civil rights, in Los Angeles; on community development, in Cleveland; on the economy and jobs, in Houston; and finally, in June, a two-day wrap-up in Washington, D.C. (Continuing their history of indifference to the wishes of the people, the Republicans never held any public Platform hearings. The Republican Convention convened in August in Dallas, where their Platform was written.)

The turnout at our hearings was extraordinary. Among the one hundred and thirty scheduled speakers at our first hearing in New York on foreign policy were Leszek Waliszewski, a member of Solidarity speaking on behalf of labor in Poland; William Ford, the brother of one of the nuns murdered in El Salvador, questioning the present Administration's policy in Central America; and Professor Dennis Brutus, a black South African exile presently teaching at Northwestern University, supporting Jesse Jackson's goal of making South Africa a central issue in our Platform on foreign policy. Historian Barbara Tuchman testified on the folly of policies that can lead to war, as did Professor Carl Sagan on the disastrous effect of the "nuclear winter" that would follow global nuclear war.

In the end, over one thousand people had poured out their hearts to us, including many who had just walked in off the street. Unlike the Republicans, the Democrats had given anyone who wanted to speak an opportunity.

*   *   *

We were braced for trouble in New York, where it was particularly important for me to have a successful hearing on foreign policy. At issue was Jesse Jackson's intention to send in the head of the American Arab Anti-Defamation Committee to testify on his views on the Middle East. The Jewish community in New York, and nationally as well, was already upset by Jackson's pro-Palestinian position in the Middle East. A confrontation seemed imminent until it was defused by Charles Atkins, who had been a student of Jackson's top policy adviser, Dr. Ronald Walters, at Howard University. Between the two of them, and helped by other staff members, a compromise was worked out: the Arab-American and Jewish-American leaders were scheduled for afternoon sessions in different rooms. Each was heard, and no confrontation took place.

The Platform hearing in Los Angeles was another potentially serious problem. In this very large media market, where it was important to do well, there was trouble brewing with Hispanic organizations over the Simpson-Mazzoli immigration bill pending in Congress. Many Hispanic Democrats were outraged that the Democratic Party leadership in the Congress, including me, did not strongly oppose the employer-sanction provisions of the bill, which imposed penalties on employers who hired illegal aliens. The tension was heightened by the many labor organizations that supported the bill at that time. And the public arena in which the Hispanics had chosen to vent their anger was the Platform hearings.

I had locked horns with Sal Alvarez, one of the Platform Committee members from California who had driven me crazy at every Platform hearing. No matter what the theme of the hearing, he would press me to include specific reference and opposition to Simpson-Mazzoli in the Platform.

We were heading for a showdown in Los Angeles, where some Hispanics had threatened to disrupt the Platform hearing on May 14. A week before we were due in that city I was given a status update by my staff during a late-night meeting in my congressional office. "Gerry, this is a major civil-rights issue for Hispanic Americans," Charles Atkins said to me. "I cannot overemphasize the depth of feeling. People in this country still have real fear they'll be treated differently because their skin is brown, because their last names are different, because they speak

English with an accent." The Hispanics, Charles went on, were afraid that with the passage of Simpson-Mazzoli they would revert to second-class status, that all their jobs could be threatened by employers who wouldn't spend the time to check out their legal status or even risk hiring them in the first place. The Hispanic position was that the illegal-alien problem could be far better handled by increasing border patrols than by putting the burden on the employer.

I understood. I knew what it was like to be labeled because of a different-sounding last name. There was much more at stake in this issue than stemming illegal immigration. And so I arranged to meet with key Hispanic leaders in Los Angeles before the hearing to work it out. I also visited a child-care center in a Hispanic neighborhood with local Hispanic women activists and did all I could to assure the community I was sympathetic.

Though the process had been difficult, it was worth it. There was no confrontation at the hearing in Los Angeles. And we ended up drafting a strong statement opposing employer sanctions in the Platform without mentioning the Simpson-Mazzoli bill specifically.

The press was becaming more and more intrigued as we traveled around the country. It was, after all, an election year. Often we were the only show in town. And always there was the oddity of me, not only as the first woman Platform Chair but increasingly mentioned as a potential vice-presidential candidate.

My parents, Dominick and
Antonetta Ferraro, October 2, 1927,
in New York.

Eager to face the world
at eighteen months.

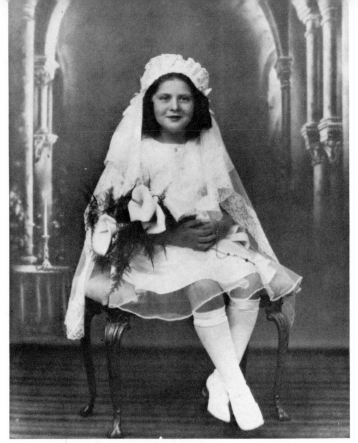

First Holy Communion: seven years old, Newburgh, New York.

Admiring my older
brother, Carl, at
his high school
graduation, 1946.

Even at nine, not Miss America
but Uncle Sam.

Teaching second grade at PS 85, Queens, 1957. Many pupils turned up to help on the campaign.

With John on our only vacation without the children, 1962.

Laura's first birthday, 1967. No, I didn't bake the cake.

1978's Christmas portrait included my mother (l) and mother-in-law (r),
Rose Zaccaro.

THE 1978 CAMPAIGN

With DA John Santucci, 1978, who later was with me when we kicked off my first vice-presidential campaign trip.

Miss Lillian launching a tough Democrat.

Bad enough they ripped up my poster, but littering!

My Donna campaigning at sixteen. Total confidence in her mom.

With Gert McDonald (r), district
leader, listening to constituents.

One of my first meetings
with House Speaker
Tip O'Neill, 1979.
Yes . . . we *did* like
each other . . . and still do!

ON THE WAY TO VICE PRESIDENT

"Don't call her baby. Call her Vice President."

—Congresswoman Barbara Mikulski, national NOW conference,
Miami Beach, Florida, June 30, 1984.

B<small>Y THE SPRING OF</small> 1984 my name was on the national political map. So was my emergence as a viable candidate for the vice-presidential nomination.

On March 21, Matthew Flynn, the Wisconsin state chair, endorsed me for the second time for Vice President.

On April 9, Barbara Kennelly gave me my first public endorsement at the Woman's National Democratic Club in Washington.

On April 15, the *Des Moines Register* called me the "Democrats' secret weapon."

And on May 4, Tip O'Neill endorsed me in the *Boston Globe*.

My base of support was broadening to include a congressional colleague, the chairman of a state party delegation, a Midwestern newspaper, and the Speaker of the House of Representatives. Labor was also coming on strong. In March, William Wynn, president of the AFL-CIO's largest union, the United Food and Commercial Workers, and Robert Georgine, head of the AFL-CIO's Building and Construction Trades Department, threw a joint fund-raising party with Tip O'Neill as honored guest for my upcoming congressional reelection campaign.

This rapid turn of events gave me something else that

counted—a new ability to raise campaign funds. Raising money had always been a problem. Five years before, I had had a fund-raiser in Washington that netted a little over three thousand dollars. Then, that was a big deal to me. But now, between the conjecture about the Vice Presidency and my position as Platform Chair of the Party, I was suddenly a draw. In March 1984, I had three fund-raisers back to back that brought in over one hundred and fifty thousand dollars. It was wonderful to know so many people were betting on my future.

Team A, I discovered later, now felt that their timing for moving the vice-presidential project from a concept to my being the specific choice was being overtaken by a mounting groundswell. But I still held the concept at arm's length. I was too rooted in Congress, too absorbed by my ongoing work on Platform, too steeped in my own pragmatism, to take the groundswell seriously.

Besides, I was exhausted. On May 15 I returned to Washington from Los Angeles, after my intense meetings with the Hispanics and a full day of Platform hearings, to appear at the early morning Godfrey-Sperling media breakfast the next day. And over the scrambled eggs, I almost blew away my candidacy for good with two responses. When a reporter asked me: If Mondale were to win the nomination, who would be his best running mate? I responded: "Hart." The next day the press reported it as a straight news comment, saying that I had called for a Mondale-Hart ticket.

Disaster, not only because the primaries were still going on but also because of my determination to remain neutral toward all the candidates as Platform Chair. Immediately I called Hart to explain—I had not called for Mondale for President but had answered a hypothetical question starting with the word "if." Hart was very gracious about it, and that moment passed. The other almost didn't.

At the same breakfast I had gone out of my way to prove that the thematic formula of the Platform would not include specific legislation for any special constituencies, even for women. The Republicans were already beating us over the head with the charges that the Democratic Party had sold out to special-interest groups, which the President had picked up and run with in the last year, and I wanted to refute them. But I went too far. When asked if "no specific legislation" included the ERA, I said yes.

Equal rights for women, I announced at the breakfast, could be in the platform without using the capital E, the capital R, the capital A. A ripple immediately ran around the room and I realized what a gaffe I'd made.

As soon as the breakfast ended, I hotfooted it to the nearest phone to call my congressional office. "Call NOW, the NWPC, all the women members of Congress, DNC political director Ann Lewis, and Bella and Steinem," I told them rapidly. "Tell them not to say anything to the press until they talk to me." I could just see the headlines: "Ferraro, First Woman to Head the Platform Committee, Comes Out Against the ERA." I could have kicked myself, realizing the whole flap could have been avoided if I had differentiated the ERA as being a constitutional amendment rather than a piece of legislation; that way the Platform could easily have included the ERA as a Democratic goal, as indeed it ended up doing.

But for the moment, the damage was done. I issued a statement to the press at noon, attempting to explain my comment. But would the women activists, all of whom had been fighting for the ERA for years, accept it? We gathered in the Congresswomen's Reading Room in the Capitol at one p.m., where I told them personally about my mistake and what I had done to correct it. And, as one, they gave me their support.

It was fantastic, really. Any of these high-profile activists could have blasted me in the press. But not one did. The women's support was incredible, yet no one ever wrote a story on how the women had backed me up. That afternoon I suggested a headline to a reporter from the *Baltimore Sun* who was disappointed the ERA flap had fizzled: "Ferraro Screws Up at Press Breakfast and the Women Join Hands Around Her." But, of course, good news was no news, and that story never ran.

While I was certainly not neutral on the subject of the ERA, I continued to go out of my way to remain neutral toward all the Democratic presidential candidates. By the spring of 1984, the field had narrowed to Mondale, Hart, and Jackson—with Mondale the clear favorite. And my job as Platform Chair was coming to a head. In the traditional endgame of presidential party politics, the representatives of all three candidates on the Platform Committee were now jockeying to get their candidate's own campaign themes written into the Platform.

The Platform would actually be written by a special fifteen-member drafting committee. The more members each candidate had on the drafting committee, the greater would be the opportunities to have his policies given priority over the others'. Numbers were critical. But so was the fairness of the Platform Committee. After the June primaries, we used a calculator to work out how many members each candidate should have on the drafting committee in relation to the delegates he'd accumulated during the primaries.

According to our figures, Mondale should get eight of his people on the drafting panel to Hart's five and Jackson's two. But Hart joined with Jackson in claiming that the delegate allocations did not fairly reflect the actual vote counts in the primaries. According to this new approach, Mondale would receive seven members, with Hart getting five and Jackson three. By joining forces, Hart and Jackson would then have been able to outvote Mondale.

No way, I said firmly to both Hart and Jackson. The issue wasn't negotiable. The numbers based on the established delegate-selection rules clearly showed Mondale's deserved control. The two accepted my decision with good grace. They had to; the rules were clear. And that potential confrontation quickly passed.

I think back now to my high hopes of making the actual Platform short, simple, clear, and readable in one day, unlike the mammoth 33,000-word tome that had weighed down the 1980 Convention. In early June I had my platform staff work with the three candidates to prepare a first draft. I then appointed Richard Arrington, mayor of Birmingham, Alabama, to chair the fifteen-member drafting committee in a marathon drafting session in Washington. After three days of nonstop work, the fifty-six-page staff draft had surpassed the 33,000-word record of 1980, swelling to ninety pages. So much for brevity.

The drafting committee then delivered its draft to the full Platform Committee, which completed the final touches in only a day and a half. We had a finished Platform. We had brought it in a whole day ahead of schedule. And there had been a minimum of fights, all the more important because we had done it in front of the national press, which had been invited to cover all our open meetings and drafting sessions as well.

Why did this matter so much? Because this year of all years we needed a Platform which brought us together, which expressed our deepest convictions, and on which every Democrat could proudly run. If we knew what we stood for, we'd have a much better chance of getting the message across to the rest of the country. It was a symbolic victory too. Democrats had overcome divisiveness for a common goal; if we could work together now, we could work together in the White House, whoever the candidates.

I had pulled it off. And when the final meeting of the Platform Committee broke, many of the members were sporting Mondale/Ferraro and Hart/Ferraro buttons on their lapels. What a kick. I couldn't contain a self-satisfied grin as I waited at National Airport to fly home.

"Aren't you Geraldine Ferraro?" one family asked me while I waited for the shuttle.

I smiled yes. They must have read about what I considered to be my triumph on Platform, I thought contentedly.

But no. All the public cared about was the mounting drama the newspapers had now dubbed the "veepstakes."

"Gee, we hope you get the nomination," they said.

The vice-presidential conjecture was everywhere. By early July, the possibilities had been rounded out to seven by Mondale: Henry Cisneros, mayor of San Antonio; Tom Bradley, mayor of Los Angeles; Wilson Goode, mayor of Philadelphia; Martha Layne Collins, governor of Kentucky; Dianne Feinstein, mayor of San Francisco; Lloyd Bentsen, senator from Texas; and me. Michael Dukakis, governor of Massachusetts, and Dale Bumpers, senator from Arkansas, were also being mentioned for the Vice Presidency, but the first seven were the hard core. In terms of titles, that added up to four mayors, one governor, one senator, and one congresswoman. Fine. In terms of specialized constituencies, it came out to one Mexican-American, two blacks, three women, and one white male. Wow. No wonder the press was having such fun with the Vice Presidency. The list sounded like a lineup for Noah's Ark.

Meanwhile, the groundswell for a woman Vice President was

rolling right along. On June 18, two members of the National Women's Political Caucus presented a very persuasive memo on the rationale of selecting a woman Vice President to John Reilly. The eight-page, single-spaced memo identified major voting groups, analyzed key electoral states—and kept coming up with the same answer: a win with a woman on the ticket.

In terms of voter turnout, the memo pointed out, a woman would be an incentive for the 695,000 blacks registered by Jackson during the primaries alone and for women, who already made up fifty-four percent of registered voters. Conceding two hundred and nine electoral votes from such Republican-entrenched states in the West as California, Oregon, and Washington, the memo went on to demonstrate how the Democrats could top the Republican tally by a narrow thirty-seven votes if the traditionally Democratic states of the Northeast came through, along with the return of such key states as New York, Illinois, and Ohio to the Democratic fold. These states had been particularly devastated by Reaganomics, and a woman Vice President was seen as winning back this crucial bloc by bolstering the Democratic messages of fairness and balanced economics.

But the real hook was Texas. No Democratic president had ever been elected without carrying Texas. And here the gender gap had been the most powerful, with the women's vote accounting for Ann Richards's election to state treasurer and the winning difference in Mark White's gubernatorial race in 1982, as well as in Lloyd Doggett's 1984 primary race for the Senate. Not surprisingly, Reilly took the memo very seriously, as did other Mondale staffers, the political community in Washington, and the press, which also received copies. Women were playing the political game very well this time. And I had been drafted as one of the major players.

On June 3, I was endorsed by the Nassau County Democrats.

On June 4, I shared the cover of *Time* magazine with Dianne Feinstein under the head: "And for Vice President . . . Why Not a Woman?"

And on June 21, Barbara Walters interviewed me on ABC's *20/20*.

Looking back, it seems amazing to me that even after being on the cover of *Time* and speculating about the subject on national television, I still didn't believe my candidacy would ever really happen. The press was full of it. In political circles it was a major subject of discussion.

It had taken a casual comment by my mayor, Ed Koch, on television one Sunday morning to start bringing me up short. On one of the rare weekends I was in Queens during the Platform work, I was using the time to clean up our bedroom when John suddenly called up from the den to turn on the television set. "Koch is talking about you and the Vice Presidency," John said. We both watched. And listening to Koch in the politically neutral sanctuary of our own home suddenly made the possibility more credible. Here was an influential public official talking about my candidacy on a responsible news program. The cumulative effect began to catch up with me.

For the first time John and I talked about the possibility of my actually becoming Mondale's running mate without laughing it off. "People are carrying on about this Vice Presidency thing all over the country," I said to John. "It may be the weirdest long shot we can imagine, but it's possible." We stood there for a moment staring at each other. John didn't say anything. Neither did I. I went back to cleaning up the bedroom and he took the dog for a walk.

That moment was a flash point for both of us. I had never really confronted the fact that I might be the vice-presidential nominee. But John had. For months he had quietly been weighing the momentum of my candidacy. He understood what the repercussions on our life would be and, unlike me, he was beginning to face up to them. We were at an age—John fifty-one and I forty-eight—when we could begin to relax and enjoy ourselves.

I'm sure he felt that I was slipping away from him, that I was going to be giving him even less time at a point when he felt he was entitled to more. The children weren't an issue. They were well on their way to focusing their lives outside the family. I used to kid that my children were the only ones in America who had found the perfect solution for getting rid of their mother during their teenage years: they sent her to Congress. But John and I had always been close, very close, and outside of his business his life had focused on me and the children. Our youngest child, Laura, was about to go off to college, and the house would soon be empty. I think John began to feel at that point that he was going to lose his Gerry, too, and that there was nothing he could do about it.

In 1977, when I was at the DA's office, John had urged me not to go after a seat on the City Council. "Don't run," he'd said. "You've already got more than enough demands on your time." So I hadn't run then, but I told him I did plan to run for public office eventually. When the opportunity came up for Congress the next year, it was John who was the first to support me. "Give it your best shot," he had told me, not wanting me to go through life feeling he had kept me from doing what I wanted to do. And he had worked as hard as he could to get me elected, so that if I lost, I'd never be able to say he hadn't helped me.

From that time on, he'd always let Gerry be Gerry, at increasing personal sacrifice. Now we were both getting swept along in the vice-presidential sweepstakes. That morning in June, John was realizing that we were getting in too deep, that it was too late to be able to walk away from it.

Though I had always tried to keep my family life and political life separate, now they were getting intertwined. On June 14, Laura graduated from high school. Afterward, John and I took her and a few friends to lunch at the New York restaurant Maxwell's Plum to celebrate before I went on to Marymount to deliver their commencement address. This was obviously a special day for the family, and I had left instructions with my staff not to find me unless it was a matter of life or death. The day should have belonged to Laura, not to anyone else. It ended up belonging to Fritz Mondale.

No sooner had we sat down to lunch than the phone calls started coming in to the restaurant from my office in Washington. John Reilly was trying to get in touch with me, a staff member said. He wants you to fly to North Oaks, Minnesota, the day after tomorrow to report on the Platform to Mondale. No, I said from the restaurant phone as people streamed by me. The next call was from Susan Estrich, my executive director on the Platform. Reilly is driving me crazy with his insistence, she told me. Again I said no, because we were just about to start drafting the Platform and if we reported to Mondale, we would also have to report to Hart in Colorado and Jackson in Illinois.

There was no time for that and increasingly less time for my family, who were getting very irritated by all these phone interruptions.

But when I finally sat down again there was another call, this time from Reilly himself. And my temper almost got away from me. Reilly was grandstanding. I knew that. Mondale had gotten through the June primaries with enough delegates to just about sew up the nomination, and his staff knew that one of the ways to show he was now the leader of the party was to have the Platform Committee chair come out to Minnesota to report to him. But my arguments fell on Reilly's deaf ears, including my reluctance to further the appearance of my involvement in the Vice Presidency. Dianne Feinstein was scheduled to meet with Mondale the next week. If I went to Minnesota now, even as Platform Chair, it would lead to more speculation. I was determined to avoid looking as if I were actively seeking the vice-presidential nomination, which I wasn't. The candidate would be Mondale's choice, not anyone else's. But Reilly was adamant about the Platform report. My family was upset. And I went to Minnesota.

It was a mistake from the beginning. As predicted, the papers had a field day with the implications. "Running Mates?" asked the New York *Daily News*'s front page the next day under a picture of the two of us. And the meeting, though Mondale called me "one of the stars of our political party," was, I thought, less than perfect. Susan Estrich had been handling the details on the platform, and I had asked her to bring me up to date on the plane going out. Between various passengers coming up to speak to me and the flurry of serving breakfast, there wasn't enough time for her to brief me thoroughly. So when I was called on in North Oaks to discuss the Platform logistics with Mondale, which dealt with the process of the hearings rather than the substance of the Platform, I chose to defer to Susan.

This did not sit well with the Mondale staff. I wasn't too happy, either. But no one knew anything about it until stories began to leak the following week. Instead, I was now on a roller-coaster ride toward the vice-presidential nomination. Mondale had contacted the AFL-CIO for labor's views on whether a woman would help or hurt the ticket. The answer came back from Lane Kirkland, the president of the AFL-CIO: it would help. Later

Kirkland also passed on the word that I would be a stronger choice than Dianne Feinstein, as I was better known to labor.

The results were also coming in from a survey of the delegates to the Convention commissioned by the National Women's Political Caucus. Seventy-seven percent of the delegates canvassed felt that a woman on the ticket would be a plus, while only nine percent thought it would be negative. Seventy-five percent of the delegates felt that a well-qualified woman candidate would help defeat Reagan; only ten percent felt it would hurt. Out of a list of seven possible vice-presidential candidates, Hart was the first choice, with twenty percent of the delegates; I was second, with ten percent; Feinstein came in at two percent; and my congressional colleague Pat Schroeder at one percent. (Write-in votes showed three percent for Barbara Jordan and one percent for Lee Iacocca.) The final results of the survey would be rushed to Mondale by his soon-to-be campaign co-chair, Barbara Mikulski, just before he made his selection in July, but the preliminary results were being leaked to the press in June by the NWPC for momentum and public-opinion building.

All was not so well, however, in the Mondale camp. Though I was not told about it, a high-level meeting was called by the women members of Congress on June 27. Everyone was there— three of my colleagues, Barbara Mikulski, Barbara Boxer, and Mary Rose Oakar; New York City Council president Carol Bellamy; Bella Abzug; NOW officials Judy Goldsmith and Mary Jean Collins; Anne Wexler, savvy Washington lobbyist and Mondale adviser; and Mondale's key adviser on women, Carol Tucker Foreman.

Carol Bellamy evidently complained that there was little or no communication with the Mondale campaign staff. Bella said she had been ignored as well. Suddenly a lot of anger at the Mondale campaign came out—and someone leaked inaccurate stories to the press. Anne Wexler was quoted as saying she had no influence in the campaign and that her phone calls were not returned. (This was not so, and later the reporter apologized to Anne for the inaccuracy.) Mikulski's leaked "quotes" were even more injurious. The Mondale campaign, said Mikulski, who ten days later would be appointed national cochair of the campaign, was ignoring women. Angry, Mondale called Carol Tucker Foreman. "Why am I working so hard for women and everyone is still mad at me?" he asked.

It is not you they are mad at, Carol assured him. These women were his strongest supporters and had been from the beginning. It was his campaign staff that was causing the trouble—not returning the women's phone calls, giving them the runaround. The women want to talk to you directly, Carol told him. But even that request had been briefly stonewalled by Mondale's campaign chairman, Jim Johnson, who had said that Mondale would not meet with anyone who demanded a meeting. Mondale then called Paul Tully, his political director, to check out the women's complaints. They held. And a meeting was scheduled with the women for July 4 in Minnesota.

There was no doubt that Mondale was the candidate of choice from women's groups for his stand on key women's issues. From the beginning, urged on by his wife Joan, he had also been receptive to the idea of running with a woman. And he still was. The gender-gap vote had been strong in the spring primaries. Political realities seemed to point to a woman on the ticket to defeat Reagan. And at the annual three-day conference of the National Organization for Women in Miami Beach on June 30, Mondale didn't let down the women's vice-presidential hopes.

"Considering a woman is a first, but it will not be a last. We have broken a barrier," said Mondale, by now the sure Democratic candidate. "Never again will a nominee make headlines by considering a woman. Next time headlines will be made only if women are not considered."

A demonstration erupted on the floor, the women members chanting, "Run with a woman. Win with a woman," some waving placards that read: "Fritz and a Ms.," "Woman Veep NOW," and "Win with a Woman in '84." But Mondale had stopped short of actually saying he would run with a woman. And emotions were running high. To press their political hopes, the members of NOW adopted a resolution the next day to nominate a woman "strong on women's issues" for the Vice Presidency from the convention floor, "if necessary." With half of all the delegates to the Convention being women, four hundred of whom were NOW members, the pressure on Mondale seemed intense.

The furor was immediate. Women's political hopes seemed to have turned into demands. Paying no attention to the "if necessary" wording of the resolution, the media interpreted NOW's call for a woman VP as a battle cry. "Floor Fight Threatened by NOW: Convention Battle Vowed If Nominee Selects a Male," the front page of the *Washington Post* headlined the next day. I had consented to the symbolic gesture of having my name put in nomination at the Convention by New York State as a "favorite daughter." Now I withdrew my consent. Under these increasingly charged circumstances, I had no intention of challenging our own presidential candidate, who had to be able to choose his own running mate. We knew from the delegate survey that we had enough votes to force the issue, even to win it, but it would have been a messy and damaging fight. What was to be gained from that? The point was to have a united party against Reagan, regardless of who was on the Democratic ticket. What else had I been working for all these months on Platform?

On the surface, Mondale seemed unperturbed by the threatened floor fight, which had been blown out of all proportion and misinterpreted by the press. But privately, I found out later, he was very hurt. What the women didn't understand, he told Carol Tucker Foreman, was that if they kept pushing him, he wouldn't be able to select a woman as his running mate at all. Hart's characterization of Mondale as a special interests candidate was still haunting him. "I think I'm a strong man and a decisive one," he told Carol after the NOW meeting. "But somehow the press always portrays me as someone who gives in to every demand. On the one most important thing I might do in my candidacy I'll be portrayed not as a man who was strong enough to make history but a man who gave in." Carol and many of the other women thought serious damage had been done and that Mondale would not—or could not—go with a woman now.

But I didn't know anything about all this behind-the-scenes tension. When I arrived at the NOW convention, three of my congressional colleagues—Kennelly, Mikulski, and Oakar—were in fact in the process of meeting with the beleaguered Mondale to endorse me as their choice for his running mate. Though NOW itself never officially promoted an individual for the slot and concentrated instead on the concept of a woman vice-presidential candidate, privately the women had decided it was time to move beyond the concept to a specific candidate. Would I be willing? Sure, I'd said to my friends in Congress. We had come this far. We had to see it through. No one knew what Mondale would do in the end, though I still thought he would go with a man. But in the meantime, our bargaining position was getting better by the minute.

As I stood behind a half-opened door, I heard my friends in Congress announce their choice to the press. It was an extraordinary feeling. Being endorsed by unions or state delegations was one thing, but these were my highly talented, highly intelligent, and highly competitive colleagues, one of whom had been seriously mentioned as a vice-presidential candidate herself. On stage Barbara Mikulski was outdoing herself, dramatically pinning a Mondale/Ferraro button on her lapel. "Don't call her baby. Call her congresswoman," Mikulski said. "Don't call her baby. Call her Vice President."

I left the NOW convention exhilarated but sobered. The chances of my getting the nomination still seemed very remote, but I realized now, as John had a few weeks before, that I was in too deep to pull out. If I withdrew now, I would betray the hard work and dreams of every woman political activist in the country by my "thanks, but no thanks." If I didn't pull out, I had to accept the possibility that I just might become the vice-presidential nominee. I felt as if I were a kid on a high diving board looking way down at the water, knowing she had to jump.

Two days after I left the NOW convention it was my turn to join the parade of vice-presidential candidates being interviewed by Mondale at his home in North Oaks, Minnesota. I had to go, though my heart wasn't in it. The approbation of my colleagues and other Democratic groups was one thing. Being part of the actual vice-presidential selection process was another. I was almost embarrassed. Mondale had gotten himself in a bind interviewing so many different colors and sexes of candidates when in fact he was only trying to emulate Carter's vice-presidential selection process. The difference was that Carter's prospects had all been white males.

Team A wanted me to take at least one staff member with

me, for appearances if nothing else. A vice-presidential candidate should not deal with the Mondale staff, as I was about to do, but only with Mondale himself, they argued. Staff members dealt with other staff members. Principals dealt with principals. But I thought that was nonsense. I didn't need an entourage to make me look important. That's the sort of puffery about politics or any profession that drives me crazy. My husband was coming with me, anyway, which was more than sufficient.

When we flew out on July 2, the numbers for my possible candidacy did not bode well. A *New York Times*/CBS poll had just found Hart the favorite vice-presidential candidate with twenty-three percent of registered Democrats, while Tom Bradley and I shared a rating of only two percent. Fearing that the stridency at the NOW convention had compromised Mondale, women's groups had also publicly agreed that Hart would be an acceptable running mate if Mondale did not choose a woman. I really felt my trip to North Oaks was wasted time, as if we were all just going through the motions.

But the results of another poll nagged at me. In the almost daily testing of the ratings between Mondale and Reagan, Mondale was not doing well. I kept hearing my own voice at the National Women's Political Caucus the year before, advising my disgruntled colleagues that no male candidate would choose a woman as a running mate unless he were fifteen points behind. And on the morning I flew to my vice-presidential interview, that's just what the spread was: fifteen points.

THE
END RUN

*"Please withdraw my name from consideration
for the Vice Presidency."*

—*phone conversation with Walter Mondale,
July 8, 1984, Forest Hills, N.Y.*

THERE WERE JUST TWO
weeks to go until the Democratic National Convention convened
in San Francisco. As we landed in Minnesota, I was convinced
Mondale would go with Hart, though they had bloodied each
other badly during the primaries. Beyond the persuasive numbers
among Democratic voters for Hart in the polls, his selection would
demonstrate a united party and bring the energy of his supporters
to the campaign. Hart had captured the newly identified "Yuppie"
vote during the primaries, which was a big plus for him. But he
had lost labor.

On the morning I flew to my vice-presidential interview, the
United Food and Commercial Workers Union, the largest union
in the AFL-CIO, with 1.3 million members (fifty percent of whom
are women), had endorsed me for the Vice Presidency. "We believe that the Democratic Party, as the party of working people,
must nominate the best, most electable ticket," William Wynn,
the president of the UFCW, had written to Mondale. "That ticket
is Walter Mondale and Geraldine Ferraro."

The other vice-presidential candidates were attractive for good
reasons. I knew Mondale had been very impressed by Dianne
Feinstein after her interview in North Oaks on June 16. And as

mayor of San Francisco, she had done a remarkable job of uniting the city's extraordinarily diverse factions. Catapulted into the mayor's office after the 1978 murders of Supervisor Harvey Milk and Mayor George Moscone, Dianne, then president of the board of supervisors, had gone on to win reelection with an astonishing plurality of 81.2 percent. She was well grounded in urban issues and had gone a long way toward resolving San Francisco's fiscal woes. But she had no experience in foreign policy or military matters.

Lloyd Bentsen would be a practical choice, coming as he did from the key state of Texas. His conservatism and his support for many of Reagan's economic policies might make him a difficult running mate for Mondale, however. Mayor Tom Bradley, from Los Angeles, had the backing of the *Wall Street Journal* and the *New Republic,* and his candidacy would be historic in that he would be the first black nominee; also he would help secure the black vote. The same could be said of Wilson Goode, mayor of Philadelphia.

Martha Layne Collins seemed like a long shot to me. She was a real newcomer, having been elected governor of Kentucky only the past fall. She was far more conservative than I, against abortion except in cases of rape, incest, and danger to the health of the mother, which would have cost her the backing of some women's groups. In addition, Martha Layne Collins opposed gun control. But Collins's star in the Democratic Party was on the ascent; she had trounced her Republican opponent for the governorship by nearly ten points. Now she was about to serve as chair of the Democratic National Convention in San Francisco, bringing with her twenty-three uncommitted delegates from Kentucky. The star of Henry Cisneros, the young mayor of San Antonio, was also rising. He had been a member of the Kissinger Commission on Central America, was very personable, and would have attracted the minority vote.

And then there was me. Publicly I said I thought I had a fifty-fifty chance of getting the nomination. But I didn't believe it. And after my three-hour interview with Mondale, I thought the odds against had increased even more. One of the first things Mondale had asked me as we sat in his living room with John Reilly was how I would address the question of crime in America, a question that really caught me by surprise. For the last two years I had been on the Budget Committee and had become fairly expert in that area. But it had been more than six years since I'd been a prosecutor. The issues then were the death penalty, and the call to appoint tougher judges on the state level and to get more cops on the street on the local level. Mondale was more interested in the federal level, and I wasn't quite sure what he was looking for. My answers were rather oblique, I'm afraid, mostly a discussion of the crime bill that Bill Hughes, a House member from New Jersey, had introduced in the Ninety-seventh Congress.

We went on to discuss the budget, the deficit, and the situation in Central America. It was really quite a formal interview, but our long walk alone afterward was very cordial. While I silently breathed a sigh of relief that I'd worn shoes I could walk in, we talked more personally about the campaign. Though I didn't think Mondale would end up with a woman as a running mate, I decided to use the time to find out exactly what the job would mean and how much my family would be involved in the process. Why not? I had nothing to lose.

"If this were to happen, what would you expect of my husband and children?" I asked Mondale as we walked through the squadrons of Minnesota mosquitoes. "Oh, we'd want them to campaign," he said. "But the amount of their involvement would be up to them." His children were political pros by now, having been through two presidential campaigns and most recently the presidential primaries, and would give mine all the tips they needed, he assured me. He also pointed out that the job of Vice President would be less work than that of a senator, since he had heard I was interested in the 1986 race in New York. "You're kidding," I said. "No, I'm serious," he replied. He seemed to be talking, at that moment anyway, as if my candidacy were a distinct possibility.

I relayed all this to John on our flight back, torn between thinking I'd blown the interview with my inadequate response about crime and yet curious about Mondale's remarks on the Vice Presidency as being less time-consuming than a Senate position. If he had given that much thought to my future, maybe he really was considering me as his running mate. No matter who ended up as Mondale's Vice President, I told John as I had just told Fritz in North Oaks, I planned to work very hard in his campaign to unseat Ronald Reagan.

But John and I had talked enough about politics, and what I really wanted to know was if he had found any good art to buy on the tour he had just taken with Joan Mondale while I was meeting with Fritz. Art was hardly a new subject between the Mondales and the Zaccaros. Our two families had met in the Caribbean in 1980 while recuperating from the election campaigns. At what turned out to be a very expensive dinner for John one night, Joan had sold him a portfolio of posters to raise money for the Democratic Party. Now we were looking for more bipartisan art, and Joan, who knew a great deal about the subject, had promised to take John gallery hopping just as she had Dianne Feinstein's husband during Dianne's interview. But John hadn't found anything he liked and we were both disappointed.

That wouldn't be the only disappointment to come from our trip to Minnesota. During the next few days, a torrent of leaks from an unnamed Mondale staffer to the *New York Times* would blast my interview with Mondale as "somewhat disappointing" and "not up to expectations. The leaks to the *San Francisco Chronicle* would label me as "a little too flashy, a little too flip." Dianne Feinstein, the leaks implied, was a much stronger candidate than I was, better on the issues, more aggressive, and more impressive. The leaks from Mondale's unnamed "top aides" to the *Washington Post* would indirectly compare my interview not with Dianne's but with that of Martha Layne Collins, who had "a very clear idea of her own agenda of state and national affairs" that she pressed on Mondale "vigorously and effectively."

That burned me on more than one level. Why were we never compared with Cisneros or Bentsen or any of the other male candidates? Were we, as women, just running against each other? How sexist can you get?

But I was far angrier on a more practical level. At a press conference after my meeting with Mondale assessing the vice-presidential selection process I had said: "If it were not done by looking at how you get the most electoral votes, I would not only be amazed, I would be nonsupportive. I want this ticket to win, and the way you win is by counting the votes." According to the anti-Ferraro campaign now being waged by some of Mondale's staff in the press, they had been "stunned" by my response. By emphasizing the numbers of votes the nominee could bring in as the criterion for the final vice-presidential selection, I had been deemed too "political." Even my prior trip to North

Oaks to report on the platform was cited as a negative by anonymous Mondale "campaign sources" in Washington.

What was all this about? I wracked my brain trying to figure out what I'd done to Mondale to bring on this attack. I had turned down his offer to become national chair of his campaign two years ago. I'd refused the pressures of his staff (as well as the staffs of the other candidates) toward my showing favoritism during the Platform process. And I had resisted the efforts of the Mondale camp to solicit my support for their candidate throughout the primaries. I had taken my neutrality seriously. Was this the price I had to pay? Or were these smears really a campaign ploy to support Mondale's impending choice of Hart and not a woman as Vice President? Such a choice might have been politically smart. But I wasn't going to be the one sacrificed for it.

Immediately I started firing back. I didn't care about a hypothetical Vice Presidency slipping away, but I did care a lot about the reputation I had built up over the last six years and my hopes for the Senate. I called Barbara Mikulski and Tony Coelho, member of Congress from California who was a good friend of mine and close to Mondale as well, and asked them to get in touch with Mondale right away. If I had called directly, it would have looked as if I were whining about losing the Vice Presidency, a position I had never sought. "I want you to get a message to them," I told Mikulski. "If they have decided not to pick me as the vice-presidential candidate, fine. That's their decision. But they don't have to put me down as not being smart enough, or capable enough to do the job. They don't need to destroy me to give them an excuse."

But the stories continued.

"What are these people doing? These leaks are killing me, and for what?" I fumed to John Saturday night as we were preparing for bed. "The Platform is good. I've worked my fanny off on it. I've delivered a good job. And this is what I get." My Italian blood was really boiling by then. "I'm going to write Mondale a letter tomorrow withdrawing my name from consideration, and I'm going to release it to the press," I raged.

John, who is far more tolerant than I am, urged me to take some time to think about it, but I was too angry. "How can they expect me to campaign for them, expect the women's groups to support them, if this is how they treat us?" I went on. "If they don't pick a woman after parading us all out to North Oaks, then they're going to need somebody to tout their ticket to the women's groups. And they're losing me." In full fury, I called my district office manager, Pat Flynn, to let off steam and then called Eleanor Lewis to start drafting my letter of withdrawal.

Politically, it would not have been smart to withdraw my name at the eleventh hour, of course. What that signals is cowardice under fire, an easy victory for your political opponents, who are searching for your vulnerability—and have found it. And I carried the extra baggage, as always, of being a woman in a man's game, of constantly being tested. Could a woman take the heat? Could a woman bear the scrutiny of her political enemies? The tiresome answer, as always, has to be that women not only have to give more to be judged the same as men but have to take more as well. This was my first test in national politics. And I didn't like it a bit. I would have expected it from the Republicans, but these attacks were from the staff of my own party's candidate. Unbelievable.

It came to a head on Sunday, July 8. Now my vice-presidential interview was being compared in the *New York Times* to a "rollercoaster spin," preceded by a "zoom in popularity" only to "plummet after sessions with Mr. Mondale." My "apparent slippage" as a vice-presidential contender," the article continued, was tied not only to my interview but also to my efforts to get the job. While I was reading this latest salvo, the phone rang. It was Mondale. "Gerry, I want you to know that I have not had anything at all to do with these stories," Mondale said. But it was too late. "Have you read this morning's *Times*?" I asked him. "No," he replied. But my steam was up.

"Well, let me tell you, Fritz, I will support whomever you choose, but you don't need to destroy me in the process. That's downright counterproductive. You're going to need Gerry Ferraro and a lot of other people, too, to try to explain to the women's groups what you've done," I said. "I respect you. At least you considered a woman. You seriously considered a woman. But this game you're playing, trying to figure out a way not to choose a woman by leaking all this stuff, is not going to work. It will not fly."

"I had nothing to do with the leaks," Mondale repeated. "I

promise you I had nothing to do with them." Read this morn-ing's paper, I suggested to him. He said he would and then get back to me.

I didn't really expect him to call me back, but half an hour later, he did. He apologized, promising that the stories would stop, that they wouldn't happen again. But I was still angry and let my emotions get away from me.

"Please take my name out of consideration," I told Mondale. "I do not want to be a part of this process anymore. I never really did want it."

But he refused. "No," Mondale said. "I am seriously consid-ering you as my running mate. And you have my word that there will be no more negative stories about you."

I believed him. After all, I knew Fritz, knew he was a good and decent man. Obviously, someone on his staff was behind this. But why didn't he fire whoever was responsible? Reportedly, it was Jim Johnson, Mondale's campaign chairman. I would not have stood still for that. If you can't control your own staff, who can you control? In all my work with Team A, and with the women's groups as well, there had never been one leak. Not one. If there had been, I would never have worked with the person responsible again. It was that simple.

Still, I felt better after talking to Fritz. I told John I felt assured that there would be no more snide remarks about me in the press and got on the phone to call off my letter of with-drawal. Then I went outside to plant what few annuals I had time to put in for the upcoming summer.

The leaks had done a lot of damage to Mondale's credibility with the gender-gap vote, however, and there is more than one theory that points to this moment as sealing the candidacy for a woman. The resulting political storm was immediate, with the women's groups protesting the rotten tactics being used by a male high in the Mondale campaign. The women were not going to stand still for any woman's qualifications being attacked in order to pave the way for the selection of a male candidate. If Mondale wanted to go with a man, that was all right. But this was a dangerous way to go about it. And the Mondale people knew it. With less than a week to go before the Convention began, no damage control could make up for the harm being done. Overnight the Mondale campaign had jeopardized the gender-gap vote they had courted so carefully.

Other theorists point to the extraordinary delegation of women—twenty-three strong—who had kept their date with Mondale in Minnesota on July 4 as the factor that clinched his decision. The apparent stridency of the NOW Convention the week before had made it appear as if Mondale was being forced to choose a woman. That was no good. The women in the delegation wanted Mondale to pick a woman if he honestly thought it would be the right political choice, but not because he had been pressured into it. If he had decided to go with a woman as a result of their pressure, then the woman could be blamed if the ticket subsequently lost. To oil the political waters, these women wanted to reassure Mondale he had their support if he went with a man—or with a woman.

I hadn't gone to Minnesota with them, of course, being one of the potential nominees. But Ann Richards, the state treasurer of Texas, had—along with others, such as former Congresswoman Patsy Mink of Hawaii; Carol Bellamy, president of the New York City Council; Sharon Percy Rockefeller, chair of the board of directors of the Corporation for Public Broadcasting; Anne Wexler, a Mondale adviser and former Carter aide (who would become my senior political adviser); and Betty Friedan, author of *The Feminine Mystique* and a founder of NOW.

"Mondale listened very carefully to each one of us," Friedan told me later. "I told him that I had started an organization that had made history and I sensed now that a woman on the ticket would give historic resonance to his campaign. It would mobilize the gender gap, embody the 'new' politics, and lead to the future. After all, women had delivered fifty-eight percent of the New York primary vote, the turning point of his campaign."

For Mondale, time was running out. Hart was still considering a challenge to Mondale at the Convention for the nomination. And last-minute rumors were flying fast and furiously that Hart was about to ask me to be his running mate. It would have been a daring political move designed to draw Mondale's delegates to support Hart instead. Mondale had to move fast if he was going to preempt Hart.

Which way would it go? I still didn't know, even after I arrived in San Francisco on July 10. All the recent signs had been positive. In the flurry of the last twenty-four hours, Mondale aides Michael Berman in New York and John Reilly in San Francisco had grilled me. The moment of truth was arriving.

I didn't know that the final NWPC delegate survey had been rushed to Mondale by Barbara Mikulski, showing that the delegates felt overwhelmingly that the Democratic Party should nominate a woman for Vice President; and that of the likely women candidates, my name was at the top of the list.

THE TIME
IS NOW

"Vice President . . . it has such a nice ring to it."

—*St. Paul, Minnesota, July 12, 1984.*

O N J U L Y 1 1 , I W O K E U P
early in the morning in the Hyatt Embarcadero in San Francisco
to call John at his office in New York. I had to talk to my
husband. After the events of the last twenty-four hours, it was
put-up-or-shut-up time.

"This vice-presidential thing is serious," I said to him, telling
him about John Reilly's surprise visit the night before. "Fritz is
going to call me this afternoon one way or the other. What do
you think?"

John didn't even pause. "Go for it," he said.

"But there will be a lot of changes in our lives if I get it," I
went on. "I've already been away for six months on Platform.
Now I'll be away for at least another four. And they'll dig into
our lives just the way they did in 1978, but worse."

"We'll deal with it," John said.

"Is there anything we have to worry about?" I asked him,
understanding that as much as you might love somebody, there
could be things you don't know.

"There's nothing as far as I know," he said. And of course,
at that time there wasn't.

"Who do you love the best?" I asked, the traditional banter that had always passed between us.

"You," he said. And we hung up.

As I look back on that conversation now, I wonder whether it was fair. Did John really have a choice? Could he have said no? I question whether I was telling him what might be about to happen to us just so that he'd know or whether I was making sure he'd never be able to say I hadn't asked his opinion. But the time for pulling out had come and gone. We both knew it. And besides, there was still the possibility that I wouldn't become the vice-presidential candidate.

After our talk I immediately put the vice-presidential drama out of my mind. After all, I had work to do, with a full convention schedule ahead of me no matter what happened. That evening I was to deliver a speech to the World Affairs Council, which still needed polishing. But then I've never been one to put all my eggs in one basket.

Reilly called at one p.m. "OK," he said.

"OK what?" I responded.

"What did you want me to call you for?" he said.

"Because," I reminded him, "you and I had a very real conversation about the vice-presidential nomination last night. I would assume I am down to the wire for serious consideration. And I wanted to talk to John ahead of time to make sure he had no objections."

"And?" Reilly asked.

I took a deep breath. "You can go with me if you choose to," I said. "As far as the Zaccaros are concerned, it's all go."

"We'll get back to you at four-thirty," Reilly said.

The phone never stopped ringing all day with calls from the press and questions on Convention business. In between interruptions I worked on my speech with Jan Kalicki and David Koshgarian, who was the legislative director of my Washington office doing double duty as a speechwriter. I felt remarkably calm about the pending Mondale call, more worried about my remarks to the World Affairs Council. The meeting was going to be carried live on local television, the fifteen hundred members were very knowledgeable, and here was my presumed weakness again, foreign affairs. I took off my shoes, curled up on the couch, and went at it.

*   *   *

I was in the sitting room putting the finishing touches on my speech to the council when the phone rang again. This time it was Mondale. I took the call in the privacy of the bedroom. "Hi," he said. "Hi," I replied. "How are you doing?" he said. "Fine," I replied. Here it comes, I thought. And no matter what he was going to say, I had my reply ready: I will work as hard as I can for the ticket. I want you to win and you have my total support. I think you will be a tremendous President.

"Will you be my running mate?" he asked. I didn't pause for a minute. "That would be terrific," I answered, and then added the extra phrase I'd been saving for my planned response: "I want you to know, Fritz, that I am deeply honored." And I still am.

But did I feel emotional, did my heart race and my palms sweat? No. I can't focus on my emotions and still accomplish what I have to. Instead I thought: Gerry Ferraro is going to have a unique opportunity to run for Vice President of the United States, and she might very well be Vice President and that's one heck of a job and she's going to have to work very hard. This man on the other end of the phone has taken one gigantic leap, not only for all women but for me in particular. He's been hearing for months, after all, that my experience isn't heavy enough for the job. And yet, he has still gone through with it, very courageously. And that in turn makes me even more determined to do the very best job for him and for all of us that I can.

I stuck my head out of the bedroom door and said to my curiosity-ridden staff members: "How does it feel to be a part of history?"

Then I called home to tell my family, who seemed to go into a state of shock. "It's really yes, not maybe?" Laura shrieked in disbelief.

I called my mother, my wonderful mother, who wasn't at all surprised by my selection. "Of course it would be you," she said. "I've known it all along. Who could be a better Vice President?"

And as I hurried out the door a little late to make my speech, I turned to Eleanor Lewis and said, smiling, "You got me into this. It's all your fault." And off we went, at a dead run.

Into the arms of the press. The scene in the St. Francis Hotel, where I was going to speak in the ballroom, was unbelievable.

The Convention was about to begin, the vice-presidential conjecture was at its peak, and there were members of the press jammed into the hallway from all over the world. Facing this phalanx of cameras and television lights, fielding questions about whether or not Reilly had been to see me about the Vice Presidency, I realized I had a long night before me and had better go to the ladies' room.

Fritz had told me over the phone that I'd be picked up right after my speech by his aide Peter Kyros to leave yet again for North Oaks. He wanted to make the announcement there. But Minnesota was a long way away, and I'm one of those people who thinks ahead. So I took a detour up the stairs, realizing for the first time that every single television camera was watching me. It was an odd and rather unnerving feeling.

I was more nervous about my speech, however. As soon as the vice-presidential announcement was made the following day, the speech I was about to make would be replayed time and again. This was a tough audience. There were going to be experts asking me questions on foreign policy. The stakes were suddenly a lot higher than they had been an hour ago. And I was the only one who knew it.

But I had nothing to worry about. I walked into the ballroom to a standing ovation that immediately set me up for my speech. And in the question-and-answer period that followed, I played a delicate game of "I've got a secret."

"Do you think a woman will be chosen as Vice President?" I was asked.

I gave the answer I had given many times before as Chair of the Platform Committee. I pointed to the fact that a woman could add strength to the ticket, veering off then to attack Reagan and his policies, while knowing full well that only I had the correct answer to that question.

"What are your plans for the future?"

Oh, how I wanted to tell them. But I was having the time of my life. This part of my candidacy was going to be fun.

And so was the next. The crush of journalists, camera crews, and photographers was so dense as I left the World Affairs Council meeting that Charles Atkins had to block to get me through. I'd never experienced anything like the crowd at the St. Francis Hotel that night and would probably still be stuck there if Charles hadn't said, "Follow me!" and shoved our way through.

*   *   *

Immediately I was caught up in an escape plan to spirit me out of San Francisco and back to North Oaks in a manner more suited to James Bond than Gerry Ferraro. Even while I'd been on the phone that afternoon talking to Fritz, a private plane had been dispatched from Chicago to pick me up. The owner, Mondale fund-raiser Tom Rosenberg, had been eager but mystified. "Who am I picking up? The blonde or the brunette?" he'd radioed from the air. Even the Mondales' oldest daughter, Eleanor, didn't know who the nominee was when she was summoned back to Minnesota for the announcement. Arriving on the red-eye from California, she peeked into her bedroom, where I was sleeping. "It's the blonde," she squealed, jumping up and down with excitement.

To put everyone off the scent, my pickup plane had landed in Oakland rather than San Francisco. When Charles and I finally made it to the sidewalk outside the St. Francis, I was shoved into the back of a black limousine with a man I'd never laid eyes on before. "See you guys," I called to my staff standing guard over the car door. The press clamored to know where I was going. "To a private dinner with friends," they were told as I made my escape. "That's why it's not on the schedule."

But who was this guy in the back of the car? He was supposed to be Peter Kyros, the Mondale aide who had suddenly appeared in my hotel suite after Mondale's phone call and taken over all my duties, including the call to John to meet us in North Oaks the next day with whatever children he could round up that fast. But he wasn't. "I'm Michael Cardozo, one of Fritz's attorneys in Washington," this stranger said to me rapidly. (Apparently, he had been in the suite earlier, but I had not met him.) "We're picking up Peter Kyros in a few blocks." OK, I'll buy that, I thought. But still, here I was in a strange limo with a strange man. Nobody knew where I was. I could have dropped off the face of the earth at that moment and no one would ever know where I'd gone.

Then suddenly the limo slowed in front of Gump's and Kyros jumped in while the car was still moving. I felt reassured, but now convinced that we were all part of a movie. Our getaway had been successful. No one had followed us. In fact we arrived at the airport before the plane had finished refueling for the return trip. We stood in line at a nearby diner to get something to eat before the long trip east. I ordered a tuna melt, wondering what in heaven's name I was doing here. "If they only knew," Peter Kyros said, looking around the jammed diner. Peter, who had taken over all the logistics, was terrific.

The plane was small, a six-seater jet, and we didn't get to Minnesota until one a.m. I'd tried and failed to get some sleep en route. Since I was sitting in the rear, the luggage was piled right behind me, and I couldn't get the seat to recline. I looked around the seat carefully, trying to figure it out, but it was impossible. And I was not about to ask someone to help me. That would have been just great. Here I was, the brand-new vice-presidential candidate, and I didn't even know how to work an airplane seat. So I just sat there thinking, "How long am I going to have to be in this thing before we get to Minnesota?" It took forever.

I was slightly concerned about how I was going to greet Fritz. I had no problem with Joan. She had been very warm and friendly on my other trips to North Oaks, and a firm supporter of a woman for Vice President. Joan had been delightful then and would remain so throughout the campaign. All she really wanted was that her husband win. And she was wonderful. If it had not been for me, she would have been the focus of attention as the wife of the presidential nominee. But here I was in the limelight, the new kid on the block. Never once, however, did she display anything but the warmest feelings toward me.

But Fritz was another story. The last time I had really talked to him I had complained bitterly about the stories in the press. And besides, there was all the fuss about kissing. He hadn't kissed Dianne Feinstein when she had come to North Oaks for her interview. The press decided that made her a serious contender. He had kissed me, though, when I'd come to report on Platform, which to the press had signaled the opposite. What a pain this gender thing was going to be, I thought, as we flew on and on. I decided that as the vice-presidential candidate I would definitely not kiss Fritz when we arrived.

We arrived. And both the Mondales kissed me. "I'm so thrilled it's you," Joan said. "I'm so glad you're with me," said Fritz. And immediately I felt welcome, especially when I met their son Teddy for the first time in the bathroom the next morning, both of us in our bathrobes. "Congratulations," he said to me continuing to brush his teeth. This is going to be just fine, I thought. Just like home.

But the business at hand was certainly not like home. The phones never stopped ringing with congratulations the next morning as the word leaked out. Mondale manned the one in the den. I was on the one in the kitchen, talking to my mother, Tip O'Neill, Ted Kennedy, Charlie Rangel, and Bella Abzug, who had immediately started passing out little cigars bearing the inscription "It's a girl." I kept worrying about when my family would get to Minnesota. This was the beginning of our new life and I wanted them there so we could all share it together. My thoughts kept straying to John alone in New York, suddenly having to get Laura packed, find John, Jr., in Hawaii, and make arrangements for Donna, who had her own apartment in Manhattan, where she was working for a securities firm. It seemed too much to expect of one person on such short order.

What I didn't know was that my family was caught up in a cloak-and-dagger intrigue of their own. Kyros had told John to fly out to Minnesota under an assumed name to bypass the press. So Pat Flynn, making the reservations under the names of John and Laura Winston, had gone to the airport herself with her husband, Bill, to pick up the tickets, just in case the press had caught on. And of course they had. There Pat stood in line, ahead of Jimmy Breslin from the New York *Daily News* and John Stacks, of *Time* magazine. Some secret. In the spirit of the deception, Pat motioned frantically for Bill to take her place, knowing she was recognizable to the press. But the game was up. When my thinly disguised family arrived at the airport, they were met with three television crews.

All I cared about was whether they were going to make it in time. I didn't relax until Laura and John caught up with me at the state capitol, where Mondale was to make the announcement. Donna, John said, couldn't just walk out of her job and would join us the next day, while John, Jr., still hadn't been located in Hawaii. Two out of four was fine by me and I felt relieved, but concerned for my husband. He looked exhausted, not having gotten any sleep all night trying to get everything organized. Here he was being ordered around by strangers, dropping whatever plans he might have had. Of course that was what political wives had been doing for years. But still, I felt for him.

And then it was time for my first choreography: "Mr. Mondale will walk out first. You will follow him. He will go to the podium, he will make his comments, and you will stand on the side to his right. After you make your comments, you and Mr. Mondale will both then wave with your outside arms; Mr. Zaccaro will come up on your right side, Mrs. Mondale on Mr. Mondale's left . . ." The arm waving made me a little nervous. I was wearing a short-sleeved dress. Would the flesh on my upper arms wobble if I waved? After all, I am over eighteen. I decided just to raise my arm and not wave it.

And then it was time. I stood where I was supposed to, listening to Fritz make the announcement that would interrupt the course John and I had set, a sudden new course that would take us into the unplanned and the unknown. As I waited by Fritz's side I felt nothing but enthusiasm and optimism, sure that this Democratic ticket would return the leadership of our country to the party that cared deeply for its citizens, whose view of the world stressed peace and opportunity for everyone. I would never have accepted Mondale's offer if I didn't think we could win. I'm not into losing or being offered up as a sacrifice. After four years of Reagan, the voters must be realizing, had to be realizing, that the current White House was without leadership, direction, or compassion, ran my thoughts.

"This is an exciting choice," Mondale was saying about my candidacy. "This—is—an—exciting—choice!" And then it was my turn to make my remarks, to accept the honor and the challenge the presidential nominee of my party had bestowed upon me. "Thank you, Vice President Mondale," I said, and then couldn't resist ad-libbing: "Vice President . . . it has such a nice ring to it."

One face stood out in the hastily assembled Minnesota audience. It belonged to Joan McLean, the force behind Team A, who had caught the first flight out of San Francisco as soon as she'd heard the rumors of my selection. And she was beaming. The challenge now would be to make the prophecy in her fortune cookie come true. I was going to give it everything I had.

THE ISSUES
AT STAKE

*"Every generation faces one overriding problem. For ours,
it is to freeze the nuclear arms race and keep the peace."*

—*oft-repeated statement as a major campaign issue.*

R EAGAN WAS FOND OF SAY-
ing that there was a clearer political choice between the two presidential candidates in 1984 than there had been in fifty years. And
for once, he was absolutely right. In 1960, the political line between the Republicans and the Democrats had been so thin that
Kennedy aide Arthur Schlesinger had to spell out what few differences there were by publishing his own pamphlet: "Kennedy
or Nixon—Does It Make Any Difference?" This time there was
no doubt about it.

The issues were clear-cut, and Walter Mondale and I agreed
on most of them. I had been a strong supporter of the Carter-
Mondale policies and had worked hard in Congress to carry them
out. It was not going to be any problem for me to go around the
country and campaign for what we both stood for. That is the
appropriate role for a vice-presidential candidate, and thankfully I
did not have to tailor my views.

But what if I disagreed with Fritz on a proposed policy once we
were elected? Fritz assured me he would welcome my perspective
while policy was being formulated—just as Jimmy Carter had
assured him.

Although all of the campaign issues were familiar to me,

I knew that I had to do some homework on Fritz's detailed position. After all, I would have to explain and promote our agenda before a variety of audiences all over the country. As a national candidate I would also have to be totally knowledgeable about the details of an issue's ramifications in each state, from the environment to foreign trade.

The setting was Lake Tahoe, high up in the Sierra Nevada Mountains of California. The time was two days after my selection as the vice-presidential candidate. And in my lap were the briefing books the Mondale staff had given me, which laid out in detail Fritz's positions on every issue from the Simpson-Mazzoli immigration bill to the MX missile. Not only were all of Mondale's public positions recorded on each issue, but so were mine, highlighted where the two of us disagreed. Fortunately, our disagreements were very few.

Nevertheless, the pressure was intense. Hour after hour I sat on the deck of our cabin with Mondale's top issues people and taped their background briefings. We concentrated on domestic issues, such as the budget and taxes, but also touched on defense and on troubled areas such as Afghanistan. John, Jr., had finally arrived from Hawaii, and he and his sisters joined us as well. The children were very attentive. They wanted to be involved in the campaign. They needed to know the issues. And they were certainly getting a crash course.

The briefing process felt familiar. I had just gone through a set of such meetings as Chair of the Platform Committee. I had kept abreast of the issues during the regional hearings and the drafting process. At a series of breakfast meetings in my congressional office, I had also had a dozen or so experts come and talk about such issues as arms control, U.S.-Soviet relations, the situation in the Philippines, and Eastern Europe. Access to some of the top minds in Washington had been one of the advantages of being a member of Congress. There was so much talent there, so many people eager to help.

The briefings continued when I returned home to Queens after the convention. Now we turned more specifically to foreign affairs and arms control. The experts were Madeleine Albright, a professor at the School of Foreign Service at Georgetown

University and a National Security Council staffer during the Carter Administration, who had been at Lake Tahoe and would later join my staff as my foreign policy adviser, and Barry Carter, a former NSC aide to Henry Kissinger and now a Georgetown University law professor. Congressman Tom Downey of Long Island made a special trip to my home one day to share his expertise. The briefings ran from dawn till dusk, and again I taped them all. At times I thought my brain would explode from all the details I had to absorb so quickly. "Let's go for a walk," I'd suggest around three-thirty p.m. But what did we do while we walked? We talked some more.

I was concentrating so hard during these walks that often I set off across a street without waiting for the light or even looking carefully. The Secret Service agents were very upset with me, even though the traffic in my neighborhood of Forest Hills is very light. "What are you so worried about?" I asked one of the agents. This is a quiet neighborhood. "Nobody's about to run me over."

"But if somebody does," he smiled back, "do you know how much paperwork it will mean?" That was a persuasive argument.

When Madeleine and Barry left for the day, they would give me additional material to read on everything from arms control to Zimbabwe. I listened to their tapes wherever I went. I played them back in the car, in the kitchen, even in the bathtub at night. "Who's in there with you?" John would call through the bathroom door. "Oh, just Barry Carter again," I'd joke back. And slowly but surely I absorbed all the information. The first time through I listened. The second time it all seemed familiar. By the third run-through, the incredibly detailed data had become part of my life.

Together all of us developed an "issues" strategy. In what areas was Reagan most vulnerable? The answers were many: foreign policy and arms control; the economy and the mounting budget and trade deficits; the ticking time bomb of hazardous wastes; the hopelessness of the poor and jobless, as well as the struggle of single-parent families and the elderly; the slashing of funds for job training and educational programs. We grouped these vulnerabilities into a loose framework of themes: war and peace, fairness and opportunity.

Fritz and I would have our issues desks side by side at campaign headquarters in Washington. And our staffs would be in daily communication with the staffers traveling with each candidate. Our speeches on the chosen themes would be coordinated as we campaigned separately around the country, working from our individual strengths.

I thought I was at my best when I could personalize the issues and make clear to my audience that we as voters had every right to have our questions answered. I had the sense that, especially on foreign policy questions, voters felt the issues did not concern them directly, or were too complicated. As a woman and a new voice, I could help demystify arms control, talk about the defense budget in plain English, and bring home the potential danger of Reagan's Middle East and Central American policies.

Under Reagan, the world was becoming increasingly unsafe. Fifty thousand nuclear warheads were already in place, and between the Soviet Union and the United States, at least five new warheads were being produced every day. Yet, consistent with his past opposition to every major nuclear arms control agreement, including the Limited Test Ban Treaty of 1963 and Salt I of 1972, Reagan was still resisting any lessening of nuclear tensions. As we started our campaign, he was the first President in thirty years not to have entered into any arms control agreement, and the first President since Herbert Hoover not to have even met with the top Soviet leader.

Arms control was a critical issue, and our position absolutely clear. If elected, we would seek to stop or at least to slow the arms race by making a mutually verifiable nuclear arms freeze our highest priority. For humanity's sake, we had to reduce the risk of war. "Every generation faces one overriding problem," I would say again and again in the course of the campaign. "For ours, it is to freeze the nuclear arms race and keep the peace."

Reagan's record on arms control was abysmal. If John Kennedy had listened to him, we wouldn't have a test ban treaty. If Lyndon Johnson had listened to him on the nonproliferation treaty, the danger would be greater than it already was that a Khomeini, a Qaddafi, or the PLO might get their hands on the bomb. If Richard Nixon had listened to him, we wouldn't have an ABM treaty, and the Soviets would be a bigger threat than they already were.

There was an alternative. This year the voter could choose a President who would call on the Soviet leadership his first day in office, not on the first day of his reelection campaign—as Reagan would in his September 1984 meeting with then Soviet Foreign Minister Andrei Gromyko; a President who would tell us his plans for controlling nuclear weapons now; a President who would do everything possible to negotiate a mutual, verifiable freeze; a President who would not only stand up to the Soviets but also have the wisdom to sit down with them in order to end the arms race. Reagan had done none of these things, but had instead heightened the risk of nuclear confrontation by declaring in 1983 his intention to launch the arms race into space and by throwing away an opportunity in 1984 to negotiate an agreement on antisatellite weapons.

Rather than seeking to limit arms, President Reagan had gone full speed ahead spending money on defense, spending it without a strategy, and on the wrong things.

Now, Fritz and I both recognized that a safer world required a strong America. We supported steady, sustainable increases in the defense budget to keep our forces strong. We especially wanted to improve our conventional, or nonnuclear, forces. Stronger conventional forces would reduce the likelihood that in a crisis or conflict a President would feel the need to resort to nuclear weapons. We also supported reforming Pentagon management and strengthening the role of the chairman of the Joint Chiefs of Staff.

But we both opposed Reagan's plan for the deployment of the MX missile, because it was vulnerable and destabilizing. We opposed the B1–B bomber because it was wasteful, and binary gas because it was dangerous—and we already had large stocks of nerve gas.

The Reagan Administration had failed to make tough choices. It lacked a coherent strategy, often ignoring our allies and planning to fight almost everywhere simultaneously with only a vague sense of priorities. The Joint Chiefs of Staff recognized that we did not have even close to enough resources to carry out this strategy.

Under Reagan and Defense Secretary Cap Weinberger, the

Pentagon had been turned loose on a shopping spree, a weapons binge. In the first three years of the Reagan Administration alone, overall defense spending had risen about twenty-five percent, *after* correcting for inflation. Even worse, the spending emphasized nuclear weapons. Spending for strategic weapon procurement in the Reagan defense budgets from fiscal years 1981–85 rose 196 percent, or over five times faster than for conventional weapons.

While the Pentagon was buying fancy new weapons, our soldiers were not being trained adequately to use them, ammunition was in short supply, and spare parts were at a premium. Under Reagan, the percentage of the defense budget for procurement skyrocketed from about twenty-six percent in 1980 to over thirty-five percent proposed for 1985, while the proportion for operations and maintenance dropped.

The public was just becoming aware of the outrageous spare parts problem. Among other well-documented examples, the Pentagon had blithely paid $9600 for an Allen wrench, $1100 for a 22-cent plastic chair leg cap, over $7000 for a coffee maker, and $640 for a toilet seat cover. I would try to dramatize this waste to my audiences by saying that, at those prices, if Reagan went to the hardware store for a tool box, he could end up paying over a million dollars for it.

My message would be that although the political leaders in Washington and the generals and admirals were charged with looking out for our national security, all of us have to live with—or die with—the results of their decisions. I believed that by stating starkly and simply the choices between Walter Mondale and Ronald Reagan on arms control and defense, I would be helping to move the national security debate out of the war rooms and the board rooms into the glare of the public forum.

Because of the freeze movement, television programs such as *The Day After,* and, frankly, because of Fritz and me, something incredible did indeed happen during the 1984 election: discussions about weapon systems and the risk of war were taking place not only among experts, but all across America. Almost every time I spoke there was at least one substantive question on defense from someone in the audience.

We believed that Reagan's defense requirements reflected his mistaken assessment of the international situation. The President's bellicose policies in Central America were also inflaming tensions rather than reducing them. While the CIA conducted a covert war in Nicaragua, American troops held military exercises in Honduras. Reagan had asked Congress for funds ostensibly to assist the Contras in stopping the flow of arms from Nicaragua to El Salvador; in fact, the Contras' declared objective was to overthrow the Sandinista government. To drum up popular support for his request for military funds, he had lauded the Contras as "freedom fighters"—while across the border in El Salvador, the guerrilla forces opposing the government there were branded as "terrorists." Reacting in frustration to legislative reluctance to invest in a military rather than a political solution in Nicaragua, the Reagan Administration had indiscriminately ordered the mining of Nicaraguan harbors. And when the World Court agreed to hear Nicaragua's complaint that the mining had been illegal, the United States announced that it would ignore the World Court's decision.

During the Democratic platform sessions, we had spent a lot of time discussing what we considered was the looming disaster in Central America. The Administration's policies were riddled with confusion and bravura. Reagan continued to commit the error of supporting authoritarian military regimes against the wishes of the people they ruled. He continued to concentrate only on the strategic importance of Central America, forgetting that the region's instability had been brought on by a history of local problems: hunger, disease, and social injustice. We knew that the area was important to us strategically, and our platform called for making this area a top priority, but to us that meant making an effort to understand what was really going on in the countries themselves.

Reagan liked to simplify the conflict there, especially in Nicaragua, in terms of the communists versus the noncommunists, the bad guys versus the good guys. Maybe that's the only way he understood it. But during my congressional trip to Nicaragua in January 1984, I had discovered firsthand that Reagan's definition of the situation was much too simple. Yes, there was Marxism there. No doubt about it. Yes, there were Soviet and East European weapons being brought in, along with Cuban advisers. Most of Nicaragua's military armaments, the U.S. ambassador, Anthony

Quainton, had told us, come from the Soviet Union. But that wasn't the whole story. There were also local and regional problems rooted in a long history of social and political inequities. How were we going to deal with all that?

Personally, I questioned whether the money we were presently pouring in to the Contras to force a military solution was necessary or was even going to work. When I had asked a group of Contras in Costa Rica whether they thought a solution could be reached by negotiation, they had replied, "Yes."

But still we were pursuing a solution by force. And even if force succeeded in unseating the Sandinistas, I doubted that the new government would be more effective—and more democratic—than the current regime. Certainly the new government would be as totally unschooled in administration as the present one. And the odds were that the cycle of civil war would keep being triggered. "What would happen if you overthrew the government and got control?" I asked one of the Contra representatives we met in Managua.

"They would retreat into the hills and become the new counterrevolutionaries," he readily admitted.

My trip helped to convince me that the United States could not achieve a military solution in Central America without involving our own armed forces—a disastrous outcome. This truth was apparent during a friendly exchange with a member of the Nicaraguan upper class over lunch at the American embassy in Managua. He was very unhappy with the Sandinista regime, a portion of his business having been nationalized and his profits restricted. Over a glass of wine before lunch he had told me his son was studying in the United States.

"No kidding?" I said. "How terrific. But how come he's there and not here?"

"Because Nicaragua now has compulsory military service, and I would rather send him out of the country than have him join the army of a regime I detest," he said.

That was understandable. "My son, too, is in college," I told him, striking the international chord of the concern all parents share for their children. And when later I asked the entire group at the table what solutions they had, if any, to the unrest in Nicaragua, it was my prelunch companion who said he had the answer.

"Let's hear it," I said. "If you can solve this now, then I can cancel the rest of my trip and go home."

"The United States should invade," he responded firmly.

I couldn't believe it. "Let me understand you correctly," I said. "What you are proposing is that the United States send in troops to unseat the Sandinistas here and establish a government that would be more favorable to your interests."

"Exactly so," he replied. "We cannot do it without military intervention from the United States."

"Do you realize what you're saying?" I asked him. "You have sent your son to the safety of the United States. Yet you are asking my son to leave his home to come here to fight your war for you." That was a price I was unwilling to pay.

I would use that exchange as often as I could in speeches, bringing home the end result of Reagan's pursuit of a military rather than a politically negotiated solution in Nicaragua in a way every parent could understand. I am not soft. But the facts showed that Reagan's policies were counterproductive. Rather than diminishing Sandinista influence, his policies seemed to be giving them more legitimacy. Rather than making sure that there was less communist influence in Central America, his policies seemed to have produced more. I used to tell my audiences that in the previous four years, the Sandinista army and security forces had increased to four times their 1980 size. There were more Soviet and Eastern bloc advisers than there had been in 1980; and there were thousands more Cubans scattered throughout Central America. In El Salvador, after four years and despite more than $1 billion in military and economic aid to the government there, the number of guerrillas had more than doubled.

I knew that we had legitimate security interests in Central America, but we would get nowhere if we did not seek a regional solution by negotiating. I was convinced that Ronald Reagan was militarizing a conflict that could be solved by peaceful means, that he was Americanizing the conflict and doing so by covert means that the American people did not want.

"It's time to end the secret war in Nicaragua," I would say over and over again during the campaign. "Let's stop the fighting and step up the talks. Let's send in the diplomats before we deploy the Marines."

I have always believed that military action should be the last resort. So, probably, do the majority of men. But during the campaign men questioned whether I as a woman could deal with tough foreign-affairs issues—issues of life and death, fighting and dying, having to push the nuclear button. In fact life requires that women face survival issues more frequently than men. We are the ones who give birth, who more often than not wait with our children for hours in emergency rooms. We understand that you don't risk life unnecessarily, that force should be used only when every other avenue is exhausted.

I was equally distressed about Reagan's lack of a coherent Middle East policy. What I had learned on my trip to Israel and then on to Lebanon in the spring of 1983 with several congressional colleagues had put me at odds not only with the Reagan Administration but with my own Speaker, Tip O'Neill.

In Beirut, we had met with our Ambassador; with the Marine commander; with Wadi Haddad, the chief adviser to President Gemayal; and with Palestinian women at the Shatilla and Sabra refugee camps, which should have been described more accurately as slums. Even after the massacre in the camps some seven months earlier, little or no attention was being paid to the welfare of the refugees there. We saw no evidence of the United Nations Refugee Assistance effort, not one person wearing an UNRA armband, not even a sign giving directions to any health facility.

We did, however, see and talk to the Marines who were in Lebanon as part of a multinational peacekeeping force. Many of them were eighteen, nineteen, twenty—about the same age as John, Jr. And what I saw made me frightened for them. Various Lebanese factions were at war in Beirut. There were sporadic sniper attacks, one of which had killed a young Marine from my district in Queens. The Pentagon's own commission later confirmed my impression that there seemed to be inadequate security for the Marines, housed as they all were in one building, protected only by bunkers and barbed wire. Wadi Haddad told us that his government would need the Marines there only for another year to train the Lebanese forces. But after talking to others and to the Marines themselves, I didn't agree with him. As we reported later to Congress, it would take at least two to three years before the multinational forces could be safely withdrawn. And meanwhile, the Marines would remain in constant danger.

When the vote on the resolution to extend the Marines' stay in Lebanon came up in the House five months later, in September 1983, I spent the day on the floor listening to the debate. But nothing I heard convinced me that the danger our Marines were in was worth the price.

"Gerry, you're with us on this, aren't you?" Tip O'Neill said to me as he passed by in the aisle while the vote on the resolution was being taken.

"No, Mr. Speaker, I'm not," I told him.

Tip pressed me. "You are a member of the House leadership, Gerry," he said.

But I had seen and heard too much in Lebanon. "I know, Mr. Speaker, but I don't agree with you on this issue," I told him. And I voted against extending the Marines' stay in Lebanon.

Having met many of them in Lebanon, I saw the Marines not only as professional soldiers but also as human beings, as sons. I had taken down the names and addresses of those from New York and had called their parents when I got back to let them know how their sons were doing. And so I was devastated four weeks after the House vote when John, Jr. woke me up early on October 23, calling me from college to tell me the Marine barracks had just been blown up. I thought he'd gotten the episode mixed up with the embassy bombing, which had occurred two weeks after we'd left Lebanon. But no.

"Mom, I just heard it on the radio," he said, all upset. "A couple of hundred guys have been killed."

I was stunned. "I hear you," I said, shaking myself awake.

"It's an act of war, isn't it?" he said. "I've registered with the Selective Service. What do I do now?"

There it was, my son calling his congresswoman mother, who was supposed to know all about acts of war, so that she could tell him what the procedure was to defend the Reagan Administration's mess in Lebanon.

The criticism leveled at Reagan for the loss of so many Marines was intense.

Three times in seventeen months, terrorists had driven their lethal cargoes of explosives right to the front of our embassies and detonated them. The first time, the embassy had no gate. The second time, the gate was open. The third time, which was to occur during the campaign, the gate had not yet been installed.

A Pentagon investigation was launched after the Marines were killed in October 1983, negligence was found on behalf of the Marine command, and Reagan would announce after the finding that as commander-in-chief he would accept the full responsibility. Great. But what did that mean, "I accept full responsibility but the American public won't hold me at fault"? No one should be allowed to get away with that, especially the President of the United States. A true leader admits he has made a mistake and takes steps to make sure it doesn't happen again. But Reagan had a different way of minimizing the criticism.

Two days after the Marines were killed he ordered the U.S. invasion of Grenada. The politics of it were absolutely mind boggling. Just a few weeks earlier I had been to a briefing by the secretary of the Army at which several hot spots—maybe thirteen— in the world were pinpointed on the Defense Department map by what looked like electric bomb explosions. Grenada was just one of them. There was no need to invade Grenada at that exact moment (or maybe ever) except for the political factor: when you have a failure, you move to an immediate success. And he had. I thought as soon as I heard about Grenada, "Reagan has changed the subject."

I was against the invasion, not only because of its seemingly political motivation but because I thought it had actually placed the American medical students on Grenada, whom the Administration was supposedly rescuing, in greater jeopardy instead. Even the invasion itself seemed pretty ludicrous. Reagan deployed about five thousand soldiers, helicopters, and a naval task force to subdue around seven hundred Cubans, only some of whom were soldiers, among a Grenadian population of less than one hundred thousand—most of whom were women and children.

Grenada was certainly not a peaceful little island paradise, of course. Cuban influence was growing. Maurice Bishop, the prime minister, had been assassinated, and a curfew had been imposed.

There was good reason to be concerned about not only the political stability of the island but the safety of the medical students as well. John Santucci, the DA from Queens County, whose son had been a student in a medical school in Grenada, had taken his son off the island after he had sized up the situation. But were the conditions there cause for a full-scale U.S. invasion at that very moment? Wouldn't it have been more prudent for the Administration to send a plane down first to remove all the medical students? It would have been so much easier.

Instead, U.S. military forces came in at night, wearing night camouflage, spraying gunfire, and scaring the kids half to death. Overnight the invasion of Grenada replaced the tragedy of the Marine massacre in Lebanon in the press. Now the Republicans had a new and positive campaign issue: President Reagan is strong. America is standing tall. President Reagan won't let anybody push us around. But still the Administration hadn't learned its lesson in the Middle East.

Eleven months later the U.S. embassy in East Beirut would be bombed and more lives lost. If the similar attacks against the embassy and the barracks had not been warning enough, for weeks the terrorists had been making explicit public threats against major American installations. Nevertheless, our personnel would be placed in a building without steel reinforcements, a strong guard gate would not yet have been installed, and earth fortifications designed to deflect explosions would not be in place. How did Reagan explain this last incident away? By comparing our nonexistent security to the common delays experienced in remodeling kitchens.

I didn't blame Reagan for the actual bombing, of course. But his cavalier reaction to the lapse of security at our embassy was inexcusable.

Then there was the economy, which affected foreign and domestic policy. Under Reagan, the economy was being held together with rubber bands. The President claimed the economy was recovering. What he left out was the cost. In only four years, Reagan had accumulated deficits greater than those of all other American Presidents combined. In 1984, the federal government was paying more than one hundred billion dollars in interest charges just to service the public debt, payments that not only did not buy any services for the American public but forced up interest rates on consumer and business loans, as well as on home mortgages. The trade deficit was growing. In the garment industry alone we were importing forty percent of our clothes and over thirty percent of our shoes. During the Reagan recession, a postwar record of 11.9 million Americans were out of work, compared with six million in 1979 and 7.4 million in 1980. Six million Americans had slipped below the poverty line (based on federal standards of family size and income) since Reagan took office. The Republican Administration had mortgaged the futures not only of our children but of our grandchildren as well.

The record trade deficit, which resulted from the strength of the dollar in world currency markets, plagued the entire country, but had different consequences in different regions. In the Northwest, there was little evidence of the heralded Reagan recovery, because the timber industry in Washington and Oregon could not compete with cheap timber from Canada. In the farm belt there was a massive credit crisis, with farmers seeing their exports declining or remaining flat. In Pennsylvania and Ohio, the steel industry was staggering, as imports from South Korea, Japan, and Brazil overwhelmed American markets.

But many people never understood the trade deficit. As a congresswoman I had tried to explain that a "strong" dollar was not a reason for patriotic pride. As a vice-presidential candidate I would try again, explaining that under Reagan, the trade deficit had grown steadily from thirty-nine billion dollars in 1981 to forty-three billion in 1982 and then to sixty-nine billion in 1983. The deficit for 1984 was expected to soar to over one hundred billion dollars. According to the Commerce Department, every billion-dollar increase in the foreign trade deficit means twenty-five thousand American jobs lost or not created. Reagan's 1983 trade deficit had already cost some 1.7 million Americans jobs, and his 1984 deficit could mean the loss of three million potential jobs.

Trade deficits do more than inhibit job growth. They keep interest rates high because industry and private citizens have to compete for credit with the federal government, which needs the money to keep the government running. The high interest rates, in turn, attract capital from foreign investors. The influx of foreign capital into the United States increases demand for the dollar, thus raising its value. Was that something to be proud of? Far from it.

The inflated value of the dollar was making American-made goods cost more both here and in markets abroad in comparison to foreign goods. "We're being socked both ways," I would tell my audiences. The budget deficit and resulting high interest rates added a thirty-percent surcharge to American goods sold abroad while giving a thirty-percent discount to foreign goods sold here. "It's not that the Japanese are better salesmen than we are. It's the budget deficit that's killing us in trade," I'd say. But people still didn't see the linkage between Reagan's budget deficits and the battering our industries were taking. Like many issues, the details had become so complex that the public could not possibly absorb quickly all the facts necessary to make an informed decision. Even the semantics were misleading, and so I stopped using the word "strong" to define the dollar and substituted "overvalued" or "distorted" instead.

The economy should have been the most persuasive issue in the campaign. But it would not be. Reagan had successfully erased it as a concern from people's minds. We would try to get the public to look back at Reagan's 1980 campaign promise not only to balance the budget, but to have a budget surplus of $93 billion by 1983. What did we have instead? A $180-billion deficit! "Well, folks, he's only a quarter of a trillion dollars off," I'd say, trying to get the point across with humor. But it wasn't funny. The budget deficit was appalling, reaching into every facet of American life.

No matter what we did, we would be unable to get the message across to the American people that Reagan's economic policies were a major cause of the trade deficit and the rising number of Americans slipping below the poverty line. Where unemployment was high, the people would understand all too well. In Youngstown, Ohio, for example, I would be cheered when I said: "It's time to replace an Administration that makes jobs its chief export. Ronald Reagan tells you to check the want ads. The problem is you don't get all those foreign newspapers where the jobs are being advertised." But nationally, Reagan's politics of "optimism" were persuasive, and personally he was very popular. Pat Schroeder had described him as the "Teflon" President, and she was right. We couldn't get anything to stick to him. Every poll we took, and they were almost daily, showed that many of the voters were with us on the major issues, but were still going to vote for Reagan.

It was hard for people to sense a risk to their future when the present seemed so rosy. The current prosperity was one such illusion. A maintenance-free environment was another. Reagan and his "environmental deputies" Interior Secretary James Watt and Environmental Protection Agency administrator Anne Gorsuch Burford had slowed or reversed virtually every national environmental program. Their record of retreat was perhaps best exemplified by the Reagan Administration's failure to protect the public from the nightmare of exposure to hazardous chemicals.

Local waste dump problems may not excite much interest on a broad national scale. But they should. To people who live near them, hazardous waste sites are a very serious health issue. And to the rest of us they are a red flag to our own communities, particularly our children. This nation has thousand upon thousand of such environmental time bombs ticking away, jeopardizing our future, yet the Reagan Administration had cleaned up only six of them in three and a half years, though Congress had created a Superfund to attack the problem. We needed to bring this home to the electorate. If Americans weren't worried about this problem now, they would be someday, if the Reagan Administration continued doing next to nothing.

So we would choose one campaign event to focus solely on this issue—Huber Heights, Ohio, not far from Dayton, where a landfill on the EPA's Superfund list was reportedly emitting noxious fumes and leaky hazardous chemicals into the ground, possibly contaminating underground well fields.

The idea was to have the event on October 4, in a family's backyard adjacent to the landfill. Four or five people from other parts of Ohio who also lived near similar waste sites were to join a panel there. The staff, for reasons of time and, I suppose, political safety because of the ever-present national television cameras, wanted the event to be fairly controlled—not spontaneous.

I was to make a few opening remarks, listen to the complaints of only the chosen panel, ask some scripted questions, then wrap it up. But I knew this issue; I had worked on it in

Congress, and I knew it was ours. No need to worry about political safety. And if we lost some time, well, we could make it up later in the day. So I abandoned the script and I opened up the discussion—not only to the panel but to the other couple of hundred people assembled around us.

I got a very emotional earful. One woman said, "I was a very conservative Republican. I'm still a registered Republican, but I will not vote for Ronald Reagan this year." She was so outraged.

A local official expressed concern that we were giving a bad name to his town by appearing at a landfill. I assured him this event was not a put-down. "There are thousands of Huber Heights throughout the country," I said. "We're here to say you're not alone in this battle. This is one of those times when you don't want the government off your back, you want it on your side."

Close to my heart, of course, were women's issues. Domestically, Reagan's record was unconscionable. Reversing forty years of Republican support for the Equal Rights Amendment, Reagan had removed the ERA from the Republican agenda. Intrusion into the private lives of women was being promoted by Reagan's determination to overturn legalized abortion. Since 1980, the Reagan Administration had accelerated the feminization of poverty at an alarming rate: two and a half million women had sunk below the poverty level, pushed there by a President who had stated: "The social safety net of programs . . . [is] exempt from any cuts." Inequities were being upheld for women in educational opportunity and in the marketplace, where tree trimmers were being paid more than emergency-room nurses, dog-pound attendants more than child-care workers. Women were being paid less because they were women. And there was no justification for it.

The words of the Equal Rights Amendment are simple enough: "Equality of rights under the law shall not be denied or abridged by the United States or by any state on account of sex." Those words had been included in every Republican Platform since 1923—until Ronald Reagan struck them out in 1980. When the passage of the ERA came to a vote in Congress in October 1983, the constitutional amendment lost by only six votes. But following the lead of the Reagan White House, two out of every three Republican members of Congress had voted against it. There were already laws protecting women, the Reagan Administration claimed; others would be enacted as needed, they said.

Yet Reagan had repudiated his own statute-by-statute approach to eliminating sex discrimination by refusing to support the Women's Economic Equity Act.

Women continued to be stuck in pink-collar jobs, making up sixty-percent of the country's clerical, sales, health, and service workers but fewer than fifteen percent of doctors, lawyers, engineers, and skilled craft workers. Many were thankful for whatever work they could find. In 1982, women were the sole support of more than 9.4 million households. By 1984, the number had risen to 9.7, representing sixteen percent of all families, but *half* of all poor families.

Three out of every five women working full-time were earning less than ten thousand dollars a year; one out of every three less than seven thousand dollars. Minority women were faring the worst. While white women workers were making fifty-nine cents for every dollar earned by men. Full-time black women workers were earning only about fifty-four cents, and Hispanic women only forty-nine cents, at the same time, unemployment among women was rising steadily—18.6 percent among black women in 1983, the highest rate in nearly twenty years. Yet Reagan failed to understand that most women go into the job market out of necessity. "Part of the unemployment is not so much recession as it is the great increase in people going into the job market, and ladies, I'm not picking on anyone, but because of the increase in women who are working today and two-worker families . . ." Reagan said with stunning ignorance and insensitivity in 1982.

Under the Reagan Administration, there was not one area where women were benefiting. In most, they were losing. Reagan's increase in defense spending meant fewer jobs across the board for women, a 1984 analysis by Employment Research Associates in Lansing, Michigan, found. The higher military budget had resulted in almost two million fewer jobs for women in manufacturing and service industries and in state and local governments. "Every time the Pentagon budget goes up $1 billion, 9500 jobs are lost for American women," the study concluded.

One way women could even the odds was through education. I felt strongly about this, and very personally. Whatever the differences in the way my mother had treated me and my brother in a traditional Italian household when we were young, one thing was always clear: as far as educational opportunities were concerned, it was never, "He can but you can't."

Despite her encouragement, I knew what it was to encounter discrimination purely on the basis of gender. When I graduated from law school, I had interviewed at numerous firms. At one firm, after the fifth interview, I was sure I had the job. It had gone so well. When it was all over, the partner broke the news: "We think you're terrific, but we're not hiring any women this year."

Only in numbers did women begin to change this mentality. Yet now the Reagan Administration was trying to reverse over a decade of progress under the 1972 Education Act. For twelve years, Title IX of the act, prohibiting sex discrimination in education, had opened opportunities for women. Women's enrollment in marketing, technology, and business-management programs had increased by 750,000. Doctoral degrees awarded to women had doubled. The percentage of women entering medical school had tripled. The number of sports available to college women had doubled. Olympic gold-medal winner Joan Benoit readily admitted that if she had not won a scholarship to North Carolina State under Title IX, she could never have run her way to victory in the women's marathon in the 1984 Olympics.

Yet Reagan's Justice Department had successfully argued to limit drastically the use of Title IX, paving the way for schools once more to place quotas on the number of women they would admit and to restrict women's access to certain areas of study. The Reagan Administration had in fact threatened the future for all students. Under Reagan, 700,000 fewer students a year could qualify for the guaranteed student loans that made their education possible.

The elderly were suffering as well. Seventy-two percent of the elderly poor were women, as were three out of four senior citizens living in public housing. To sixty percent of these women, Social Security provided their only significant source of income. Yet in 1981 Reagan tried to eliminate the $122 a month floor on Social Security benefits, designed to assure that no one received less than that amount—money that kept three million of these elderly women alive. Congress restored the minimum benefit, but only for those presently receiving it. That floor would no longer hold for newly eligible Social Security recipients after January 1982.

Health coverage for the elderly was also being severely curtailed. In his proposed budget for 1984, Reagan wanted to shift one billion dollars in medical costs from Medicare to the elderly patients themselves. Sixty-one percent of the recipients of Medicare were women. As with all the other cuts, women once more would be affected disproportionately.

Reagan's record on the family was no better. Though the President and other Republicans would spend a lot of time extolling traditional family values during the campaign, thereby giving the impression that his Administration was "profamily" while the Democratic ticket was somehow "antifamily," his record said quite the opposite. Due to Reagan's budget cuts, 700,000 children had lost their medical care benefits under Medicaid, while another 750,000 had had their benefits reduced. One million had lost their eligibility for food stamps. Three million children had been dropped from school lunch programs. Despite the fact that six to seven million children under the age of thirteen have working parents, seventy-five percent of day-care centers had been forced to cut back their services because of federal cuts.

Reagan's cuts were intolerable. One hundred thousand poverty-level pregnant women and young children lost the diet supplements and health care provided under WIC—Women, Infants and Children Program. Far fewer than half of those who needed WIC were receiving it.

Nowhere was the hypocrisy of the Reagan Administration more apparent than in its position on abortion. While Reagan was professing a dedication to get the government off people's backs, his position on abortion would deny women the right to make their own decisions about whether and when to have children and instead would have government make that decision for them. Federal funding for abortions for poor women had been cut off in 1977, an action that already discriminated against the poor. But instead of increasing federal funds for family planning as an alternative to abortion, Reagan had in fact cut them. Title X, a major source of funds for the Public Health Service, had had its budget slashed by more than twenty-five percent in fiscal 1982, to $125 million. In fiscal 1983, appropriations for Title X were lowered even further—to $124.4 million.

For years in Congress, I had been outraged by the callousness of these budget cuts, cuts that singled out the most vulnerable in our society—the poorest, the handicapped, the youngest, the oldest. I had worked hard to restore as many benefits and programs as I could, and had campaigned against candidates who supported Reagan's budget. As the vice-presidential candidate now, I would have an even greater opportunity to speak out against the inequities this Administration not only supported but advanced.

Were these women's issues? Yes. But did we expect women to vote for me just because I felt so strongly about these issues, because my candidacy could be seen as representing women's concerns? No. The women's vote is not a monolithic one. Our campaign did not assume that it would be in 1984. We would have to win the support of women. My place on the ticket would certainly draw women's attention, but it would not guarantee their vote.

I did not feel a concentration on women's issues would be advantageous or even appropriate. All issues, not just those pertinent to gender, are women's issues. As Vice President, I would represent the interests of all constituencies, not just one.

Later I would be criticized by some feminists who felt I should have spent more time developing the women's vote. But I didn't agree with them then—and I still don't. I wanted people to vote for me not because I was a woman, but because they thought I would make the best Vice President.

There is no doubt, however, that I ran as a woman, and brought a different perspective. How better to illustrate the harsh reality in Reagan's threat to cut back Social Security and Medicare benefits, even emergency fuel assistance to the elderly, than by telling the story of my mother? She had gotten no Social Security after my father had died, no pension. I didn't want other women to struggle that way—or other daughters to watch them.

The discrimination toward women in my lifetime alone had been outrageous. And I had felt it every step of the way, from my disappointing job interview as a young lawyer to my lower salary as a bureau chief in Queens to my inability to get credit in my own name during my 1978 congressional campaign.

After my election to Congress in 1978, I hoped that was behind me. But when, as a member of the Aviation Subcommittee of the House Public Works and Transportation Committee, I applied for a WINGS card from Eastern Airlines so that I could be billed separately for my weekly shuttle flights to Washington, I was turned down. Not until I brought up the subject at an ERA luncheon—needling the Eastern Airlines lobbyist present—did I receive one.

Even after three years in Congress, I could not get a VISA card from Citibank the first time around, despite dutifully listing my salary, my employer, my excellent credit references with American Express and Eastern Airlines (finally), plus my savings. And I was a woman with clout. What about women who were not members of Congress?

Under the law, women were finally beginning to make progress. But Reagan was trying to turn back the clock. So of course I personalized the issues. I had a lot to personalize. I would tell the stories everywhere, sometimes to my campaign staff's discomfort.

"Personally, as a Catholic, I accept my Church's teaching on this issue. I am opposed to abortion as a Catholic. But if I were raped I'm not sure I'd be so self-righteous," I would say throughout the campaign.

And at the beginning the male members of the campaign would wince every time. Personalizing abortion was too strong, too upsetting for them. "Do you have to?" they'd ask me. "It's so jarring."

"It's more jarring to be raped," I'd reply. I had seen enough of rape victims and unwanted children suffering from abuse during my years in the district attorney's office to sear my memory forever. There was nothing abstract about rape or the agony of those unwanted children. Of all the issues, abortion was the one that had to be explained in the most human terms, however uncomfortable it might have been for the audiences or my staff.

*   *   *

We certainly were strong on the issues. But I knew I would be tested as the first female vice-presidential candidate—and not only on substance.

Shortly after the Convention ended in July, the State Department phoned to offer me a security briefing as they had for Mondale. We could ask for anyone in the State Department, I was told; I need only call Secretary of State George Shultz's office to arrange it. This I did, talking to Shultz personally. "I'd like to take advantage of your offer, Mr. Secretary," I told him. "I'll get back to you to arrange the time and place of the briefing in September."

But whom to ask for? Secretary Shultz, who had been very cordial, had suggested the number-three man in the State Department. But I knew Fritz had asked for—and gotten—Robert C. McFarlane, Reagan's National Security Adviser. McFarlane had gone to North Oaks to meet with him.

What, then, would be proper for me? My staff and I batted the possibilities back and forth. Should I, as the vice-presidential candidate, meet with a lower-ranking State Department official? Should I make it easier for whomever by going to Washington to meet with him, or should I ask for the same home visit Mondale had been given? Our holding the meeting in my congressional office in Washington did have its problems. This would be top-secret stuff, and the traffic in and out of my office was unbelievable.

For the first time we faced the question that was to run throughout the campaign in every decision we made. What appearance would it give? Was I getting the same treatment a male vice-presidential candidate would have expected? As the first woman vice-presidential candidate there were no precedents for me to follow. So I created my own by adopting the model of a little old white-haired senator from the South as my alter-ego. However I thought "he" would have been treated became the standard for my expectations. And in this case, anyway, "he" solved everything.

I, too, asked, for McFarlane to come to my house in Queens, which he did. Inasmuch as Fritz had had Jim Schlesinger, former Secretary of Defense and head of the CIA, and Ambassador Max Kampelman, later to become President Reagan's chief arms control negotiator, with him during his briefing, along with two staffers, I asked my good friend Pat Moynihan, the senior senator from New York and member of the Senate Intelligence Committee, and Tom Foley, the whip of the House, to sit in on my meeting along with Madeleine Albright.

So many factors come into play in presidential politics. There are the candidate's substantive positions on the issues—the only criteria that should really count. But there is also the campaign strategy to pinpoint the vote and capture it. Then there is the stump style of the candidate, the all-important image that he or she projects to the voters. And throughout this campaign, there would be an untested and unknown element—the first candidacy of a woman. There was so much I wanted to get across to the public—and so little time.

NOBODY SAID IT
WOULD BE EASY

"Can you bake a blueberry muffin?"
"I sure can. Can you?"

—*exchange with Mississippi agriculture commissioner Jim*
Buck Ross, Jackson, Mississippi, August 1, 1984.

FIFTEEN WEEKS. THAT'S all the time we had from the middle of July to Election Day in November. A little over three months. We had even started early. Though presidential campaigns traditionally kick off on Labor Day, the last few campaigns have seen the start-up time move further and further back. Our campaign was no exception—for good reasons. One, the latest Gallup poll, in mid-July, showed Reagan leading by ten points. And two, I wasn't a well-known national figure. Not only did I have to introduce myself to the American public, but I also had to establish where I stood on the issues. We'd need every minute we could get.

In the eyes of the public the campaign got off to a smooth start as Fritz and I took a trial run on July 31, starting in Queens and on to Ohio, Mississippi, and then to Texas. Behind the scenes, however, it was a zoo. I needed time to straighten out my congressional offices in Washington and New York, cast my last votes on legislation, prepare for the campaign, and, most important, select my campaign staff. But there was hardly time even to get started—and too much to do.

In Congress, my private pension reform bill was at last coming up for a vote on the floor in August, and I was negotiating at

140

the same time with the chairman of Public Works, Jim Howard of New Jersey, to bring my Tandem Truck Safety Act to a vote before the campaign began. This act, which was finally signed into law on October 30, 1984, permitted states, with the approval of the Secretary of Transportation, to ban the huge trucks from sections of interstate highways deemed unsafe to handle them. It was very important to my congressional district, where these trucks were tearing up the Brooklyn-Queens Expressway. I felt a responsibility to my constituents to see through the legislation I had worked on, though it was probably naive of me as the vice-presidential nominee to try to keep doing my job as a member of Congress. It was hard enough just trying to keep my head on straight.

The frenzy around my candidacy was almost out of control. The national press was now camped outside my office in the hall, and the Capitol Hill police had to put up ropes around my office to keep them back. It was bedlam. Our communications system was strained to the breaking point, and four new phone lines had to be brought in.

Besides the Secret Service agents, who never left my side, a uniformed officer and an undercover agent from the Capitol Hill police became permanent fixtures in the reception room. On several occasions when we received threats, the Capitol Hill police went through my offices with dogs trained to sniff out bombs. When gifts started pouring in—books, hats, pins, even a boxing glove and a robe with a salami in it—everything had to be x-rayed. The salami looked so suspicious that the bomb squad was called in to dismantle it.

The volume of mail quickly became so overwhelming that the Speaker gave us an extra room on the fourth floor just to handle it. When I had first taken over my congressional duties in 1979, we had gotten maybe nine letters a week. During my six years in office the volume of constituents' mail had grown to two hundred and fifty a week. But nothing had prepared us for the avalanche of mail that followed my vice-presidential nomination.

All of a sudden, we were getting two thousand to three thousand letters a day! Over the next four months, I would get over fifty thousand pieces of mail—over five thousand birthday cards alone. Unless a letter asked about legislation, we considered it campaign mail, and the campaign paid the postage. Every gle card or letter would be answered by one of the eighty volunteers, many from the Women's National Democratic Club, working from eight-thirty a.m. to eight p.m. five days a week. Obviously, I couldn't read all the letters, but I was very moved by the particularly touching ones that were brought to my attention, and by the fact that so many people had taken the time to share heartfelt best wishes.

Now, I couldn't go on to the floor of the House without ten people stopping me, saying, "Gerry, I need you to come out to my district to do this or to do that." It was all very exciting. A stream of people, from elected officials to congressional employees, came by my office to congratulate me. There was one interruption after another, including requests from more than a hundred and thirty Democrats in Congress to have their pictures taken with me for their campaign literature. We lined them all up in the hall one morning, and from nine-thirty to eleven-thirty I smiled at the camera with each of them. (I drew the line in the case of a freshman Republican who evidently didn't know where he was.)

Meanwhile, I had to get going on my campaign staff. My congressional staff in Washington and in my district office in New York were very talented, but all of us were novices in a national campaign. There we were, a group of seventeen in both offices trying to do the work of a member of Congress representing the Ninth Congressional District in Queens while suddenly having to respond to all this vice-presidential clamor as well. It was total craziness. And I knew it couldn't go on.

"You're great, but we don't have the time to learn the national scene together," I told them. "I'm going to take on professionals as senior campaign aides, because none of us, including me, knows how to deal with a national campaign and we don't have the time to learn." Several of my congressional staff would come on the campaign part-time at lower levels, and the rest would work extraordinary hours as volunteers, after their long days fulfilling their duties to the people of Queens.

I soon discovered we were already out of time. Without wasting a minute, the Republicans launched their first salvo to discredit my candidacy. I knew the campaign loans the Federal Election Commission had questioned in 1978 would come up again. That was fair game. What I did not expect was the sudden rush of news stories about the financial disclosure statements I'd been filing in Congress for six years, on which I had taken the statutory exemption not to include information about my husband's finances. Seventeen other members of Congress had taken the same exemption in 1983, twenty-three members in 1982, twenty-one in 1981, and twenty-two in 1980, while nearly twice that number had failed to indicate whether they were taking it or not. All in all, the "spousal" exemption had been claimed by others on 101 different occasions in the five-year period from 1979 through 1983. No member had ever been challenged or even questioned about taking the exemption. Until my nomination.

Bam. Bam. Bam. Suddenly I was getting hit from all sides. And so was John. In one ten-day period spanning the end of July and the beginning of August, my ethics in having taken the spousal exemption would be publicly challenged, while John's own ethics in handling a court-appointed conservatorship of a widow's affairs were being questioned, and several of his real-estate transactions were being smeared with innuendo. The honeymoon following my nomination was over. And I had been the vice-presidential candidate for only two weeks.

Instead of focusing on getting the campaign off the ground, I had to deal with the mounting storm about our finances. As the vice-presidential nominee I was required to file a financial report with the FEC, which I was preparing to do. Under the law I had until August 20, thirty days after my nomination, to submit this report. But with the daily speculation in the media about the Ferraro-Zaccaro financial picture, the press was not content to wait the thirty days.

"When are you going to respond?" the press hawked at me every time I stepped out of my office. "When are you going to file?"

"When I have my papers together," I would answer again and again. "I have thirty days to file."

I wished it could be faster, but our accountants, Arthur Young & Company, were very thorough, wanting to check and double-check every detail. This took time, because, among other things, the disclosure requirements were very extensive. We had retained Arthur Young to assist us only on August 2.

Meanwhile, the press never let up. And so my own staff

started pushing me. "We've got to give the press something," they insisted. But still I resisted, wanting to wait until the forms were filled out correctly. With all the furor about our finances, a simple mistake would be magnified tenfold.

And, of course, that's just what happened. On July 24, in the midst of all the chaos in and out of my office, my staff handed me a press release about my financial disclosures. I read it quickly, too quickly, and it was released. In my haste I hadn't picked up the clause that not only stated that I would release my income-tax returns on August 20, but that my husband, John, would release his as well. "My husband and I believe it is in the public interest to do so and because the office of Vice President is one of high public trust," the statement read.

"What's all this about releasing my tax returns?" John said to me. "I told you I'd release a financial statement, but not my tax returns."

"I know. It was a mistake," I told him. "Don't worry about it. I'll take care of it."

Just how I was going to handle it I didn't know. But I knew it was my problem. After all, I'd gotten us into this mess and it would be up to me to get us out. I could clearly see John, sitting at the kitchen table with Michael Berman, saying he would release a financial statement but not his tax returns. Now I'd announced he would.

What a week. I seemed to be having one confrontation after another. And none of it was advancing the campaign—specifically, the selection of my campaign staff. I wanted to include as many qualified women as possible in top positions, so that they would be visible, as I was. That was part of what my candidacy represented. I had started the process at the Convention in San Francisco and was now scrambling for the time to pursue it in the few days I had in Washington. After bouncing around names with my own staff and Mondale's, who were seasoned national pros, I called Anne Wexler. Anne was not only a friend, but had been Assistant to the President for public liaison in the Carter White House, knew the Mondales, and had worked on the national level. She was thrilled, coming on as my senior political adviser. One down. I turned then to Ranny Cooper, a senior aide to Ted Kennedy—and member of the original Team B—to act as a consulting adviser to help select the rest of my campaign staff. She, too, accepted. Two down.

At the Mondale staff's suggestion I then talked to John Sasso, who was chief of staff for Mike Dukakis, the governor of Massachusetts. John had a reputation as a talented political organizer and an excellent strategist. He was also very formal, never seemed to smile, and insisted on calling me "Mrs. Ferraro," both in our preliminary meetings in San Francisco and in Washington.

"Now, John," I finally said to him, "after the election, you will have to address me as Vice President Ferraro. But we've got too much to do beforehand to let titles stand in the way. Try saying 'Gerry.' Just try it. Watch my lips: 'Gerr-eee.' "

It worked, and Sasso, though he must have thought me a little strange, signed on too, taking a leave of absence from the governor's office to become my national campaign manager. Three down.

And another confrontation. Where were the blacks in my campaign staff of three, Jesse Jackson thundered to a meeting of Operation PUSH—and to the press—in Chicago on Saturday, July 28. My appointments of two white women and one white man, I read the next morning in the paper, were "unfair and unacceptable." After only three appointments I was already condemned—in public and by a fellow Democrat. I couldn't believe it. What had happened to the unity we had built up at the Convention between the candidates? Why was one Democrat trying to do in another?

I couldn't let Jackson's criticism stand. If the first woman vice-presidential candidate was going to be seen as weak, we might just as well stay home. I wasn't about to let anyone think I could be marched over by black, white, male, female, or anyone else. I never had allowed that impression in my entire time in Congress, and if I had to prove that I wasn't going to allow it at any point in the campaign, this was the time to start. Politics is filled with all sorts of power games, right down to secretaries placing phone calls and demanding that you get on first so that you are the one to wait until whoever is calling is ready to talk. I don't play those games, and I don't want anybody playing them with me.

After reading Jackson's blast in the Sunday newspaper I went to mass in Forest Hills. During the homily my mind wandered (it happens sometimes) and I planned my response to the Jackson situation. "Jackson is inaccurate," I said after church to the press, who by now were following me everywhere. There were many more campaign slots to fill, I pointed out, and Jackson had been too quick to criticize me. Yes, it was true I hadn't consulted with him—or with any constituency groups—before making my first appointments. And I wasn't planning to start now, especially since Fritz had already been falsely accused of bowing to special interests. "I don't have a hundred and one days to make decisions. I have a hundred and one days to win the election, and I intend to do that," I said to the press. "Jackson should know better."

I was sorry to have to confront a fellow Democrat. And inadvertently I had temporarily made the situation worse. I had made my remarks to the press too fast, forgetting they had not caught up yet with my Queens speech. The next day the *Daily News* headlined: "Gerry Tags Jesse As 'An Actor.'" So much for my pronunciation of "inaccurate."

Fritz, however, was evidently delighted with my counter-punch, I was told later. "Jackson let her have it and she clipped him right in the eye," he laughed. But some damage had been done, and the phone calls started pouring in, criticizing me for my apparent trashing of Jackson as "an actor." It was all getting too much. Bogging down the Democratic Party in internal squabbles was not going to help us defeat Reagan. Jackson and I had to get it straight between us. So I called him up.

"One of the things you and I have to understand," I said to him, "is that we're going to have to work on this campaign together. Please don't beat me over the head in public again. If you have something to say to me, do me a favor: call me first and don't say it through the newspapers because I'm going to have to respond in kind."

Jackson reiterated his complaint about the absence of black women from my campaign staff. I had eight more positions to fill, I pointed out to him, and though I intended—and wanted—to have black women working with me, I resented his public and premature criticisms. It was my campaign staff we were talking about, after all. Not his. And so we came to an understanding.

No sooner had I finished working it out with Jackson than Fritz and I took off on our first swing through the South.

The campaign staff thought it would be a good idea for us to go out together to test the waters, to have Fritz introduce me to the Southerners. It was a relief to get away from the frenzy in Washington, to do what I knew I could do well: campaign. And the response to our first political trip was overwhelming.

Fritz was ecstatic about the crowds, seven thousand in front of the governor's mansion in Jackson, Mississippi, ten thousand in front of the statehouse in Austin, Texas. He hadn't had many crowds like that before. And, of course, neither had I. A lot of women turned out to see us, women of all ages and backgrounds. For the first time I felt the intensity that many of the women brought to my candidacy. "Gerr-eee, Gerr-eee," they continued to chant, putting all their emotion into one word. They wanted me to succeed so much. And I wanted so much to succeed for them. "Wow. Do I have to worry about the South?" I asked the crowd in Jackson. "No," they shouted back.

But *did* I have to worry about the South? Maybe. On a trip to a soybean-and-cotton farm in the morning with agriculture commissioner Jim Buck Ross, the subject turned quickly from the difficulties of farmers to my success with blueberry muffins. Mississippi was developing four new crops, the seventy-year-old Ross said, catfish, crayfish, grapes, and blueberries. I hadn't ever eaten catfish, I confessed, but blueberries did grow wild on our property on Fire Island.

"You grow blueberries?" Ross grinned. "Can you bake a blueberry muffin?"

Everyone cracked up. "Sure can," I finally managed to respond. "Can you?"

Ross shook his head. "Down here in Mississippi, the men don't cook," he said.

It was fun. The headline the next morning in the *Clarion Ledger* read: "Mondale Woos, Ferraro Wows Mississippians." And we made blueberry history. After the election I would receive a cookbook entitled *Down Here Men Don't Cook,* that included both of our blueberry-muffin recipes side by side.

Our reception in Texas was even warmer—literally. It was as hot as it could possibly be in Houston, Austin, and then hotter still in San Antonio. Texas was an essential state for us. And on our first trip all the signs pointed to go. The mayor of San Antonio, Henry Cisneros, who had been considered for the vice-presidential nomination, introduced me as his "cousin" to a cheering crowd of 6,000, citing the shared ancestry of Italians, Spaniards, and Mexicans.

It is impossible for me to describe the emotion of those rallies, the intensity of feeling, the bond among the people, and the way they reached out to me.

"*Mano y mano, venceremos,*" I said to them. "Hand in hand, we will win."

The crowd must have taken me literally. In San Antonio, I experienced a phenomenon that was to follow me through the campaign. Many people in the crowd had brought small children with them, especially girls. One man with a baby on his shoulder reached out to me and said: "Touch her." That was very heavy stuff, as if he were asking me to bless her in some way. It happened wherever I went, people holding up their daughters to me to be kissed or touched somehow by this historic candidacy.

I never could get over it. I was a mother and well aware of how easily babies can catch cold or anything else that is going around. Even in the fall, the parade of babies being held out to me wouldn't slow down. "This is flu season," I'd caution the parents, "and we all have colds." But it didn't seem to make any difference.

On Wednesday, August 1, I flew from Texas to North Oaks with Fritz to sit down and plan the rest of the campaign. He was thrilled by our trial run.

"Did you see all that energy and enthusiasm in the crowds?" he said. "How can we keep it all going?"

"Just leave it to me, Fritz," I said.

I was kidding, of course, but among other things I truly hoped to increase the gender-gap vote throughout the campaign, to reach out to women, especially those who had not been involved in politics before, to have women really make a difference. If the enthusiasm in our first crowds was any indication, the women were with us. The campaign had gotten off to a very good start.

Until our first strategy meeting that night. My skeleton campaign staff was traveling with me—Anne Wexler, John Sasso, and the indispensable Eleanor Lewis. There were too many of us to spend the night at the Mondales' house, so we were staying at a nearby motel. The plan was for us to gather at the Mondales' in order to lay out the upcoming campaign. But it quickly developed that there was nothing to lay out. Everything had been done.

The evening started off very cordially. Fritz seemed relaxed, surrounded by his top people brought in for the meeting. His press secretary, Maxine Isaacs, was there, as was his senior adviser, John Reilly; his campaign chairman, Jim Johnson; his communications director, Dick Leone; and Paul Tully, Fritz's political director. Over our glasses of wine, Jim Johnson suggested we talk about the schedule for the next month. Good, I said, anxious to get started. I wasn't prepared for what happened next.

Johnson brought out two charts with our schedules blocked in, one chart marked in red ink, the other in green. "How come the chart isn't in pencil?" I asked. It looked as if there was to be no discussion at all about my part in the campaign. There were the next three months of my life, finalized in ink. The inference seemed clear. I was supposed to do as I was told.

"Evidently you do not want any input about the campaign from me," I said to the group, who looked somewhat startled.

"I just thought the charts would be easier to read this way," Johnson said.

According to my ink, I was scheduled to leave for California on my first solo campaign swing the very next week. But I wasn't ready. I knew I would attract a lot of press, I needed time to prepare, and I didn't even have my staff organized.

"You have me scheduled to go to California on Wednesday, the eighth of August, a week from today, and I can't," I told them.

"Why not?" they asked.

"I need the full work week to put together a campaign staff, get my congressional affairs straightened out, and go over the issues first," I told them.

"You have to go to California," they said.

"Fine," I replied. "I'm delighted to go to California. But I will not go on the eighth. Give me until Sunday, the twelfth. I'm not leaving until I have my staff in place. I'll do whatever you want in this campaign, but I will not make a fool out of myself. The last thing we need is for us to go out prematurely, make a mistake, and have people say of the first woman's vice-presidential campaign: 'Look, they're already bumbling.' This campaign has to be professional from the beginning."

Fritz hadn't said a word as we went around and around. He just sat there listening while Reilly, then Leone, and then Tully got on my case. I had made my decision, but they refused to hear me. This was not a great way for the campaign to start. But a precedent had to be set. If I'd already had a campaign staff, this whole situation would have been handled staff to staff, not candidate to candidate. What I was confronting was even worse. This was one candidate's staff ordering the other candidate around.

I had had it with all of them. And Fritz Mondale had had it with me. By now he was beet red with anger. "I guess that ends the conversation for tonight," he said. And he walked out of the room.

I was right behind him, but I went out the front door to the car. "Let's get out of here," I said to John Sasso, and off we went. I was so angry I even left Anne Wexler and Eleanor behind. They came running down the path, but it was too late to catch us. Instead they caught the Secret Service. The mosquitoes were so ferocious in Minnesota that the Secret Service had had to build a sentry box to protect themselves from the bugs. In the pitch dark, Anne and Eleanor hadn't seen it, and when the agent stepped out to see what all the fuss was about, Eleanor nearly had a heart attack thinking he was a bear.

Even after they finally arrived back at the motel in a staff car, I was still pretty angry. "If that had been Senator Bentsen sitting there in that seat, no one would have dared open their mouths," I said. "First of all they wouldn't have come in with that chart, and second they would not have gone on insisting once he had said 'no.' They would have said 'OK, Senator. We'll see what we can do to accommodate you.' "

We were scheduled to go back to the house in the morning, which was fine with me. I had to talk to Fritz. After all, we were all going to be working together for the next three months. When we regrouped the following day there wasn't a word about scheduling. Instead we talked amiably about issues that had been on the agenda for the morning. My chance came when Fritz said, "I'd like to talk to you alone." Immediately the staff vanished.

"I was a little upset last night," Fritz said.

I nodded. "I was aware of that, Fritz. But let me tell you, so was I," I said. And I told him exactly how I felt. "I want this to be a campaign where we can work together. I want you to win more than anything else. And I think you will be a wonderful President. But as your running mate, I still want to be consulted, rather than listen to your staff telling me what I *have* to do.

"They're not used to dealing with a woman, but they're going to have to learn," I went on. "To help them along, let me suggest that until they can get used to recognizing I'm a partner in this thing, they should pretend every time they talk to me or even look at me that I'm a gray-haired Southern gentleman, a senator from Texas."

Fritz seemed surprised.

I explained that his staff would not have been so presumptuous had they been dealing with a senior male senator—or any man.

"Oh, they didn't mean anything by that," Fritz replied.

But he must have understood. From that moment on, Fritz's staff transmitted all their messages and inquiries to me through my staff. At least now our two campaigns would give the appearance of understanding each other.

I had picked up the four extra days I needed in Washington before going to California. But on August 7, in the midst of the press clamor about my family finances, my final committee work on my congressional affairs, and my nonstop meetings with legislators and interviews with potential campaign staff, an unexpected bombshell hit.

"There is someone here to serve you with a complaint," one of my frazzled congressional staff said to me that day. Complaint? For what? I was stunned. But although as a lawyer I knew I had to accept the service of the complaint, I also knew that as the vice-presidential nominee I sure wasn't going to be served in my congressional office in front of the national press. "We're not going to give any process server a photo opportunity," I told the staff member. "Tell the Secret Service not to let anyone inside this door."

My mind was whirling trying to figure out why I was being served. I didn't have long to wait. Almost immediately the national media carried a press release from the ultraconservative Washington Legal Foundation, an organization with admitted ties to the White House, announcing that it had filed a complaint against me with the House Committee on Standards of Official Conduct. At issue was my alleged violation of the Ethics in Government Act in failing to list my husband's assets, liabilities, and transactions on my congressional disclosure statements and to list the same for my children. It also contended I had misreported or failed to report fully my own.

I believed that the Washington Legal Foundation was fronting for the Republicans. A Republican congressmen, George Hansen of Idaho, had just been disciplined by Congress in June on four counts of filing false statements on his congressional disclosure forms. It had been a great scandal for the Republicans. Now they wanted to create one for the Democrats. I was disgusted. Hansen was a convicted felon. I hadn't broken any laws. Yet immediately the press would play right into the Republicans' hands and start comparing me with Hansen.

I was getting one unpleasant surprise after another those last four days in Washington. The next day, August 8, I was scheduled to meet with a group of black women from Jesse Jackson's campaign, a meeting I was looking forward to because I wanted to straighten things out. The last time we had met, at the Convention in San Francisco, had been more confrontational than constructive. Instead of seeing my nomination as a breakthrough victory for all women, this group of black women had felt resentful. They were angry that no black woman had been seriously considered. And during the Convention, they had taken out their resentment on me.

In putting together my national campaign staff, I had planned to bring on qualified black women in top level positions. The black community needed us in the White House as much as we needed its vote to get there. Reagan had been remarkably insensitive to minorities—witness the support of his Justice Department on behalf of tax exemptions for segregated private schools; and the lack of support for the Voting Rights Act of 1982, as well as the Civil Rights Act of 1984 on the part of his appointees to the

Equal Employment Opportunity Commission and to the Civil Rights Commission, turning away from the traditional policies of those agencies. I wanted the active help of the Jackson women on the campaign. I didn't seem to be getting it.

In San Francisco I had met first with the black women delegates for Mondale and then separately with those for Jackson to hear their suggestions for top staff jobs. Unfortunately I couldn't meet with them together. The Jackson women would have nothing to do with the Mondale women, feeling the latter had sold out to a white candidate. Meanwhile the Mondale black women had put themselves on the line within their own communities to support Mondale and deserved the first rewards. I wanted input from both groups for my campaign staff appointments, and also to start healing the wounds.

But I wanted to be fair to the Mondale women. When you're building a campaign, you start by reaching out to the people who have supported you all along. Then you do the best you can to bring in others.

"I don't care what color they are, what sex they are. I want the best talent in the country for my campaign staff," I had said to both groups, adding to the Mondale women: "You've been loyal to Fritz from the beginning. Now I'm reaching out to you." Why the addition? Because they were afraid that Mondale, in an effort to bring Jackson into the campaign, was going to bend over backward to bring in all of Jackson's people to the exclusion of the people who had worked for him from the start. I wanted to assure them this would not happen.

Jackson had top women supporting him: former Congresswoman Shirley Chisholm; president of the National Council of Negro Women Dorothy Height; labor leader Addie Wyatt; C. Delores Tucker, the former head of the American Association of University Women; and Donna Brazile, a Jackson campaign organizer. They were all terrific. To them I had added a different message: "We don't win this if we're fighting with each other. Let's come together." But my attempts for cooperation and conciliation hadn't worked. Shirley Chisholm had even flown out of San Francisco the day before our scheduled meeting rather than meet with me. I was very sorry about that.

And I was just as sorry about the meeting three weeks later in Washington. "Do you have the recommendations I asked you for?" I said to the Jackson women when they gathered in my office.

But the answer was no. For two hours they sat there alternately lecturing me and criticizing the three campaign staff appointments I had already made. I had gotten it once from Jackson. Now I was getting it from the women in his campaign.

"You did not consult with us," they complained.

"I haven't consulted with anyone, not Judy Goldsmith of NOW or Hispanics or labor, and I'm not going to consult with you either," I countered.

To try to make peace, I decided to tell them in confidence what had not yet been announced. Barbara Roberts Mason, who had seconded my nomination, was already in the process of clearing up her commitments to come on the campaign as my senior policy adviser.

"You want a black woman?" I asked the women in my office. "Yes," they said. "Good. You've got one," I said. "Who?" they asked. "Barbara Roberts Mason," I said. They shook their heads. "That's not what we mean."

It was outrageous. Barbara Roberts Mason was well qualified and she was black. But she wasn't the right black woman. She had been a dedicated supporter of Mondale, not of Jackson. She wouldn't have shown Jackson's power in the Mondale/Ferraro campaign.

Even when I had to go out of my office to cast a vote on the floor of the House, the women still wouldn't leave. We were getting nowhere. As I walked out the door, they were preaching to me about the importance of the black vote as if I didn't know anything about it. It was so counterproductive.

Mercifully, I ran into Congressman Charlie Rangel, cochair for the Mondale campaign and my friend from Harlem in New York. Charlie had been one of the first people I had called from Fritz's house in North Oaks after I'd been chosen for the nomination. "My heart is full," he had said then, a lovely sentiment I'd gone on to quote in my acceptance remarks in St. Paul. Now I was overjoyed to see him. "You've got to handle these women or I'm going to blow," I said to him. And he did, coming back to my office with me after the vote on the floor. The Jackson voice would be heard, he assured the others. Both black men and women would be instrumental in the campaigns.

But even Rangel's assurance and my repeated request for suggestions, which indirectly offered a staff position to any among them if they'd only come halfway, wasn't enough. Though I never did get any recommendations from the Jackson women, I went ahead with what I'd intended to do in the first place. Some really great Jackson women would come on my campaign, such as Donna Brazile, who joined us as a valuable member of our political staff. Charlie Rangel would arrange for Addie Wyatt, another prominent Jackson supporter, to be one of the vice-chairs for the general Mondale-Ferraro campaigns. And Shirley Chisholm was appointed to the Women's Senior Strategy Council for Mondale-Ferraro.

Still, it was sad to start off the first candidacy of a woman this way; members of the very constituencies that should have been the most supportive were fighting among themselves instead.

With my first campaign swing to California just a few days away, I continued to fill out my campaign staff.

At the suggestion of Maxine Isaacs and Anne Wexler, I signed on Pat Bario, a former Carter White House aide now doing public relations in Washington, as my press spokesperson. Charles Atkins from my Platform Committee staff came on, too, as my deputy campaign manager, as did Steve Engelberg to handle domestic issues and Madeleine Albright to deal with foreign policy. Samuel R. (Sandy) Berger, a former speech writer for Secretary of State Cy Vance and now a D.C. lawyer with the firm of Hogan and Hartson, agreed to write speeches through Labor Day and to help recruit a full team of speech writers. Fred Martin, a Mondale adviser, later headed up my speech-writing team. Tony Podesta, president of Norman Lear's People for the American Way, volunteered to help with scheduling through Labor Day and pulled together a team of schedulers for the remainder of the campaign. Addie Guttag, whom I'd recently hired to raise money in New York for my congressional reelection, would continue in her role, but now as a national fund-raiser. And Kate Schaeffer rounded out the team as a trip director.

A few of my congressional staff also went national with me. Eleanor Lewis, my administrative assistant, would have the title of executive assistant, but be known in campaign jargon as my "body person" because she never left my side and was responsible for everything from coordinating my daily staff meetings to keeping my glasses unscratched. David Koshgarian, my legislative director, would be part-time on the campaign to write speeches and issue papers, as would Marsha Ackermann, my congressional press secretary. Betty Hegarty, my secretary and scheduler, would be traveling with me much of the time, typing my speeches and assembling my briefing papers until the early morning hours.

Joan McLean, the force behind Team A, had wanted to come on as my trip coordinator, but she had had limited experience on a national campaign and so she joined as part of my issues staff. It was nice to see another familiar face.

There were many others. A national campaign is run by more than a handful of people. But these were the people who were going to take the lead over the next three months. Now my staff was more or less in place. On August 8, four days before I left on my solo swing to California, House Majority Leader Jim Wright invited me to lunch with the Texas Democratic delegation in Washington. The lunch was off the record, a precondition I had always taken seriously. And to assure the Texas delegation that they could have faith in my candidacy in spite of the storm about my family finances, I told them that I was releasing more than the information required by law and that there would be a detailed financial disclosure, including a complete financial statement from John. He would not be releasing his tax returns, however.

At a press conference at Washington's National Airport just as I was about to take off for California on August 12, I was taken aback by a question about John's decision not to release his tax returns. The only place I had mentioned it was at the off-the-record lunch with the Texans. Someone must have walked out of that luncheon and leaked my comment to the press.

Like a political novice, I answered the reporter. This time my candor would backfire.

"I requested my husband to do that and he feels quite frankly that his business interests would be affected by releasing his tax returns," I said. "John told me: 'Gerry, I'm not going to tell you how to run the country. Don't tell me how to run my business.' " I knew as soon as I saw the ripple run through the press corps that I'd made a major mistake. But there was no way to take back the words. Instead I tried to change the subject—and only made it worse. "You people who are married to Italian men, you know what it's like," I quipped.

My candidacy had been struck an almost fatal blow before the campaign had hardly begun. And I had done it to myself.

MY FINANCES,
JOHN'S FINANCES,
AND POLITICS

"He's not the candidate. I am."

*—press conference, ballroom at the Viscount Hotel,
Queens, New York, August 21, 1984.*

THE NEXT WEEK WAS A nightmare. With one spontaneous answer to an unexpected question, I had created a monster. After the ill-fated meeting with the press at the airport in Washington, I flew off on my first campaign swing to California and Oregon. My vice-presidential financial disclosure statement was due eight days later, on August 20. And during my five days on the West Coast, the furor about John's tax returns and my congressional disclosure statements followed me everywhere, dominating the beginning of the campaign.

While I went ahead with my speeches to senior citizens in Sacramento and to the National District Attorneys Association in San Diego, winding up the week with a huge rally in Seattle, every question I was asked, every news story that ran, centered on our finances.

"Ferraro's Hubby Won't Bare Taxes" screamed the headline in the New York *Daily News*. "He must have something to hide," sniped George Bush's press secretary, not mentioning the fact that Bush had not released *his* tax returns since 1981, when he had placed his assets in a blind trust.

I had known from the beginning that my candidacy would draw unusual attention. As the first woman vice-presidential candidate, I would be the subject of curiosity. As the first Italian-American on a national ticket, I, along with my family, would be vulnerable to the inevitable and reprehensible attempts to link us with organized crime. As a two-career family in which the woman was running for national office, our personal affairs would also come under microscopic scrutiny. I'd known all these things, but I hadn't been worried. We had nothing to hide. And having survived the dirty tactics of my right-wing opponent in my 1978 congressional race, I knew we could take the heat.

But this wasn't the Ninth Congressional District in Queens. This was a national contest. And never did I anticipate the fury of the storm we now found ourselves in.

Even my quip about being married to an Italian was blown completely out of proportion. All I had meant to point out was that Italian men tend to be private about their own affairs. But instead, my remark was interpreted as an ethnic slur. Of all things. My father was an Italian man. So are my husband and my son. I love all three. How could I ever have been thought to smear them? There was a double standard prevailing here, a double standard I would have to face throughout the campaign. The day before I'd made my remark about Italian men, Reagan had warmed up for his regular Saturday radio broadcast by saying: "My fellow Americans. I am pleased to tell you I just signed legislation which outlaws Russia forever. The bombing begins in five minutes." No matter how you look at that remark, it was outrageous and dangerous coming from the President of the United States. Yet Reagan's unbelievable aside that a bombing attack on the Russians was about to begin was given less media attention than mine about being married to an Italian.

Hundreds of letters poured in from women telling me they understood exactly what I had meant. But the press kept the totally inconsequential remark alive. And even those people with a vested interest in the success of the campaign, who could have kept their thoughts private, didn't. I was especially saddened that the governor of New York misunderstood what I had said. "It's never good to use ethnic stereotypes," said Mario Cuomo, who was also the state chairman of the Mondale-Ferraro campaign, on a public-radio talk show. "I will not applaud her remark."

On one level, my first solo trip to the West Coast was triumphant, the crowds and enthusiasm overwhelming. Every time I faced the press, however, I was besieged with questions about our finances. It was brutal. I had four or five television and print interviews scheduled in each city we visited. One reporter accused me of stonewalling. Another asked me if John had paid his taxes at all. Still another pressed me on whether the Mondale-Ferraro campaign hadn't mishandled the whole situation.

Rationally I knew the members of the press were just doing their jobs. But personally it was getting to me. I am a polite person and I'm not used to people yelling at me.

"For goodness sake, can't you give us the time to get our finances together? You'll have them when they're ready," I finally said in desperation to one especially pushy reporter. That night on the national news I was reported as getting "testy."

And the fire was spreading. Taking the spousal exemption on my congressional disclosure statements and not detailing John's finances caused speculation to grow that I really did have something to hide, that by taking the exemption I had done something unethical if not illegal. But that was not true—nor was it the reason I had taken the exemption. The exemption criteria have to do with knowledge of a spouse's financial affairs and with the intermingling of assets and incomes and the exchange of economic benefits within the marriage. I thought I satisfied those criteria. John and I led separate professional lives. Our finances were separate. I kept my books. He kept his. I paid my bills, my rent on my apartment in Washington, my congressional expenses. He paid his bills in New York, and the routine family expenses. He filed his income-tax returns. I filed mine, even though filing separately cost us more in taxes than joint filing would have. But the mounting conjecture about John's business affairs, fueled by my remark about his decision not to release his income-tax returns, made the exemption claim on my congressional disclosure statements look suspicious.

Then a new bombshell hit. Three days after I'd left for California, the banner headline in the *New York Post,* owned by right-wing conservative Rupert Murdoch, read: "Gerry's Hubby in New $torm: Charge Zaccaro Lied on Campaign Funds." What was all this about? There I was on a boat tour on the Willamette River in Portland, Oregon, stressing our campaign points on the environment, while a new scandal was being manufactured by the conservatives in New York. And our accuser now was a lawyer named David Stein.

Our 1978 campaign loans were a matter of public record. They had happened because of my difficulty in raising funds for my first congressional campaign and my misunderstanding of the new Federal Election Campaign Act. Not wanting to do anything improper, I had welcomed the advice of David Stein, a former lawyer for the Federal Election Commission. He had been in our living room in Queens in the spring of 1978 and advised me and John, my campaign treasurer David Blanksteen, and a host of others that under the new election laws it would be perfectly legal to borrow the campaign funds from my immediate family and to pay them back later. What a load off my mind it had been at the time to hear that. Stein was supposedly an election-law expert, a lawyer who had served on the staff of the very body that would review my campaign's financial reports, and he was volunteering his help to boot.

On his advice, I had gone ahead and borrowed $134,000 from my family. I desperately needed the money, being a comparative unknown in my district challenging both the Democratic organization in the primary and facing Al DelliBovi, a three-term assemblyman, in the general elections afterward. Women were not considered viable candidates then, particularly in my conservative neighborhood. If I was going to win, I would have to do it on my own. And I did, confidently reporting the family loans to the FEC, sure that I was within the law. As it turned out, I wasn't.

To my amazement and chagrin, just before the primary the FEC informed me by letter that the loans from my family had been improper. I could have contributed as much of my own money as I wanted to my campaign, but other people including members of my family, could contribute or loan only up to one thousand dollars each. So I was instructed to pay back the amount of the loans exceeding the legal limit, which I did promptly by selling my interests in two properties in Manhattan. I was furious at David Stein for misadvising us then. But I was beyond anger for what he was saying now.

First in the conservative newspaper *Human Events* and then to the national press, Stein was claiming that his advice to us in 1978 had been exactly the opposite—that he had advised us *against* borrowing campaign funds from my family. I couldn't believe it.

Why was anyone listening seriously to David Stein? His word wasn't credible now, and it certainly hadn't been correct in 1978. In fact, after its 1979 investigation of the family loans, the FEC had levied fines totaling only $750 on the basis of our undisputed representation that we had acted in reliance on Stein's mistaken legal advice. "I know David Stein, and I didn't find it improbable that he would have given that advice," said William Oldaker, who had been the FEC general counsel in 1979, according to comments quoted later in the *Washington Post* on August 15, 1984. Stein, we had discovered, was a "former" FEC lawyer because he'd been let go by the FEC a few months before he'd met us. Stein's work had not come "up to the standard I felt was necessary as a minimum for an FEC lawyer," Oldaker went on to say. But no one was reading the small print in the heat of the 1984 vice-presidential fury, only the headlines. Stein's credibility wasn't being questioned. Ours was.

I had imagined the campaign would be tough. But I never expected it to be so dirty. Besides the Washington Legal Foundation's complaint lodged with the Committee on Standards of Official Conduct in Congress and the Justice Department against me, two more complaints—one from the Fund for a Conservative Majority and the other from John Banzhaf, a gadfly professor at the National Law Center of George Washington University— quickly followed David Stein's surprise about-face attempting to get the FEC to investigate again the financing of my 1978 campaign. All these highly publicized charges would hang over my head throughout the campaign and would not be resolved until after the election, when the FEC would determine on the basis of its review of the charges to close the file without conducting any additional investigation. On its part, the House Committee on Standards of Official Conduct would absolve me of any deliberate wrongdoing or deception after reviewing thousands of cancelled checks and other bank records and reams of other documents pertaining to real estate and other transactions over a six-year period, and a wealth of other data laboriously collected by John and our attorneys, plus amended financial disclosure statements, which I filed on October 1, correcting inadvertent errors and omissions on my prior statements. (As of this writing, the investigation opened by the Justice Department in response to the complaints of the Washington Legal Foundation, the Fund for a Conservative Majority, and John Banzhaf has not been concluded.)

Though I would certainly feel vindicated, both these decisions came too late to clear up the problems that plagued my candidacy. I had never thought of myself as a neurotic person, but during the campaign it was hard for me to decide whether I was developing a persecution complex or whether, indeed, I was being persecuted.

Instead of concentrating on campaign strategy, my staff and I were forced to spend much too much time keeping the details of the financial furor straight. On the California trip, I pointed out to the press that my vice-presidential disclosure statement would exceed what any other candidate had ever filed. I kept repeating it. And repeating it. And repeating it.

The tension began to get to me. I started to bite my nails, a habit I'd gotten over as a kid. And to eat. I'd always been able to leave a meal with food still on my plate. Now I started to eat almost compulsively—and to gain the thirteen pounds the campaign would eventually put on me.

There was nowhere to get away from all the questions. Instead of being able to relax on my campaign plane or to work on the speeches I was giving all over the West Coast, I had to constantly counter the questions about our finances, even at thirty thousand feet. On this first trip, there were sixty-one members of the press aboard, sitting in the rear of the plane. The fifteen members of my staff, my two children, Laura and John, Jr., and I sat in front of them with the Secret Service in between. The only bathroom was in the rear. To use it I had to run the gauntlet of the press every time; they, of course, seized the opportunity to ask me more questions. The pressure was intense.

I had two options. One was to stop drinking water so I'd never have to use the bathroom. Or, two, to make any remarks I made on the plane off the record. I chose the latter. I needed some time, any time, to be able to let off steam, to joke around, to forget our problems for just a few minutes. But the members of the press had their job to do as well, and our agreement to keep any remarks I made on the campaign plane off the record was very unpopular—and short lived. I went back to not drinking water.

For the moment, my candidacy was out of control, the ripple effect from my remark about John's tax returns reaching out to include Fritz as well. I felt awful. Fritz hadn't asked for this. And he sure didn't need it, either. On the day I left for California, a CBS News/*New York Times* poll found Reagan ahead by sixteen points. Instead of hitting Reagan on the issues, Fritz was being hit himself by the press on the Ferraro-Zaccaro finances while he campaigned in Iowa, in Arkansas, everywhere he went that week. We spoke to each other briefly during our first campaign swings, but we avoided talking about finances.

Publicly, Fritz was defending John's position, insisting his nondisclosure was perfectly legal. "It is his right under the law, and I'm not going to second-guess him," Fritz said at a press conference in North Oaks on August 18. But the leak now was that Fritz felt a personal "sense of betrayal" for not being told in advance that John was not going to release his tax returns. I don't know about the "sense of betrayal" part, but Fritz was right about his not being told in advance. He'd heard about my reversal on releasing John's tax returns as everybody else had. To be honest, I never thought it would become such a big issue. I felt terrible.

Did I want John to release his tax returns? Of course I did. But was I going to ask him to? No. There was no legal requirement for him to release them. And from the beginning, he had said he wasn't going to. I trusted him and felt he had nothing to hide. He just didn't see why his business should be the focus of or even a criterion for my candidacy. He's a private man, almost old-fashioned in some of his ways. And I was the one who had chosen to run for the Vice Presidency. He hadn't. I wasn't about to pressure him. And neither was Fritz. Never once did Fritz lean on me—or John—to reverse his decision. He was too much of a gentleman to interfere in John's personal affairs. But none of us had anticipated the fire storm that was now sweeping my candidacy.

The press sensed a good story, and they wound up getting one. I had supplied it. And the Republicans went out of their way to fan the flames.

Their tactics in New York were shameless. In the midst of all our other troubles in this one week in August, Rudolf Giuliani, the U.S. attorney and a Reagan appointee, suddenly called John down to his office to be questioned as a witness about a six-year-old real estate transaction John had had nothing to do with. John had been interviewed in his office two years ago by an investigator on this case. He had given all the information he had then and had never heard a thing since. There was nothing new to say now.

What was Giuliani's motive? I won't judge that, but this latest episode certainly did discredit John, because many among the public were not informed enough to make the distinction between John's being called down to aid an investigation and his being investigated himself. It wasn't enough to be street smart in this campaign. I had to be gutter smart as well.

One cheap shot after another was being thrown at John. On August 20, *New York* magazine ran an item claiming that thirteen years ago John's father, who had also been in real estate, had rented space to an alleged organized-crime figure.

How ridiculous and how irrelevant? John's father had died in 1971. John had sold the building in question immediately after to pay taxes on the estate. What did any of this have to do with whether or not I was qualified to be the Vice President? But in the open season some among the press had declared on us, four days before the magazine hit the stands, *New York* had rushed this smutty item with no named source in it to all the newspapers in the city, probably hoping to win praise—and a credit line—from those papers that picked it up. I was sickened.

I was nearing the end of my four-day trip to the West Coast, trying to steer the campaign back to the issues critical to the future of the country. That was the dialogue we should all have been involved in. But we weren't. Instead, the headlines coming out of New York now implicated John in the mishandling of the estate of Alice Phelan, an eighty-four-year-old widow. I didn't know much about it, only that in 1982 John had been appointed by the court in Queens to handle Mrs. Phelan's affairs after she had been declared incapable of handling them herself. John's job as conservator was to pay her bills and debts while investing her money wisely.

What I was finding out now was that John had borrowed money from the estate in October 1983, personally guaranteeing the loan and repaying it five months later, on March 9, at 10¾ percent for October and twelve percent thereafter, more than a point higher than the 10¾ percent the money had been earning in a money-market account. He reported this when he filed his 1983 accounting of the estate. In February 1984 John borrowed money from the estate again, paying an interest rate of twelve percent. That loan was repaid March 27, 1984. Both times the investment secured more money to the estate than if the money had been put into a savings account. But this time Jonathan Weinstein, the Queens court-appointed referee who had written the vague rules governing conservatorships, on reading the reports advised the court that the loans might be improper. A hearing had been scheduled for June. Since not all the lawyers could make it, a new date had been set in July. But Morty Povman, the attorney for the estate, had asked that the hearing be adjourned until August. Morty, a city councilman and Democratic district leader, was attending the convention in July and then going on to Hawaii for a vacation. Later I'd be asked why John had not disclosed this matter to Michael Berman or to me that morning in our kitchen. At this point in July, the conservatorship was considered a matter that had already been cleared up save for the technicality of a court hearing procedure, because John had repaid the money and reinvested it for the estate in an approved investment months ago. And so he had gone off to the convention unconcerned.

I was stunned to hear about the loans in the midst of everything else. "What's this all about?" I now asked John.

"Harold Farrell told me that it was perfectly legal to borrow the money for business and that in fact the loan would make more money for the estate," John told me. "He was a lawyer so I took his advice."

Harold Farrell. My blood ran cold. Harold Farrell was no longer a lawyer, a sorry fact John had found out too late. Farrell was a con man who had been disbarred in 1966 based on allegations of extortion. Six years later, in 1972, he was convicted of conspiracy to violate a section of the Racketeer Influence and Corrupt Organizations Act. But in late 1982, when John had met him—and felt sorry for him—John hadn't known any of that. Farrell had answered an ad John had placed in a New York newspaper regarding the sale of a piece of property. During their discussions Farrell mentioned that he needed office space close to Manhattan because his wife was being treated for cancer. "I have a free desk in my office if you want to use it," John had told him, a not unusual offer for John to make. He had extra space and had always been very generous in letting people use it. But this time his generosity backfired. When John discovered the extent of Farrell's misrepresentation in December 1983, he'd thrown him out of his office. But Farrell's "legal" legacy had lived on, surfacing now in John's being called into court.

I wasn't particularly worried about the hearing. John was a businessman, after all. Not a lawyer. And Weinstein's written rules concerning conservatorships did not even mention, let alone spell out, the impropriety of taking loans for personal use. Besides, in his same report to the court, Weinstein had also requested an increase in the bond protecting the estate because under John's management the estate's value had risen substantially. John had done his job very well. And the cases our attorneys had found showed that the drastic remedy of removal of a guardian was appropriate only where there was some detriment to the estate.

But the politics of it nagged at me. John's going to a court hearing would draw the press, lots of press. The hearing had every possibility of turning into a media circus, with the decision being unnecessarily harsh under all the public scrutiny. I didn't want John, as the high-profile husband of the vice-presidential nominee, to suffer on my account. I just wanted him to be treated fairly. Unfortunately, that wasn't what would happen.

On Thursday night, August 16, I returned exhausted from my campaign swing. John's hearing was a week away. The deadline for my financial disclosures was only four days off. Friday had been set aside for a marathon meeting with the accountants, who had been working for two weeks with John on the vice-presidential disclosure. And while I was away, John had changed his mind. "I can't stand seeing you beaten up in the press this way," John said to me in the kitchen. "If they want my tax returns so badly, let them have them. Who cares."

Was I relieved? Sure I was. But it was his decision, and his alone. We decided not to tell anyone about the new decision until we had talked to our own lawyers. And so began what became known in our family and the campaign as "disclosure weekend." I've never been through anything like it in my life. And I hope I never will again.

On Friday, we went into total immersion with our new accountants, Arthur Young & Company, a top accounting firm brought in at the suggestion of Michael Cardozo. Disclosure time was only three days away now, and for the next eight hours I would have a crash course in the intricacies of our family finances and my disclosure statement. Seventeen accountants, lawyers, and campaign aides crowded into the room while pages from my disclosure statement were flashed up on a screen. I had to learn it all—and fast.

To add to the tension of the weekend, I was also scheduled to appear on *This Week with David Brinkley* on Sunday morning, a date that had been made before the financial uproar. That made the stakes doubly high. First, there would be the financial stuff to prepare for. Second, I had to be totally prepared for Brinkley, my first major national news program. ABC's White House correspondent, Sam Donaldson, and conservative columnist George Will would be questioning me on domestic issues and foreign affairs. It was going to be a weekend and a half.

John was already exhausted, having worked nonstop with the accountants, Mondale's campaign lawyers, and our personal lawyers to make certain the vice-presidential disclosure statement for the FEC was complete and correct.

Though the statutory requirements called upon me to release only my sources of income, property interests, liabilities, positions held and arrangements as to future employment, and continued payments for past employment, I had decided not to claim any spousal exemption and to report similar information on John and my dependent children, John, Jr. and Laura. In addition, I included, even though it was not required, information about our property transactions, gifts, and reimbursements. We decided, again going beyond any legal requirements, to release our separate federal tax returns for 1979 through 1983, as well as our joint return for 1978, and to provide current statements of our net worth.

No other candidate in history had ever gone so public with his or her financial affairs. But at the same time, no other candidate had ever had to undergo such a siege, both from political opponents and from the press.

No wonder John was exhausted. He was a small businessman who had never expected his business records to be the focus of the entire nation. Some of his transactions had been sealed with a handshake or by a personal letter instead of written contracts. Some of the records he did have were difficult to locate. But the accountants were not interested in our bookkeeping habits. They wanted substantiation for everything.

John had spent long days trying to locate the pertinent records. He was not alone. Members of the press were also searching, looking through real estate records of past transactions involving John or his family, obviously hoping to find some irregularity. Though John had refused Secret Service protection when it was offered to him at our meeting with the Mondales in Lake Tahoe, now he needed it just to move through the squadrons of press who followed him wherever he went. His life was no longer his own.

It belonged to the press. The Ferraro-Zaccaro finances were the hottest story of the year, much of the interest centering on John's business transactions, his clients, and his colleagues. During the time of the vice-presidential disclosures, *Newsday* admitted that it had ten reporters assigned to ferret out stories—but the number was probably closer to twenty. The *Philadelphia Inquirer* went even further, claiming seven but actually assigning as many as twenty-seven reporters to our affairs, I heard during the campaign—or even forty-four, the number I was told in a visit to Philadelphia the following June. More than a dozen major stories were written in the *Philadelphia Inquirer* as a result, two on the front page trying to link John to alleged organized-crime figures (they didn't), another a half-page spread on our homes in Queens, Fire Island, and St. Croix, as if just owning real estate were some sort of crime in itself.

A few newspapers, at least, questioned with the *Inquirer*'s overkill. "They went after it like a crusade, not a news story," Abe Rosenthal, the executive editor of the *New York Times,* was quoted as saying in an article in the *Los Angeles Times* after the election that addressed the role of the press during the campaign. "Never in a million years would we have emulated what the *Inquirer* did." Other editors ascribed the Ferraro-Zaccaro media onslaught to our Italian heritage. "I don't think the press . . . would have put that kind of energy into it if we'd been talking about somebody named 'Jenkins,' " said Ben Bradlee, executive editor of the *Washington Post.* "You'd have to be on another planet not to think that."

But we weren't on another planet. At this unfortunate moment the objects of all this attention were very definitely on earth. And time was running out. By the time of our all-day meeting on Friday, the accountants still didn't have all the information they needed. But we had to get going on my instant indoctrination about our family affairs anyway. "Disclosure Monday" would be the most critical day in my professional life. My whole career, let alone my candidacy for Vice President, was on the line. And I was a little uptight.

"Who is that?" I snapped at the accountants' office, looking at Francis O'Brien, Mondale's former campaign press secretary. He had been sent by the Mondale campaign to help with the press on finances, I was told. "I don't want him in the room," I said. I didn't know Francis and couldn't afford to trust him. I'd been reading the leaks from the Mondale staff about Fritz's unhappiness with me as his running mate. "I want my lawyers here, who are subject to privilege," I said. "I want my own accountants. And nobody else." I was suspicious of everyone at that point. I didn't want any strangers in that room.

The lawyers from the Mondale campaign were another matter. I had worked with all of them before the finance issues had come up, and I not only liked them enormously but trusted them as well. Michael Berman had even called me in California as a friend to urge me to get my own lawyer as we headed toward the financial showdown. "The Mondale campaign will represent you totally, Gerry," he'd told me. "But there may come a point in the campaign where there is a conflict of interest and you're not going to be protected sufficiently. We think you should get your own lawyer to protect the interests, first and foremost, of Geraldine Ferraro." He'd even suggested a name, Washington lawyer Stephen Pollak, whose only conflict was that his law partner, Anthony Lapham, who would be working with us, had worked with and was a friend of George Bush. "I'm presuming Tony won't discuss my affairs with George Bush on the tennis court," I'd said, and signed them on.

Now Steve took me aside. "Gerry, you have to understand that any privilege regarding this meeting is just shot anyway. Too many people are here." Reluctantly, then, I let Francis O'Brien back in the room—the smartest thing I ever did. He ended up as my very competent press secretary for the rest of the campaign, replacing Pat Bario.

It became increasingly clear as the meeting wore on and on that our extensive financial disclosures were not going to answer all the questions being asked. How could I justify taking the spousal exemption on my congressional forms, for example, claiming that I knew nothing about John's business, when I had listed myself as an officer of P. Zaccaro Co., Inc., and as part owner?

Because my involvement was merely titular, I explained. I owned one of the three shares of P. Zaccaro Co., Inc., a real-estate management company that held no properties at all. Its net worth was less than twenty thousand dollars, based mostly on the value of the office furniture and fixtures. The annual income from my one share varied from zero to three thousand dollars—in some years there had even been a loss—which I had reported on my income-tax returns.

The main reason I was listed at all was simply this: John's older brother, Frank, had died very suddenly of cancer in 1968. One week he was alive and well, or so we thought. Seven weeks later he was dead. John's father had died soon after of cancer himself. John had been devastated by these two losses in a row. His father had worked at the office right up to the end. John had literally had to pick him up and carry him home, where he died two days later. Talk about intimations of mortality. John was staring it in the face and immediately made me an officer of P. Zaccaro Co., Inc. If something were to happen as suddenly to him, the business could continue because, as a lawyer, I was entitled to deal in real estate in New York State. As a further guarantee of continuity, John wanted me to get an insurance license, which I did by going to school two nights a week, so that the family business could continue uninterrupted. But I had never used it. Once more, I had merely been preparing for any contingency by having a plan in place. It was a simple explanation that on paper now looked suspect.

There was also going to be some confusion about our joint 1978 tax return. Our own accountant, Jack Selger, was a lovely man in his seventies who had started working for John's father over forty years ago. After John and I got married, we'd asked Jack to handle our accounting work as well, including my tax returns and John's returns and later my congressional disclosure statements. My only complaint about Jack had been that we paid a high percentage of our income in taxes, over forty percent of our combined incomes each year. "Can't he come up with some sort of tax shelter?" I'd say to John. But John would say that Jack didn't trust shelters. "What is he, an undercover agent for the IRS?" I would joke.

I had never doubted Jack's competence. Why should I? In all the years he'd done our financial work, we'd had no reason to question whether Jack knew what he was doing. Jack was the CPA. I wasn't. Besides, he was a friend of the family, and it never occurred to us to go to anybody else. If all this hadn't come up, I'd still be using him today.

Poor Jack. I really felt for him now, sitting in that room full of accountants and lawyers. Besides various errors in my congressional disclosure statements, Jack had also made a mistake on my taxes, I was now finding out. Jack had miscalculated the profit I'd made on the half share of the building I'd sold in 1978 to enable my election committee to repay the campaign loans made by my family. This meant I now owed the IRS $29,709 in back taxes, plus interest of $23,750, as well as taxes to New York State. That was nowhere near the $200,000 the press was estimating that I owed. But still, that error wouldn't look too hot.

There were so many questions, so many things I just didn't know about the ins and outs of John's business. Some matters were difficult to sort through because I'd never gotten involved in John's business. I knew precisely how much I was worth. But I hadn't known until this minute how much he was worth. Even so, for the rest of the campaign I would be hounded by the accusation that of course I knew every investment, every transaction, he and his companies had made. That was simply not true. I hadn't known any of the specifics about John's business.

For almost six years we had been a two-career couple, working in two different cities. When I managed to get home, I guarded what little time I had together with my family. I never let anyone call me at home on routine business, even my staff. Very few people had my home number. If anyone wanted to reach me, I was available during the day in my office. "If there's an emergency or if you're dying, give me a call at home," I'd said to my staff. "Otherwise, don't do it."

With so little time together, John and I rarely talked about our respective careers. He didn't know the specifics of my congressional work any more than I did about his real-estate transactions. Did he say to me: "What is your position on the tobacco-subsidy legislation pending in Congress?" No. Did I say to him: "Tell me, John, what properties are you buying or selling this week?" No. We talked the way any family does, about the happy things—the kids and their plans, when we'd be able to get away on vacation—as well as the unhappy ones—our housekeeper who was losing her sight due to cataracts, and what to do about the dog, who was having difficulty moving her hindquarters.

Our professional lives were separate. And so were our finances. It was very important to me to be financially independent. My father had died unexpectedly, and all of a sudden my mother had been on her own. I had seen firsthand how important it was for a woman, any woman, to have money of her own, just in case. When John and I married, he had a lot more money than I did, and everything we had belonged to the Zaccaros. I didn't like being dependent on John—not that he minded. He'd always been very generous. But being financially dependent made me uncomfortable. I wanted to earn my own way. And besides, after the FEC ruling on the family loans to my campaign, I had learned a lesson. If ever again I needed money in a career emergency, be it for Congress or the Senate, my assets would have to be liquid—and in my name.

There had been such a hassle in funding my 1978 campaign that I had decided never to tie up my money where I couldn't get at it when I needed it.

"Do you know what you're doing?" John used to say to me. "Please don't put your savings in bonds. It's not as good an investment as real estate." Maybe not. As I found out later, he had even bought back the property I had had to sell in 1978 to pay back the family loans to my campaign. That created a controversy of its own. But real estate is his business. But I wanted my assets to be immediately available. And I wanted greater financial independence. From that moment on I put whatever money I could save in municipal bonds, although John was right; I could have made more in real estate. But the lesson had stood me in good stead. When I found out during "Disclosure Weekend" that I owed the IRS over fifty thousand dollars in back taxes and interest, I was able to convert my bonds in a matter of hours and pay what I owed speedily.

There was more to it than that. Gaining financial independence was a matter of pride to me as well. Now I could help out my nephews if they needed something, give my mother money if necessary. They were my side of the family, and I didn't want to have to ask my husband for the money. Even with our own kids, if I wanted to buy something for them, or for John, it came from me. I was finally paying my own way. And I knew about every penny that came in or out of my accounts.

The public may have wanted me to be superwoman and all-knowing about John's business transactions. There was a presumption that because I was a lawyer I should have known the ins and outs of his business dealings. But I didn't. I wasn't John's lawyer. I was his wife, and just like any other time-short partner in a two-career marriage I was certainly aware of what my husband did for a living but didn't know most of the details. How I wish we'd had four years to prepare for my candidacy the way many politicians have. We'd had forty-eight hours.

The FEC deadline for filing my vice-presidential disclosure statement was five-thirty p.m. on Monday, August 20, in Washington. We decided at the meeting on Friday that the accountants would follow the filing with a technical briefing for the press. What to do about all the questions that would remain? After all, it was more than our financial affairs the press was questioning. My credibility was being challenged as well. "Why don't I have an open press conference?" I suggested. "Let every single member of the press come and ask me every single question they can think of until they're asked out, until they're convinced I'm not hiding anything. It's the only way to finish this issue once and for all so we can get on with the campaign."

It was a risky move to put myself on the front line, but to me it was the natural way to go. If I were open and honest with the press and through them the public, perhaps the suspicions about my credibility would be laid to rest. And Francis O'Brien agreed. The setting should be near my home in Queens, we decided, and big enough to accommodate every member of the press who wanted to come. We settled on the Viscount Hotel at the Kennedy Airport and sent out the word not only about the press conference but about John's decision to release his tax returns as well.

When we got home Friday night, the kitchen phone was ringing. "I'm glad you and John made the decision to release his tax returns," Fritz said. "It was the right decision." Was he relieved? Of course he was. He was getting hit hard. Here I was, supposedly the perfect vice-presidential candidate to give the ticket a fighting chance against Reagan. Instead, the campaign had been badly snagged by my personal affairs.

I really hurt for John. And I also hurt for Fritz. I have since said that if God had shown me a videotape the day Fritz asked me to be his running mate of what the next months would be like, I would have said, "Thanks, God, but could you do me a favor and choose Dianne?" You don't deliberately hurt the people you love. But it was too late now. There was nowhere to go but forward.

Fritz was also being heavily criticized in the press for not supporting me more on my finances in public. That wasn't fair. He couldn't. He was in a very awkward situation having a woman as a running mate—and in trouble. Had I been a male candidate, Fritz could have come forward and said, "I'm behind him one hundred percent, and we'll see this one through together." That would not have been seen as a put-down. But how would it have looked if he had come forward to try to protect the little lady? The white male vote we needed so badly would have seen his gesture as Fritz bailing out the helpless woman. The feminists would have come down on him, charging him with acting the male stereotype of being "paternalistic" and "protective." No. This was my battle and my battle alone.

If Fritz couldn't defend me himself up front, he had certainly sent the best of his campaign staff to help me behind the scenes. Those guys were phenomenal, having worked day and night the whole week I was in California. They were all high-priced lawyers, and anytime I asked one of them for help, he could have said: "Hey, Gerry, I'm not working for you. I'm working for Mondale." But no one ever did.

I've never understood why the press didn't understand the bind Fritz was in. Even columnist Murray Kempton, whose insights I admire, came down heavily on Fritz. "The moment Ferraro's troubles began, Mondale lapsed into silence and left it to his staff to leak word that he felt he had been betrayed," Murray wrote in *Newdsay*. ". . . He was leaving a wounded soldier to hobble out of the line of fire as best she could."

I couldn't bear it and asked Barbara Mikulski to call up Murray to explain. "Tell him he's wrong and why he's wrong," I told her. "Get some of the women's groups to call him, too. They can tell him how Fritz cannot go put his arms around the poor vulnerable woman. That's not what women want for a vice-presidential candidate. No matter how big her problems are, she'll take care of them on her own."

I don't know whether Barbara ever called him, but ten days later when I saw Murray at the Labor Day parade I ran over to him on the side of the street and asked him to walk with me for a bit. I explained the awkward position Fritz had been in and that there was nothing he could have done. But if Murray wrote a column correcting his initial impression, I never saw it.

The tension on "disclosure weekend" never let up. On Saturday, John was still collecting information for the accountants while some of my aides came to our house to help me prepare for my appearance the next day on *This Week with David Brinkley*. In the morning I concentrated on domestic issues with Steve Engelberg; in the afternoon, on foreign affairs with Madeleine Albright. Fred Martin, my speech writer, was there all day, playing the role of David Brinkley as moderator. Steve and Madeleine alternated playing Sam Donaldson and George Will. Most of the lawyers— Steve Pollak, Tony Essaye, and others—were in Washington, completing the financial disclosure statement and putting together the papers for the press conference, but there was a stream of other campaign aides in and out of the house all day as the time for the financial showdown came closer. I was being pulled in eighteen directions at once.

By Saturday night we were all exhausted. I went upstairs to find John still putting together some last-minute information for the accountants. John had pulled out some of his records from the top of the closet. And he looked awful. "I've just found another item of income, and I don't see where it's entered on my tax return," he said. I went over to him.

"It has to be somewhere," I said. "Let me see."

But we went through the whole form and couldn't find it. "My God, I don't see it anywhere," John said.

We were so worried that there had been yet another mistake.

John and I looked at each other. We both panicked. And suddenly his eyes filled with tears.

John crying? I'd seen him cry only once before, when he'd found out his brother was dying. I couldn't stand to see him suffer so. "Please don't do this to yourself," I said, putting my arms around him. What had he done to deserve all this? This good man who had never hurt anyone in his life, who had supported me in everything I'd ever done, was being destroyed. And all on account of me. Suddenly I was in tears as well. We stood there in the bedroom, surrounded by pieces of paper, clinging to each other. And John, Jr., walked in.

He was devastated. Here were his parents, his models of strength and protection, crying. It was an awful moment for him as well as for us. And he grew up on the spot. From that time on until the campaign was over, John, Jr., never left our sides except to campaign on his own or to substitute for one of us when our schedules conflicted. When we were home, he chose not to go out with his friends. If either one of his parents ever needed him, he was going to be there for us.

The panic over the missing item was resolved by a late-night phone call to our accountant, Irwin Ettinger, who reassured us that the amount was in the return and told us where to find it. But the morning did not dawn any easier. Nothing was going smoothly. Half the time on *This Week with David Brinkley* was taken up with my defending either my 1978 campaign loan, my claim of the spousal exemption on my congressional disclosure statements, or our Italian heritage because of the *New York* magazine story. "A lot of us have grown up with a vowel at the end of our name," I said. "The implication that just because we're Italian-American we're connected to organized crime is appalling. I have no words to describe my anger at someone attempting to imply that," I said, meaning Rupert Murdoch.

But inevitably, the subject kept returning to our finances. I couldn't resist facing down columnist George Will, who had just written a particularly cruel column in the *Washington Post*. "The hesitation to release her husband's tax returns may mean he has not paid much taxes," he had written that very morning. I'd had it. We had paid over forty percent of our combined income in taxes. He just didn't know it yet. "George Will, tomorrow afternoon you're going to call me up and apologize for your column of today," I charged him on national television. I was fed up with the press prejudging matters before all the facts were known.

Momentarily I felt better. But it was a false dawn. By Sunday night there were still so many details to be pulled together. Fred Martin had been working all day in Washington on questions I might be asked at the press conference, and he returned to our house that night with my campaign manager, John Sasso, and one of John's lawyers for this phase, John Koegel, to look for even more information that would be helpful to release on Monday. Just how much more in taxes had we paid by choosing to file separately? What was my exact voting record in the House on real-estate matters? Then there were all the technical details to absorb on John's purchase of various properties in the names of several different corporations.

It all began to fall apart on "disclosure Monday." By ten a.m. the press was jammed into the Georgetown Holiday Inn in Washington for their first shot at the Ferraro-Zaccaro finances and the scheduled technical briefing. The Associated Press even had three accountants hidden away in a hotel room, all ready to tear apart our returns. But the moment came and went with no disclosures—and no briefing. The Arthur Young accountants had discovered that additional information was still needed. They were not ready to file the disclosure statement. The filing and the briefing were delayed until one p.m. But still the Arthur Young people weren't satisfied.

I was frantic. While the drama with the accountants and the press was being played out in Washington, I was being grilled at home by the lawyers on the questions I could expect at my press conference the next day. Even people who did not have legal or accounting expertise were full of advice. Take the responsibility for one of Jack Selger's errors, Fred Martin suggested, citing four examples. No, I said firmly. They weren't my errors.

Maxine Isaacs, Fritz's press secretary, arrived to monitor the showdown for Fritz. You should never have taken the spousal exemption, she told me. You're going to have to release all the financial information that would have been included if you hadn't claimed the exemption. I won't do it, I told her. First, I hadn't been wrong in claiming the spousal exemption. And second, it would take weeks to collect all that information and I wanted to get this behind me. "Don't you feel it all slipping away?" Maxine pressed, meaning the momentum from the convention and our chances for victory.

I was sure it could all be recaptured in my press conference the next day. But would there be a next day if we couldn't file the disclosure statement before the deadline—now just three hours away? Through the windows I could see the television lights and the cameras trained on the house. I felt desperate. In between the lawyers' questions I made phone call after phone call. "You've got to go. You've got to do the briefing," I urged Irwin Ettinger and Charlie Reynolds of Arthur Young. But no matter how hard I pushed, they wouldn't budge.

My lawyer Steve Pollak tried to calm me down. "They're not going to go with it until they're absolutely sure they have everything they need," he said to me over and over. Finally the accountants were satisfied, and at five-nineteen, eleven minutes before the official deadline, we filed the disclosure statement with the Federal Election Commission in Washington. The technical briefing with the accountants was moved to eleven-thirty the next morning, an hour and a half before my press conference at Kennedy Airport was scheduled to begin.

By nine a.m. Tuesday, our house was overflowing with all the accountants, lawyers, and members of my campaign staff as the time for my press conference approached. There were over twenty people jammed around our dining room table, which seats eight comfortably. We had bagels and coffee laid out, but no one had an appetite. Some of these people had been working on the disclosure statement for weeks in Washington, but didn't know me and didn't know how I'd react under fire. For a couple of hours I had questions hurled at me about every aspect of our finances, from the seeming discrepancies of being listed at times as secretary, treasurer, or vice president of P. Zaccaro Co., Inc.— "It's sloppy. I'll grant you that"—to my defense of the spousal exemption. "If you take the separation of a couple's finances to the extreme," I said, "you have to have separate refrigerators."

Soon many of the accountants and lawyers had to leave for the technical briefing. It would be my turn next. As I walked up the stairs to change my clothes I knew that the next two hours could mean the end of my career. If I made a mistake at the press conference, I was going to call Fritz immediately and withdraw from the ticket.

I wasn't worried about getting rattled. As a trial lawyer I'd handled myself in adverse situations before. I wasn't worried about what I was going to say, either. I was going to go out there and tell the people honestly and directly what had happened and what I knew about it. What I was worried about was the press. The outcome would all depend on their response.

"Say a prayer for me," I said to my mother over the bedroom phone. "Everything I've worked for will ride on the next few hours." On the way out the front door I added a prayer of my own: "OK, God. Please help me." That was all that was left. I had prepared and done as much as I could. The accountants and the attorneys had done all they could. Now He was the only expert left who could help.

I drove over to the hotel with Fred Martin, Steve Pollak, and my son. Donna was working in Manhattan, and Laura was going to stay home with my husband. John wanted to be with me for moral support, but the lawyers felt that with the upcoming hearing on his conservatorship, his presence could be a problem. "You can do it," he said as he hugged me good-bye. "We're all rooting for you."

"Gerry Back on the Grill Today," read the headline in the early edition of the *New York Post*. And for once the newspaper was right. I've never seen anything like it. In fact, nobody had. There were over two hundred and fifty journalists jammed into the ballroom of the Viscount Hotel, along with thirty-six television cameras and their attendant crews. There was no need for so many members of the press to be there, of course. You don't reach more people just because there is more press. One interview on the Associated Press wire reaches every newspaper in the country. I was not flattered by the size of the group. They'd all had eighteen hours to tear apart my disclosure statement and our tax returns. Now I would be the target. At one p.m. sharp I walked out to face them, my jury, my prosecutors, and my judges. I was as ready as I was ever going to be. And the sound system didn't work.

The microphones had all been wired into what's called a "mult box," an amplifier that feeds back the sound from a single microphone to all those broadcasting the session. Not surprisingly, the mult box had succumbed to overload and a fuse had blown. The technicians fiddled with this and that while I sat there staring out at the members of my inquisition, but nothing worked. I couldn't believe it. Here I was all ready to go—and nothing. "I'll come back when you're ready," I said to the technicians. And walked off.

Backstage the tension was palpable. Everybody—my staff, the attorneys, my son—was a nervous wreck. The minutes ticked by and still nothing. No one knew what to say to me, which was just as well because there was nothing to be said. I wanted to move out there fast, get on with it, and get it over with. I'm never nervous when I'm on. But the waiting can be murder, especially this day when my career was on the line. I faced the possibility of going down in history as a second Tom Eagleton, George McGovern's running partner, who had been dropped from the ticket in 1972.

After ten interminable minutes, the technicians came in and said they still couldn't fix the mult box. "Fine," I said. "Set up all the microphones instead and let's go."

"Wait a minute," my staff cautioned. "You'll have one hundred microphones in front of you."

"Good," I said. "I want the American public to see what I'm going through." Now there would be sound. And the public would see the fury. Perhaps that's how God helped me, by knocking out the mult box.

For the next ninety minutes I answered every question imaginable into the forest of microphones in front of me. I didn't think about anything except hearing the press out and answering their questions until they got tired of asking. I tried to call on everybody at least once, but one young man from the *Washington Times,* an ultraconservative paper owned by Sun Myung Moon, kept popping up no matter who I pointed to. "Let me get to everybody once and I'll come back to you," I said to him. But still he kept jumping up and down, attempting to grab the spotlight.

For everybody who was trying to nail me, however, there were others who never left my side. There were people who hurt every time I got belted, who bled when I got cut. One of them was my friend Peg Swezey, the president of the Queens Chamber of Commerce, who, inexplicably, I now saw tucked away in the

© ANN BURROLA

Our campaign was for her.

The candidates.

With Ray Kopp, retired detective from my DA days, one of many full-time volunteers.

Poor Eleanor Lewis, withstanding the elements to track my speech in Merrill, Wisconsin.

Ferraro the peacemaker: Councilman Ed Vrdolyak (l) and Mayor Harold Washington on one stage, Chicago.

A network of elected women officials: Minnesota Secretary of State Joan Growe (l) and Lieutenant Governor Marlene Johnson.

© ANN BURROLA

Congresswoman Barbara Mikulski, National Co-chair, standing tall.

Pat Flynn in Queens negotiating the schedule with Washington.

Press conferences, whenever, wherever.

© ANN BURROLA

Women making a difference. With Bella Abzug (l); Donna Shalala, president of Hunter College; Assemblywoman Geraldine Daniels, my mother; City Councilwoman Carol Greitzer; Irene Natividad, newly elected president of NWPC.

Women's meetings: we did them all over the country; this one is in Harrisburg, Pennsylvania.

It was nice to see some friendly faces.

"Can you tell me why you're voting for Ronald Reagan?" UAW/Chrysler plant.

We didn't have a prayer in North Carolina, but we sure tried for Governor Jim Hunt (l) and Congressman Robin Britt (r).

With Bishop Joseph Sullivan (l), who spoke up for the homeless and hungry.

Columbus Day, New York City. All the crowds we missed on Labor Day.
With Mayor Ed Koch (l), Fritz, Governor Mario Cuomo (r).

Columbus Day, Newark. With another proud Italian, Congressman Peter
Rodino (center), and Senator Bill Bradley, who pretended he was.

back of the room. How had Peg gotten in? On a borrowed press pass from a local Queens paper, she told me later. She just wanted to be there to give me support.

The questions went on until they became repetitious. That's just what I wanted. At every press conference there are always reporters who have more questions to ask—and not enough time. No one would ever be able to say that about this press conference, the longest any reporter could remember. "Let's wind this up in five minutes," Francis O'Brien suggested after an hour and a half.

"How about fifteen?" I countered. But I knew I had won over at least some of the press. When an editorial writer from the *Wall Street Journal* asked me a question and then yelled, "Answer it!" after I was a little slow in responding, his fellow members of the press booed him.

"It's a ten!" yelled Maxine Isaacs, when finally the press conference was over. She'd called up Fritz immediately to tell him the positive news, since the television station in Minnesota had not run the last forty-five minutes. Right away he held his own press conference reinforcing his support for me. The normally taciturn Secret Service were no less jubilant. "You know, we are not supposed to comment on the people we're protecting, but, Congresswoman Ferraro, you were just wonderful in the press conference," one of the agents said to me on the way home.

John and Laura met me at the front door. "You were fabulous," John said.

I called my mother. "Are you all right?" she said, ever the worrier.

Yes I was. But just. It was incredible how close the call had been. John Stacks, then the New York bureau chief for *Time* magazine, later told me that *Time* had an article all ready to go with a title something like: "Ferraro Lets Down the Women of the Country." Stacks was at the press conference to finish off my obituary, but afterwards he ran to the phone to pull the article. Instead of my obit, *Time*'s cover the next week read: "Ferraro Fights Back," with the subtitle inside, "Under pressure, Ferraro passes a vital test." I was thrilled.

There was only one thing outstanding. Instead of George Will's calling in his apology on Monday after he'd learned that

John had indeed paid his taxes, he had sent me a dozen roses. "Has anyone told you you are cute when you're mad?" the card had read. I hadn't had time to call him and thank him for the flowers before the press conference. At home now, I did.

"You did a superb job," he said from the press room at the Republican Convention in Dallas.

We chatted for a few minutes about the reaction of the delegates to my press conference. But that wasn't what I was calling about. "Thank you for the roses, George, but there is something I think you should know," I said.

"What?" he responded, probably thinking I was about to give him a scoop.

I let him hang for a minute. "Vice Presidents aren't cute," I said. And hung up.

The campaign had certainly taken a turn for the better. From that moment on, the national press, anyway, stopped harassing me and started taking my candidacy more seriously. And I sure was relieved myself. I truly thought all the questions and innuendo about our personal lives would stop and I could finally deal with the substantive and critical issues this country faced under Ronald Reagan.

My optimism soared. "Today is the first day of the rest of the campaign," I told three thousand cheering members of the American Federation of Teachers the next day in Washington. "Normally, I begin a speech by saying, 'I'm delighted to be here.' After this week I have to tell you, I'm absolutely thrilled." Now, finally, I could get on with it.

ON THE ROAD

"Only 103 More Days."

—*Mondale-Ferraro campaign-countdown calendar.*

P EOPLE. OF ALL THE PHE-
nomena that would be a part of my candidacy, the crowds that
surrounded me wherever I went would become the most vivid
and fulfilling campaign image I carried—masses of people stretching up city streets, jammed into town squares, hanging out of
windows, clinging to telephone poles, standing on top of cars,
perched in trees. There were over twelve thousand at my first
solo rally, in Seattle, on August 16, and equally large crowds at
rallies the following week in Camden, St. Louis, and Nashville. I
can still hear the cheering, whistling, and foot stomping; the
political chants—"Ronald Reagan is no good. Send him back to
Hollywood."—and my own personal cheering section: "Gerr-
eee! Gerr-eee!" Never has a political candidacy drawn so much
curiosity—and rarely so many enthusiasts. From sea to shining
sea, it seemed, everyone wanted to get a look at the first woman
vice-presidential candidate.

I was just as fascinated to see all these people as they were to
see me, to look at the endless crowds while I stood on hastily
constructed podiums, auditorium stages, the steps of town halls
all over the country. As far as my eye could see were the faces of
America; young, old, well-to-do, poor, of every possible ethnic

descent, business executives, blue-collar workers, often people in wheelchairs—and women. "I never thought I'd live to see this day," one eighty-year-old said to me in Minneapolis. At a fund-raiser in St. Paul a week later I repeated her comment. As I was leaving, an elderly woman beckoned me over and said: "You know the story you just told about the eighty-year-old woman? Well, I'm ninety-one and I never thought I'd live to see this day, either."

The pace was backbreaking. In the next three months I would travel over fifty-five thousand miles, campaign stumping in eighty-five cities in eighty-seven days. It wasn't always easy. At one rally in Portland, Oregon, the pouring rain dissolved my best lines, which I had just penned into my remarks, prompting the Oregon Historical Society to request the soggy papers as a souvenir. At a September picnic in Bayonne, New Jersey, the platform nearly collapsed, the sound system was terrible, and there was no podium. I asked the man standing next to me to take the pages of my speech as I finished delivering them. The only trouble was he became so engrossed in reading the speech over my shoulder that he started taking the pages out of my hands before I'd finished with them. I almost ended up delivering the speech while reading it over *his* shoulder. Total craziness.

There were other funny moments. After a long, grueling day in Montgomery, Alabama, I arrived exhausted at my hotel room only to watch the Secret Service agents try unsuccessfully to get my door open. "What's with you guys?" I twitted them. "Just shoot the lock off with your guns."

But they were above that. "Congresswoman Ferraro," one agent said to me gravely. "Would you happen to have a hairpin?"

The Secret Service agents were one of the best things about the campaign. They were fabulous, professional and courteous— both my details, headed by Paul Hackenberry and William Wasley, and John's, headed by Benny Crosby and Mike Johnston. It was not Gerry Ferraro they were guarding so much as the office I was running for. And they took the job very seriously. When I reached out to one crowd the Secret Service was a little worried about, I looked up to see Mike Goehring moving through the crowd parallel to me, using his own body as a buffer between me and anyone who might try to do me harm. Every time I got out of the car, the agent would hold his hand over my head; I'm not sure if it was so I wouldn't bump it or because people getting in and out of cars are most vulnerable, and a head is an easy and almost always fatal target. Cars and airports made the Secret Service particularly nervous. From the first airport, in Lake Tahoe, the agents would scan the rooftops as I moved from the plane to the car or vice-versa, keeping their fingers on the triggers of their automatic Israeli submachine guns, called Uzis, which they carried on their shoulders like pocketbooks.

It was hard at first to get used to. At Lake Tahoe, John and I had been awakened in the middle of the night by voices right outside our window. In Queens that meant one thing. You were about to be broken into. "Relax," John had said. "It's just the Secret Service." In the morning I explained my Queens paranoia to them, and we never heard another word. Whenever we got home during the campaign, I never felt more secure in my life. The Secret Service doused the light on our front porch so they wouldn't be direct targets, and stationed themselves around the yard and the street. That was just fine with me. Throughout the campaign I was the only person in New York City who went to bed without thinking of locking her front door.

I got impatient with them only once. In early September I had been campaigning on the West Coast, and John, immediately after a hernia operation, was with me on the trip, just to get away. But it had been a mistake for him to travel so soon, and he was really in bad shape. I had to make a stop in New Jersey and urged him to go directly home.

After the event I was naturally anxious to see him. But instead of following the direct route home, which takes only twenty minutes on city streets, the Secret Service wanted to take the longer highway route. It was safer, they explained to me. The stopping and starting at traffic lights made me an easier target. And there was no way they could get the entire motorcade filled with staff and press through all the lights together. I was angry because we always seemed to take the most time-consuming ways to get home. Outside of New York I didn't feel it, but this was my city, and I wanted to be in my own house. So I crabbed and fumed in the backseat en route. They did it my way, but of course, they were right. And I felt terrible about it afterward.

They were wrong, though, in the number of women agents the Secret Service employed, and my candidacy proved to be

somewhat embarrassing to them. Since 1971, the Secret Service
had assimilated only around eighty women into its force of close
to eighteen hundred (the Secret Service never releases exact numbers), and often there wasn't a woman agent available for my
detail. The lack of women agents was highlighted by my trips to
public rest rooms. Every time we would look for one, it created a
minor crisis. The agents would then have to "secure" the ladies'
room, going in and peering under the stalls to make sure there
was no one lurking inside. It was a ludicrous situation. After a
while I started going into the ladies' room ahead of them, bending
down to check out the stalls myself and then yelling, "All clear!"
But the agents were behaving correctly. Their job was to protect
me. And there always was the possibility that someone could
have been in there who wanted to do me harm.

Only once did the Secret Service mess up. And it wasn't my
security that was lost. It was my luggage. On September 15, Fritz
and I were scheduled to attend the biannual National Italian American Foundation dinner in Washington, along with Ronald Reagan
and George Bush. It was a formal dinner and the only time all
four candidates would be seen together during the campaign. But
when I flew into Washington from Elmira, New York, where I
had spoken to a student group, the dress bag containing my
evening dress and John's tuxedo was not there. Instead of being
sent to Washington, the dress bag was locked in the trunk of a
Secret Service car in our driveway in Queens.

My staff was getting hysterical. Protocol called for the presidential and vice-presidential candidates to enter the dinner first, to
be in place when the incumbent President and Vice President
arrived. But without our evening clothes, we couldn't go anywhere, and time was running out. Three substitute dresses owned
by various staff members were rushed to the hotel, as was a
tuxedo for John. Nothing fit. "I'll just wear my business suit,"
John said agreeably, but that was vetoed. So were the emergency
dresses—by me. "I will not appear on a podium with the other
three candidates on national television feeling uncomfortable," I
said firmly to my staff, who were leaning hard on me.

This was nothing new. They had heard it before in San
Francisco. I wanted my speech to be delivered well, and I wanted
my people to be proud.

While our dress bag was in the air, the NIAF dinner began—

without us. I used the time to meet with two of my lawyers and go over the Washington Legal Foundation's complaint lodged with the House Committee on Standards of Official Conduct about my congressional disclosure statements. And Fritz was wonderful about the dilemma, quite content to wait until our luggage came through, which it finally did. Then we went down to the dinner together, well after Reagan and Bush had arrived. I began my speech by saying, "It is wonderful to be here with that other Italian on the ticket, Fritz Mondali." I was back in stride.

The campaign trail was never dull and often challenging. The first thing I had to learn was to get over my reluctance to do giant rallies. I'd always disliked them. I was far more comfortable giving speeches in more intimate settings, enjoying the give-and-take between the audience and myself, as in my town-hall meetings in my congressional district. Involving the audience in a dialogue, I've always thought, is far more instructive both for me and for them.

These rally audiences were different. The ten, twenty, or thirty thousand people who showed up usually weren't there to be enlightened, but to have an emotional experience. After waiting for two hours in the rain or jammed into a high school gymnasium, they didn't want to hear a long speech. They wanted to feel part of a political event, to be excited, to applaud and cheer. At a rally, the speaker is not supposed to talk at the people but with them, to interact with the crowd. I needed to have short, punchy lines and to know how to deliver them. At the beginning, I didn't have either.

So I had to bite the bullet and learn. Rallies, after all, were the politics of numbers. At first I practiced my lines in my hotel room with my staff, muttering all the time, "I hate this," while they applauded at the proper times. But still I talked too fast. I swallowed my syllables. At a rally in Providence when I finished a sentence with "we educate our children" it was heard by some as suggesting we "chuck our children." I really bewildered them in Youngstown, Ohio. Taking a shot at our Republican "critics," it sounded more like our Republican "critters," which was what they really were, anyway. Even the press, who were getting more used to my rapid Queens speech, were taken aback when they thought they heard me accuse Reagan of having a drug problem. It took a copy of my text to clear up what I meant when I said: "The President has a habit of taking bows while the heroine is still tied to the tracks."

I wanted a professional's perspective and asked Dayle Hardy, a public-speaking instructor now at Trinity University in San Antonio, Texas, who had worked as a fellow in my congressional office for six months to join me on the road for three days. She showed me how to mark my speeches for emphasis and to set up key lines. "Where other Presidents worked to clean the air, help the poor, and pass the ERA,/Ronald Reagan has fogged the air, helped the rich, and passed the buck," my text read for a rally in Chicago in early September. A few days later, at a rally at Hunter College in New York, my text was marked: "Ronald Reagan says/ we should cut education funds, and wants to launch a teacher into space. But I say/ let's help the students and teachers here on earth."

It was getting easier and my delivery was getting better. "Bring your voice up at the end of a sentence," Dayle advised me. "You keep turning away from the microphone, and you can't do that," she said. "You are losing your voice."

The crowds themselves were often invaluable teachers. In my first rally, in Seattle, the crowd was so huge that there was a time lapse of maybe two seconds between the sound of my voice and the reaction of the people standing way back on a hill. The delay sure slowed me down. And I began to have fun. In Spokane, Washington, I spotted a sign in the crowd, stopped my remarks, and began to chuckle. "Jane—Wyman—was—right," I read slowly, to the crowd's delight. Other times, signs in the crowd highlighted points I was making. In Wisconsin, a little girl was standing in front of the crowd holding a sign reading: "My daddy needs a job."

"Stand up here and show your sign to these people," I said to her. "If Mr. Reagan thinks the economy is so great, why are there so many people like your daddy unemployed in this country?" The crowd was moved.

Fritz and I were rarely in the same place at the same time after the convention, appearing together at only a half dozen rallies, several dinners and parades over the entire campaign. When we were together, I spoke first, and then Fritz would speak. He always insisted that I not introduce him, but that someone else should introduce me and then him. "You are an important candidate," he would say to me. "It would be putting you down to have you introduce me to an audience. I don't want to place you in that position."

The only exceptions were my introduction of him to the rally after the first debate and his introduction of me to the crowds after my debate.

Both our campaigns were directed from national Mondale-Ferraro headquarters in Washington—the groups we were to speak to by the schedulers (literally side by side) and the themes we were to address by the issues staff. Besides the rallies, there were fund-raisers and parades to attend and, of course, serious speeches to be made. The themes for these speeches were coordinated so that they would complement each other. On several occasions, we spent a whole campaign week on a single theme.

I tried to keep to a strict personal schedule, pacing myself so that I wouldn't burn out. The day usually started at seven a.m. local time, wherever we were, with a staff meeting and ended at night with my last event, which I tried to schedule no later than eight p.m. But because we were rarely in the same time zone we'd been in the day before, no one was ever quite sure what time it was. I wanted to have at least one "down" day a week. Contrary to the original schedule, which had me on the road over the weekends, my schedule was rearranged as much as possible to put me home on Sundays, my church day and the one day I could be with my family.

In the morning staff sessions Francis O'Brien and John Sasso would bring me up to date on news of the campaign—what was happening with Reagan and Bush, what kind of press Fritz was getting, and how the campaign looked in newspapers around the country. We would also go over the questions I might be asked by the pros that day and refine my answers.

One of our first staff meetings in Seattle, during our swing the week of August 12, was the undoing of my initial press secretary, Pat Bario. The press had heard about these meetings and had asked to sit in on one. So there we were with the tape whirring when the subject of issues came up.

Pat spoke up. "I don't know what the local issues are here that we might get hit with," she said. "Does anybody?"

I couldn't believe it. "I do," I said immediately. What a great impression to leave with the public, that I was both unknowledgeable and unconcerned about local problems and that my staff was unprepared and didn't know what was going on. The national press, of course, picked up Pat's gaffe, running that segment of our meeting while calling the campaign still "somewhat disorganized." And Pat, who continued to handle the press in a way I felt was ineffective, was later replaced by Francis O'Brien.

I hated the playacting of those morning mock press conferences. I do fine on my feet during the real thing. But the rehearsing seemed so superficial and silly that when the press wasn't there I often gave off-the-wall answers to my staff just for the fun of it. They were not always amused. "Congresswoman Ferraro, why did you vote for the Boxer amendment in Congress?" they asked, also on a trip to California.

Instead of going into the merits of Barbara's amendment dealing with the sale of power generated by the Hoover Dam, I joked, "Because Barbara Boxer asked me to. And because she's a friend of mine."

So many groans ran around the room that we had to develop a system so my staff would know when I was kidding. A tug on one ear was the secret signal to relax. As the stress of the campaign mounted, I sometimes needed to use both ears before my beleaguered staff got the point.

And on we pressed. Certain states were targeted as critical. The midwestern states of Ohio, Pennsylvania, Illinois, and Michigan were important industrial states and Democratic strongholds. I made eight separate campaign swings through Ohio, and seven through California. The campaign saw my candidacy as the unknown magnet that might just draw the bold and new spirit Californians thrive on, though California was definitely a long shot. Not only was it Reagan's home state, but only one Democratic presidential candidate had carried California in the last thirty-two years. Moreover, Mondale had lost the state to Hart in the primary. But California had forty-seven electoral college votes, more than one-sixth of the total of two hundred and seventy needed to win the presidency, and the demographics showed large groups of Yuppies, voters of Italian descent, Catholics, and women.

I also had specific constituencies targeted for me. Peter Hart, Mondale's chief pollster, was constantly testing the political waters, calling the shots on which pivotal groups could be most swayed by my candidacy. We had already been endorsed by many black groups and labor organizations. But there were some constituencies we weren't sure of at all, and Fritz suggested, "Gerry can bolster us with those groups."

The high-tech vote was one, since my candidacy was seen by the campaign as symbolizing the politics of the future. I spent a lot of time in computer centers and electronic companies all over the country, prepping myself beforehand on such high-tech newspeak terms as "REMS" and "disk drives."

"It's a great pleasure to be here at Apple, which is helping to show us the way to the twenty-first century," I said in Cupertino, California. "After all, it was not so long ago that people thought that semiconductors were part-time orchestra leaders and microchips were very, very small snack foods," I joked, always attempting to inject a little humor.

Many college students and young professionals had aligned themselves with Gary Hart's "politics of the future" during the primaries, attracted by his emphasis on "new ideas" and economic growth for the young. We were afraid, now, that these same young people might either sit out the election or go for Reagan. My candidacy as a woman, symbolizing new leadership and a fresh approach toward the Vice Presidency, along with my voting record in Congress, was seen as bringing in the young vote. So students became mine at Syracuse University; the University of Texas at Arlington; Hunter College, in New York; the University of Oregon; the University of Washington; Northwestern University, in Evanston; Michigan State University; the University of Iowa; the University of Massachusetts at Amherst; Valley College, in Van Nuys, California; San Diego State University, Community College of Rhode Island, in Warwick; and my own alma mater, Marymount College, in New York. I spoke at many high schools as well, to members of the community in Sterling Heights, Michigan; Hinsdale, Illinois; Waterbury, Connecticut; Green Bay, Wisconsin; Germantown, Pennsylvania; and many other places.

I loved talking to the kids. After I had completed my remarks on arms control at Truman High School in Independence, Missouri, a student who was getting ready to vote for the first time asked if he should register as a Republican or a Democrat. I asked him what he thought about the nuclear arms race, and he told me that he was too busy with his homework to think about it. I then said that, considering his priorities, he should register Republican.

The exchange was published in the press. Then the Reagan campaign picked it up. George Bush's reply was subsequently reprinted in the *Kansas City Star*. "Do not let the politicians make you think you must neglect your homework only to worry about nuclear war," Bush wrote.

Obviously, the point I was making was that though self-advancement is important, we have an obligation to ourselves and to society to be concerned about the survival of humanity. I thought the distortion was a cheap shot.

Naturally, women were also seen as my special constituency. But the decision was made early in the campaign that I would, of course, speak to women's groups, but not solely on women's issues. I didn't have to prove my credibility to women on the ERA, pay and pension equity, fair insurance laws, programs and support for single heads of households and their children, while I did have to prove myself with other groups.

Given the results, perhaps that was the wrong decision. I don't know. But women certainly weren't ignored. In every major metropolitan area we went to, I met privately with between fifteen and two hundred women activists, elected officials, and community leaders.

Our message to the women at these closed meetings was really quite simple. First, we finally have a woman candidate, and we've got to show that she'll move the ticket forward. Second, we need to register as many new voters as possible to show that women can make a difference. And third, we've got to motivate people to go to the polls in November and vote.

Often the enthusiasm coming out of these meetings was infectious. In California, I asked one woman from the state chapter of NOW how voter registration was going.

"Terrifically," she said. "We set up ironing boards everywhere as a gimmick to draw attention. And they're just the right height for people to fill out their voter registration forms." "Great recycling idea, since none of us use them for ironing anymore," quipped a state legislator in attendance.

I passed the idea and the quip on to other women at subsequent meetings in Chicago, New York, and Philadelphia.

Wherever we went, the new women's network was having a clear impact on the old politics. Up until 1982, one of the party leaders in California told me, he'd always called on labor groups to build up a crowd for political events. For the first time this year he had also reached out to the women's groups. They had helped produce the biggest crowds of all.

The local and state chapters of NOW were always there for us with their green and white signs. The American Nurses Association was there, as was the American Federation of Teachers, the National Education Association, the Business and Professional Women's Association, the National Women's Political Caucus, the American Association of University Women, and many others. Some people in the growing crowds weren't affiliated with any organization. They were there because the network of women had reached them, excited them, and energized them to come. It was great.

In my speeches I spoke to whatever condition prevailed in the area we were in. But Reagan's foreign policy was a national, not regional, issue, and I challenged his actions as often as possible. "In the last four years, tensions with Russia have risen," I said to crowds in New Jersey, Connecticut, Illinois, and Tennessee. "Will this President, unrestrained by the need for reelection, heighten the risk of war?"

Certain days dictated themes of their own. On National Crime Day, I spoke to the Chula Vista Police Department in San Diego and to the National District Attorneys Association citing Reagan's budget cuts, which hampered the FBI, the Drug Enforcement Agency, even Customs, in the fight against drug trafficking. With two former prosecutors on the Democratic ticket, I pointed out, we would be tough on crime. "We not only understand crime, we've fought it," I said. "We not only condemn criminals; we've put them behind bars." And I got a standing ovation from the DAs association, many of whom were Republicans.

Woman's Equality Day, August 26, celebrating the sixty-fourth anniversary of women's right to vote, also provided a natural theme—and a cause for celebration, as it was my forty-ninth birthday. It was amazing how many key dates in the campaign coincided with other anniversaries. The first day of the convention in San Francisco was also my twenty-fourth wedding anniversary. The day of the vice-presidential debate would fall on Eleanor Roosevelt's one hundredth birthday. None of these conjunctions was anything but a coincidence. But all boded well for the ticket.

And at this woman's rally on my birthday on a steamy hot day in Fort Lee, New Jersey, I felt terrific. "In 1906, only a month before her death at eighty-five, after a lifetime devoted to women's rights, Susan B. Anthony addressed a women's suffrage convention in Baltimore. 'Failure,' she said, 'is impossible.' She's right—failure is impossible," I said to thunderous applause.

The day before, at a voter-registration rally on Long Island, it was my daughter Laura, not Susan B. Anthony, who was the subject of my remarks. "Back in June, my daughter Laura celebrated her eighteenth birthday. And I gave her two presents. One was a Walkman. She loved it. But the other gift, which cost me nothing, was far more valuable, and far more long lasting. It was a voter-registration form. I did what any fair, reasonable mother would do. I told Laura she couldn't have the Walkman if she didn't send in the voter-registration form. She did."

When I wasn't giving speeches at rallies or special audiences, I was speaking at fund-raisers. And history was being made there as well. One of the unknowns of my candidacy was the campaign contributions it might attract. No one knew if a woman on the ticket would bring in more money to the Democratic Party than a male candidate, less money—or any money at all. Men had always been the big contributors to political campaigns, either individually or through the organizations they represented. Would my candidacy be not only a professional breakthrough for women candidates, but serve as a financial one as well?

Yes. And yes again. For the first time in the history of the Democratic Party, the vice-presidential candidate would raise as much money as the presidential candidate. And women would contribute money in much larger numbers than ever before. It was astonishing. I ended up raising a record $2.1 million from women-sponsored events, another record two million dollars from direct-mail requests, and another two million from general events. Many contributions came from people who had never contributed to a political campaign before. All in all, the Democratic National Committee ended up with twenty-six thousand new names to add to its list of supporters, a legacy no other candidacy has ever produced.

The success of our fund-raisers caught us all by surprise. But it made sense. To the public, I was the draw. All the traditional Democratic donors had seen Fritz time and again during the primaries and had already contributed a lot of money to him. But I was new. We were getting two or three requests a week for my appearance from all over the country and ended up doing thirty-two fund-raisers in twenty-eight cities.

Fund-raisers were the lowest priority in terms of scheduling, leaving the staff in Washington to scramble for any time slot available. But it didn't seem to matter. Seven a.m. was the scheduled kickoff in Dallas for what turned out to be one of our most successful fund-raisers. Seven a.m.? I thought the schedulers were nuts. To get to it, people had to leave their houses by five-thirty a.m. But at six a.m. we had two thousand people, mostly women, lined up to get in. Four thousand eight hundred people paying forty dollars a head ended up jamming into the hotel, forcing us to take a second ballroom at the last minute. I don't think they even got the breakfast they were paying for, and we raised $176,300. It took the office in Washington three weeks just to process the checks—over a quarter of which came from Republicans!

Sometimes it was hard to take the money. We had a two-tiered event in San Jose, California, the top tickets going for two hundred and fifty dollars, the others for sixty-five dollars. And women who could hardly afford sixty-five dollars paid anyway. One group of waitresses had come together, writing out their checks to the campaign because they wanted to, because it was so important for them to be part of this historic candidacy. One woman told me she had asked her husband for her ticket as a fortieth-birthday present. Other women had asked for tickets—or had given them away—as early Christmas presents.

Fritz's fund-raisers at a thousand dollars a head pinpointed the traditional Democratic donors. My low-ticket fund-raisers, often held over great opposition from the Mondale campaign fund-raisers—because there had been no history of major fundraising at low-ticket events—raised money from many people who had never made a political contribution before. Whole families—mothers, fathers, and daughters—came. In Pittsburgh, three generations—daughter, mother, and grandmother—came together. Women of all ages wanted to bear witness to the first candidacy of one of their own.

My candidacy had struck a chord deeper than anyone had anticipated. "I'd vote for you if I could, but I'm twelve years old," one girl said to me in a hotel lobby in Atlanta. An eighty-two-year-old woman who had never before registered to vote sent us a two-dollar check and asked the procedure for registering. The subsequent phone calls back and forth to Oregon where she lived cost us more than her contribution, but it was well worth it to us, knowing that my candidacy meant so much to her. Ironically, the activist women's groups who everyone thought would be the most natural to raise money were not the mainstays of the fund-raising effort. The bulk of the contributions came from middle-class women who did not think of themselves as feminists or part of the women's movement. "I did not know how much it meant to me to have a woman run for the Vice Presidency until you got the nomination," was a common sentiment.

Were these fund-raisers unorthodox? Definitely. But the enthusiasm was incredible. Rather than the campaign going after people to hold a fund-raiser, people were coming to us and asking if they could. Often, not only were the Mondale people very skeptical but so was the Democratic National Committee. When California State Senator Diane Watson and Assemblywoman Gloria Molina wanted to hold a breakfast for me, the DNC said no. They won't deliver, the DNC warned us; don't do it. They are unproven, and have never been involved in fund-raising before.

How short-sighted. Though Diane and Gloria had committed to raise only fifty thousand dollars, the breakfast brought in $82,130 at thirty-five dollars per ticket from over twenty-three hundred women.

Many checks, often unsolicited, came from women who wanted to make a contribution to my candidacy but added a note that said, "Please don't acknowledge this contribution. My husband doesn't know about it." Whether these women had very little money or were married to Republicans, I never discovered. Other women sponsored fund-raising events on their own and did not ask us to send a speaker or even campaign material. Suddenly another sixty or seventy checks would come into campaign headquarters, in amounts of anywhere from five dollars to twenty dollars.

There was always confusion about who the checks should be written to. The correct title was "1984 Democratic Victory Fund." But a lot of unsolicited checks came in from women written either to "Ferraro for Vice President" or even to me personally. The campaign couldn't accept those checks and had to deposit them in the compliance fund the DNC used for staff salaries and legal expenses. As for the unsolicited checks that were written out correctly, we never knew for sure what part my candidacy had played in the contribution. The record-breaking six million dollars we know we raised was probably much less than what my candidacy actually brought in.

For all the success we were having on the campaign trail, there were constant disagreements between the Mondale campaign staff and my own, especially at the beginning. Though theoretically everyone was working under the same Mondale-Ferraro campaign umbrella, the campaign staffs really broke down into three different ones: Mondale's staff; the people I had hired on winning the nomination; and the small group I had brought with me from my congressional staff. In addition, there was a fourth group still operating my congressional Washington and district offices. Because of the different directions each group was coming from, there was bound to be some tension among them.

The problems that arose seemed to center around scheduling. Well before I had accepted the vice-presidential nomination, for example, I had promised Judy Hope, the town supervisor in East Hampton, on Long Island, and a Democrat, that I would speak to the East End Women's Alliance there on Woman's Equality Day in August and combine the visit with a fund-raiser for my congressional reelection campaign. I didn't know that after the nomination my appearance there was canceled. It would have been wrong for my image, scheduling finally got around to telling me. East Hampton was a posh summer resort. Too many rich white people. Republican-looking people, not Democrats. And the campaign wanted to downplay my identification with women's groups as well.

By the time I heard about the controversy, my appearance in East Hampton had been canceled, reestablished by Addie Guttag, my fund raiser, and canceled again. Naturally Judy Hope was furious. And so was I when in desperation Addie finally called me about it at home at eleven p.m. I couldn't believe this was happening. I had given Judy Hope my word that I would be there. And someone else had changed my mind for me, without even telling me.

"I made a commitment to Judy Hope and I will not break it," I said. "I will not do that to an elected official." Immediately I called Judy to tell her we would be there. And we were. We also did a fund-raiser at the magnificent home of then New York Deputy Mayor Ken Lipper and his wife, Evie, raising over $100,000, the most money ever raised in the Hamptons.

The very next day, I had been invited by Billie Jean King to the finals of the U.S. Open tennis matches at Flushing Meadow. And I did not even know it! The scheduler had told Kevin Donnellan, my Washington office manager, to throw out the invitation and not even to tell me about it. Again, they felt the image was wrong, too rich. Tennis was a Republican sport. Kevin sent the invitation to my district office, and Irene Sullivan, a caseworker who was handling my mail, slipped it into the pile of mail being delivered to my house, knowing that I had been going with my family to the tennis matches for twelve years, that I had that day off, and that I'd probably like to go.

Not knowing anything about the controversy, John and I went to watch the tennis after I had delivered a speech in Fort Lee, New Jersey. We were delighted to relax for a few hours. And so were the Secret Service, who thought it was one of the better ideas of the campaign. I still wasn't used to my new celebrity, however, and was terribly embarrassed when our arrival caused such a buzz and then applause in the stadium that the play had to stop momentarily on the court. I also wasn't prepared for my first threat.

"I want to speak to you," read the note passed to me, scribbled on the back of a card from a *Wall Street Journal* reporter. "If you will not speak to me, I will be forced to print things about you that can be uncomfortable." There was obviously no

way we could ever get away from the campaign, even sitting in
the sun at the U.S. Open.

Though the schedulers never discovered how I had found
out about the tennis invitation, Addie and Kevin were told they
were no longer to discuss the campaign with me, that they and
the rest of my congressional staff were causing a lot of trouble.

"Whenever you people don't get your way, you go directly
to Ferraro," Addie and Kevin were told by Jack Corrigan, my
deputy campaign manager, who had been hired by John Sasso.
"You can no longer do that. There are channels of communication that you'll just have to accept."

Addie refused. "Gerry is the one who hired me," she said.
"When she becomes unhappy with what I'm doing, she'll be
the one to do something about it."

Scheduling seemed to be the most controversial technical
aspect of the campaign, and occasionally my schedulers had to
take on Mondale's. When we looked at the schedule for September 3, for example, and saw that Fritz and I were supposed to lead
off the Labor Day parade in New York at nine in the morning, I
said to John Sasso, "Are they kidding? It's a holiday. No one
could get a crowd in my city to turn out at nine a.m., not even
for Mondale-Ferraro. Maybe you can push back the parade to
eleven o'clock. But nine o'clock? No way!"

But the schedulers on the Mondale staff insisted. And what
happened?

There we were, the Democratic presidential ticket, the great
supporters of labor, walking through empty streets. It was embarrassing. "The canyon that is Fifth Avenue in Manhattan was
disappointingly spare of spectators when the candidates were there
in the morning for a Labor Day parade," the New York Times
dutifully noted on the front page the next day, "but a midday
rally in a small town in Wisconsin was ebullient." Of course the
rally we went on to in Merrill, Wisconsin, was "ebullient." You
don't have to go to graduate school to figure that one out. By
noon, everyone in America was awake and ready for a Labor
Day parade!

I was never sure whether I was being treated the same way a
male candidate would have been. All the early memos from the

Mondale campaign concerning the vice-presidential candidate's projected fund-raising schedule started with the pronoun "he," for example. That was understandable. No one in the Mondale camp had faced the possibility that the nominee might be a woman. What was questionable, however, was that after my nomination, it had taken the campaign staff six weeks—almost half the length of the campaign—to change the pronoun to "she."

Another area in dispute was our plane. From the beginning, we had been told we would get our own campaign plane, outfitted with word processors so that we could work on my speeches in the air, and with a communication system to enable us to remain in close contact with the operation on the ground.

With so much time in the air and so much pressure, any campaign plane becomes your home away from home. Ours was no exception. The press was exhausted. The traveling staff was exhausted. And so was the candidate. In such an atmosphere, little niceties become lifelines, making the pressure more bearable. But instead of being increasingly pampered as the pace of the campaign ground along, we seemed to be less so. The working conditions of Ozark Airlines, the charter company the campaign used the most, were difficult. It wasn't Ozark's fault. The airline personnel were terrific, and Ozark provided good food and good service, but there simply were not the facilities aboard that we needed—and that could be provided only if we had our own plane—such as telephone hookups for our portable-computer terminals. As a result, my speech writers had to work until three or four in the morning after we landed because there were no facilities in the air, and the secretaries were working all night.

The press was as disgruntled as I was. After all, they had to pay first-class fare plus a half. For that they got a seat on the campaign plane, buses to carry them to each event in the motorcade, and their luggage looked after. The cost added up, especially for the television crews, whose companies often paid for an extra seat to hold their equipment. When do we get our own plane? Next week, I was told. And next week. Would a male candidate have gotten his own plane? I wonder. We never did.

Clothes were another area that became a subject of discussion because I was the first female candidate in a national campaign.

Everybody seemed to have an opinion about what I should wear, including some of the press, who would often start off the day by saying: "Don't wear that color. It will blend into the background in pictures. You need a bright color." Wear suits, not dresses, came the constant advice from Barbara Roberts Mason, my senior policy adviser. According to the Business and Professional Women's Association, Barbara kept telling me, suits made any woman look more professional. I didn't think looking professional had anything to do with the suit versus dress controversy.

In at least one city, the laws of probability turned against me. In Pittsburgh, I was asked to autograph a picture from my previous trip to that marvelous city. When I looked down to sign it, there I was, wearing the same skirt and blouse I had on then. The people in Pittsburgh must have thought I had only one outfit.

Flowers, too, made their debut in national politics, though my staff had much more of a problem with them than I did. I love flowers. But there was some feeling in the campaign that my being given flowers, as happened constantly, was a kind of put-down. What nonsense, I told them. In no way was I going to deny my femininity during the campaign, and being given a dozen roses almost daily was one of the little pleasures on the campaign trail. I would take them back to the hotel and stick them in a vase so I could at least enjoy them overnight.

What to do with the flowers immediately after they were handed to me was a problem, however. On the one hand, there was Geraldine Ferraro, a person who loves flowers. On the other hand, there was Geraldine Ferraro, the vice-presidential candidate who was not going to walk around looking like a bridesmaid. So I'd thank the donor very much and instantly hand the flowers to Eleanor to hold. I drew the line, however, at wrist corsages. I didn't want to look like someone going to a prom.

Corsages notwithstanding, the whole issue of my being the first female candidate made other people feel far more awkward than it did me. There had been such a fuss in the campaign and the media about Fritz and me not touching at all, not even raising our joined hands, that it put everybody else off as well. Whenever we landed at an airport there would be fifteen or twenty official greeters, both men and women, lined up in the rain, in the cold, any time of the day or night. Often they were old friends, con-

gressional colleagues, Democratic mayors, senators, or governors. And always, they would hesitate when they first saw me.

"I really wish I could give you a hug," they'd say.

"Go ahead," I'd tell them. "The only one who can't is Fritz
Mondale."

I was also running a thin line being careful not to promote
one group at the expense of another. Wherever I went, in addition to flowers, local people would give me a T-shirt to wear, a
hat, or a sweatshirt. If it was presented as part of the official
program, I would put it on. The audience would usually roar
their approval, as in Boston, when I wore the Celtics T-shirt
Senator Ted Kennedy gave me. But if it was handed to me by
someone in the crowd, I reluctantly had to decline, not wanting
to single out any specific group. It was hard. At one labor rally, a
union member gave me his chapter hat to wear. "Thank you," I
said, and put it on my lap.

"Wear it," he urged me.

"No," I said, not wanting to offend him, but not wanting to
alienate anyone else at the same time.

His was a specific union within the whole group that makes
up labor, many of whom were represented at that rally. How
could I put on his hat and not one from the nurses or teachers or
NOW? The only times I wore hats given to me were during the
pouring rain in Wisconsin and Oregon, when I needed them to
keep the rain off my glasses so that I could see my speech.

My kids were turning out to be amazing campaigners, on the
road almost as much as I was. Donna was still working at Salomon
Brothers in New York and didn't hit the campaign trail herself
until after Labor Day, the last one on but also last off. But John,
Jr., and Laura, who at first had traveled with me, struck out on
their own in August.

The standard line on our local evening news—"It's ten o'clock.
Do you know where your children are?"—took on a new meaning.
I didn't even know what state they were in. I had their schedules
with me and all their phone numbers, thanks to their very capable
scheduler Chris Burch, and would track them down at night,
often not knowing where I was calling. I loved to leave the
message: "Could you ask them to call their mother?" It drove the
kids crazy—and rattled the hotel personnel a bit, too.

Each of them traveled with an escort, but at the very beginning they each went with one of the young Mondales. The Mondale family was fabulous. In fact, the kids all got along so well that they became known to each other as the Mondaros. They wrote their own speeches and did themselves proud. Who would have believed it? John, who had been president of his student council, had been too shy to deliver the graduation address two years earlier and had gotten somebody else to do it. Laura, who had just graduated from high school, had been a nervous wreck when she had to address a school assembly. When I had been invited to address her school after I had been made Platform Chair, and the television cameras were following me everywhere, Laura had asked me beforehand not to call her to the front of the room. The television cameras made her too embarrassed, she told me then. Now she was turning into an old pro.

Laura had delayed her freshman year at Brown in order to campaign and ended up speaking on college campuses at Yale, Vassar, and Northwestern University, and to groups in Oregon, Washington, New Mexico, and Texas, to name a few of the states she visited. At one point I met her in a North Carolina airport with a suitcase of fresh clothes for her from home, which I traded for her suitcase of dirty clothes. On her first trip she traveled with Fritz's younger son, William, to learn the ropes—and in New Mexico was mistaken for his wife.

But she soon became a real trouper. Laura had to be evacuated at three a.m. from a hotel fire in Boston. There she was befriended by a wonderful couple from California whose name and address got lost in the excitement of the campaign, so I never got to thank them. On the other hand, her face was spat on in Ohio, and she was almost reduced to tears in Oregon in front of an audience of four hundred when one girl, referring to my views on abortion, yelled: "Your mother is a murderer." But Laura never gave in. Instead, she became more poised by the moment, once handling a press conference in Connecticut in front of thirty reporters, one hundred spectators, and fifteen microphones with no briefing at all (the person who was to meet her at the airport failed to show, and because they were running behind she went directly to the press conference). Another time, she nonchalantly introduced me to an audience of thirty thousand at the University of Massachusetts.

Not surprisingly, Laura also made a lot of friends on the campaign trail, staying up to talk with Dick Celeste, the governor of Ohio, until one a.m. at his house and swapping campaign stories with other politicians' kids. At one fund-raiser in New York, which I missed because I was getting ready for my debates, she ran into the son of Tom Eagleton, the Missouri senator who, in a blizzard of publicity, had had to withdraw his candidacy as George McGovern's running mate for health reasons. "I truly empathize with what you're going through," he said to her shortly after I had faced the press on our finances. At another fund-raiser Laura and Kara Kennedy, who had worked in her father Ted's 1980 presidential race, agreed that campaigning on college campuses was tough. College students tended to test them.

John, Jr., was just as enthusiastic a campaigner, delaying his junior year at Middlebury College to go to forty states, thirty-six of which he'd never been to before. Here was this shy kid suddenly writing his own speeches, calling our national campaign headquarters in Washington to double-check our stands on issues, speaking to student groups, labor, and senior citizens. He loved it. We've created a monster, I thought, as I watched him work crowds and handle the press. At the Pulaski Dinner in New York, John, Jr., representing Mondale-Ferraro, held his own in the company of Governor Thomas Kean of New Jersey, who was there for Reagan-Bush. One rare day he was home in Queens, he switched on the television set to discover that our grocery shopping that day had been filmed—$101.82 worth of food, including ice cream, roast beef, and turkey. "All right!" he said, and raced to the kitchen to start eating everything he'd just seen we'd bought.

The campaign was hardest, I think, on Donna. During August she was still working on Wall Street, traveling back and forth on the subway. Almost every afternoon the *New York Post* would have another smear story about her father, and she'd have to sit opposite a rowful of people reading the two-inch-tall anti-Zaccaro headlines. "It was horrible," Donna told me. "It was my family people were talking about and reading about right in front of me. They didn't know who I was. I just had to sit there."

Donna kicked off her participation in the campaign at a big rally for Senior Health Action Day in New York, bringing with her her two favorite senior citizens—my mom and John's mom. Delivering her first speech was a little hard, but she was thrilled the next day when the *New York Times* described her as "the luminary" among speakers who included Andrew Stein, Borough President of Manhattan, and Carol Bellamy, our City Council President. Several days later, Fritz topped off Donna's excitement by quoting her in a speech—a great compliment.

Then there were other occasions. Donna had her share of harassment on the road. At a fund-raiser for the National Foundation for Children in Florida, she was asked to give a ten-minute speech for the Democratic ticket. There were both Republicans and Democrats in the audience, and Donna pointed out how Fritz had been a long-time supporter of children's interests and had led the fight for expanded day-care and child-development and nutrition programs. Two people started booing her, which was rude enough, but the rudeness became unconscionable when an employee of Citibank, one of the event's sponsors, turned up the music on the PA system and attempted to drown out the rest of her speech. Donna finished her comments and left with dignity. But later she called me, quite upset.

Life was just as rough off the campaign trail. On September 12, the House Committee on Standards of Official Conduct decided to conduct a preliminary inquiry on the Washington Legal Foundation's reporting of violations in my congressional disclosure statements. I wasn't that worried about the House investigation. I knew it wouldn't look too good to the public, but I also knew that any errors in the forms were technical matters, not ethical or criminal violations. I was concerned that once more the burden would fall on John. He had supplied all his business records for nineteen months for the vice-presidential disclosure. Now the committee was calling for his business records for all six years I had been in Congress. And he had only scant weeks to produce them.

I was chilled, however, by the court's decision on August 30 to remove John as the conservator for Alice Phelan's estate. All my apprehensions about the political implications of John's hearing had proved valid. Before the hearing John had offered to resign from his court-appointed position, but he had been told that it was unnecessary. Now Judge Kassoff had removed him. "Zaccaro Booted" the headline read the next day in the *New York Daily News*. The *New York Times* was at least kinder in its subheading on the newspaper's front page: "No Dishonesty or Malice Is Seen in Borrowing."

I was stunned. And very worried about John's reaction to being so publicly—and unnecessarily—disgraced. Campaigning in Hartford, Connecticut, the day of the decision, I said to the press: "This is not the first time I've disagreed with the decision of a Queens judge." But privately, I felt that once more John was being punished for my candidacy and that if there had been no television cameras at the courthouse, John would have been advised that his actions were not within the accepted bounds of propriety for conservators and would have remained on. The Office of Court Administration in New York State even admitted there were no statewide guidelines for conservators to follow.

John was devastated. I've never seen him so depressed. Even before the judge's ruling, he had been so embarrassed by all the stories about the conservatorship that he hadn't even wanted to go out to dinner on my birthday in August. "Can't we just stay home?" he'd said. "I don't want to be seen." I felt terrible. I could see what all this was doing to him. Everything hitting at once, everything being played out mercilessly in the press.

What could I do? I was sorry, and increasingly worried. Back on the campaign trail in Wisconsin and California in early September with John, Jr., and Laura after John's dismissal from the conservatorship, I had to share my concerns with them. "Your father is very depressed and he needs you," I told them over dinner. "Whenever you're with him, put your arms around him. Tell your father you love him. He's going through a very rough period and he needs all of us right now. We're a family first and we have to stand together."

The kids, too, were devastated by what was happening to their family. They were shocked at the endless innuendo in the newspapers. They had never seen their father criticized before. Never. It wrung my heart. I valued their close relationship with their father so much, because my own relationship with my father had been cut short.

For the next two weeks I called John three or four times a day from San Diego, California; Eugene, Oregon; Kansas City, Missouri; Portland, Maine; Lexington, Kentucky; wherever we were. I could tell by his voice how low he felt. "How's it going, John?" I'd say in a cheerful voice.

But my heart always sank at his listless responses. "I've been trying to get the records for the lawyers," he'd say.

"Things are going to get better," I'd say.

But no. "How is it going to get better? It's just getting worse," he'd respond.

It was murder. Every night the kids would call from wherever they were campaigning and I'd rehearse with them what to say to the press in response to any questions concerning their father. I felt for them, for John, for all of us. I would have done anything for the campaign just to be over, to be out from under so I could be with John. Instead, I gritted my teeth and kept calling, not knowing what I'd find on the other end, and then going out to the cheers of "Gerr-eee! Gerr-eee!" Somehow I did the speeches, cracked the jokes, gave the interviews—then got to the next phone to call John again. By the time I got to Nashville, Tennessee, on October 2, it was really getting to me.

The first sign I saw in the crowd there was "Zaccaro-Ferraro Crime Organization." And something inside me broke. That night in my hotel room I did something I haven't done since I was a little girl. I got down on my knees by the bed and prayed. Dear God, please, please, You have got to help us. Please let us get through this campaign. I am not praying to win. Just let us get through it.

I couldn't quit now, couldn't let Fritz down, couldn't betray the confidence the people of the country had placed in me. No one was ever going to be able to criticize me for not knowing the issues, for not putting the time in, for not trying hard enough. I had said early on that I was going to go to bed the night before the election knowing I had done everything I possibly could to defeat Ronald Reagan. That was my primary goal. My second was to show that where I had control I was going to be the best candidate possible. No one was ever going to be able to say that under pressure, a woman would fall apart. But it was rough. I never let on to anyone how worried I was about John. Instead I was determined to campaign ever the harder, do a better job, show that I wouldn't be broken.

God must have heard my prayers. The next time I called John I heard the change in his voice right away. "How's it going?" I said to him.

"Fine," he said firmly. "I've decided it's time to get on with my life. We've been through a lot and we're going to get through this one, too."

What had happened? Who knows. But from that time on, no matter how hard it got, we would be OK.

Now I could put every bit of energy back into the campaign as we moved on to stops in Atlanta, Georgia; Memphis, Tennessee; and Dayton, Ohio, all in one day. There were signs everywhere I went, mostly positive signs, like "Give 'em hell, Gerry." Displaying political signs at a rally is really a publicity stunt, designed to catch the attention of the television cameras. And it does. The people with the negative signs try to push to the front of the crowd so that their messages will get the best coverage, while the people with the positive signs try to keep the others back. Often the rallies would end up in subtle crowd bashing as the two forces struggled for center stage.

But even though there were always more positive signs than negative ones, my eye would pick up the anti-Ferraro signs. I sure wasn't looking for them, but I saw them. In Ohio, a man was standing right in front of the podium, banging his sign up and down: "Gerry is Bi-Sexual." That went too far. It was libelous. I turned to Dagmar Celeste, a good friend and the wife of Ohio governor Dick Celeste, and said, "Find out who he is."

So she went down into the crowd. "What is your name?" she asked the man.

"I'm not telling you," he told her.

"Why not?" Dagmar said. "If what your sign says is true, you have nothing to worry about."

But running true to form, just like people who write threatening or insulting letters, he, too, hid in anonymity and refused to give her his name.

I never got over my disgust at the people following me everywhere with antisigns. None of them ever had the courage to stand up to tell me who they were. They were—and are—spineless. The hate mail we were getting—"Go back to Italy, dago" and "You are a crook"—was always sent in anonymous envelopes, with no return addresses and no signatures. That said someting about those people. You could spot the envelopes with their misspellings and their spite a mile away. I never opened any mail personally, and I told my staff not even to bother showing these letters to me.

*　　*　　*

It was amazing how much appearances seemed to be important to the campaign and to how we were being perceived by the public. The print media had space to spell out the more substantive messages we were trying to get across. But the twenty seconds to a minute the campaign received on the nightly news was more vulnerable to misrepresentation. Fritz was being perceived as dull and uninspiring, very different from the witty and convincing man I knew him to be. When he spoke extemporaneously, he was terrific. But in reading his remarks, he was much less effective. While Dayle Hardy, my public-speaking coach, was traveling with me, I called Fritz to ask if he would like her to travel with him for a couple of days. But he said no.

If Fritz was being perceived as dull, I, on the other hand, was being seen as feisty and irreverent, especially by television audiences. Instead of running the substantive part of my speeches, the networks were more apt to run my anti-Reagan one-liners. When Reagan took Harry Truman's campaign train out of mothballs to stump on it himself, for example, I marveled: "What better symbol is there of this Administration? There he is on the back of the train without a clue about who is at the controls or what direction he's going in." And my ratings in the polls fell. What the public saw was the one-liner to represent a fifteen-minute speech. And it was hurting me. Reagan was, after all, a very popular President. Who was this pushy woman from Queens to criticize him?

While the polls were sometimes negative, the crowds clearly were not. It was very bewildering reading one thing in the papers while seeing quite another in person. Everywhere I went people reached out and tried to kiss me, to hold on to my hands, to touch me. It made the Secret Service nervous, but I knew how important touching had been in my congressional campaigns. I would have touched everybody's hand in the country if I'd had time. Sometimes people grabbed my hands so hard it hurt. I had to stop wearing rings except for my wedding ring. The Secret Service tried to keep their hands over mine to prevent my being jerked into the crowd, but one day someone wrenched my hand so tightly that it broke the skin. "I warned you that would happen," the Secret Service agent, Paul Hackenberry, said to me reproachfully. And he gave me a Band-Aid.

The only time I was nervous about getting close to the crowds was at night. Often we'd land at our final campaign stop after dark, and the television lights at the airport would totally blind us. If I couldn't see, I knew the Secret Service couldn't see, either. Who was to know who was in the crowd that always gathered at the airports, what might be aimed at me? Sometimes I just waved to the crowd and walked directly into the terminal.

There were very few times I actually worried. I was scheduled one day for a meeting in Atlanta followed by a rally later that afternoon in Memphis with Jesse Jackson. At noon we had done the first rally in Atlanta's Central City Park, with Mayor Andrew Young, State Senator Julian Bond, civil-rights activist Coretta Scott King, as well as twenty thousand of our closest friends—the biggest crowd ever to assemble in that city. It was upbeat, exciting. Then we moved on to Memphis, where I was to speak with Jesse Jackson. Jackson was considered to be high-risk by the Secret Service, and I knew he'd received a lot of threats. Now here we were in the same city where Martin Luther King had been murdered. I had a terrible feeling and was apprehensive. I don't know why.

Ted Kennedy was also very high risk, but when I did a rally with him in Boston, I did not feel threatened. I'd been offered a bulletproof vest by the Secret Service at the beginning of the campaign, which I'd refused. To appease them, I'd accepted a bulletproof raincoat instead, which I'd never worn. I almost wished I had it with me that day in Memphis. Luckily, nothing happened.

In the end, of course, there is nothing the Secret Service can do to protect an individual completely. We have certainly learned that lesson, not only in this country, but in almost every country around the world. But if I had worried about being assassinated, or anguished over the threats my campaign was regularly receiving, then I couldn't have campaigned at all. You just have to put the possibilities out of your mind. I knew full well when I accepted the nomination that my candidacy would be more controversial than others might have been. What I did not anticipate was the violent and sometimes frightening reactions my candidacy would provoke—and from what unexpected directions.

THE CONSERVATIVES, THE ITALIANS, AND THE ARCHBISHOP

"To me, my religion is a very personal and private matter. But when some people try to use religion for their partisan political advantage, then the freedom of us all is at risk, and I feel compelled to respond."

—last-minute insert into a speech on fairness and opportunity, Scranton, Pennsylvania, September 12, 1984.

I NEVER WANTED RELI-gion—anyone's religion, including my own—to be an issue in this campaign. Personal religious convictions have no place in political campaigns or in dictating public policy. I have always felt that the spiritual beliefs of elected representatives are between them and their God, not their government.

The separation of church and state is one of the founding principles of our own Constitution. And a very successful one. We are a religious nation because we do not have a state religion, because the government guarantees freedom of religion but has no role in religion, because not only do we tolerate our religious differences, we celebrate them.

Until 1984. For the first time in over twenty years, religion became a political football in a game that should never have been played. In 1960, President John F. Kennedy, our first and only Catholic President, said: "I do not speak for my Church on public matters—and the Church does not speak for me." I agreed with him entirely. But there was a difference. The fear in Kennedy's time was that his Catholic beliefs would influence his public policy. In my candidacy, the opposite fear was being played out. In 1984, the fears of a very vocal minority were that my Catholic

211

faith would *not* play a part in public policy. The issue should never have existed.

From the first moment of the campaign, I was disgusted with the religious implications the Republicans were using as political ploys. At the Republican Convention in Dallas, evangelical preacher Jerry Falwell, the founder of the Moral Majority, proclaimed Ronald Reagan and George Bush "God's instruments for rebuilding America." In essence, Falwell was claiming that God was a Republican—in fact, that He was the endorsement behind the Republican ticket. That was a bit much, but nobody blinked an eye. And it got worse.

Senator Paul Laxalt, general chairman of Reagan's campaign, sent out campaign literature to forty-five thousand ministers calling Reagan's supporters "leaders under God's authority," as if the Republican campaign were a moral crusade against all who didn't share this particular Administration's religious convictions. Reagan himself went way out of bounds, accusing those who opposed his controversial call for a constitutional amendment permitting school prayer as "intolerant" of religion.

I provided a natural target for these religious extremists who were trying to get God on the ballot. I was a Catholic woman who supported a woman's right to abortion. That was a sin of faith. To other extremists, I was an Italian-American woman who had stepped out of her traditional role as homemaker, wife, and mother to run for high office. That was an ethnic sin. In the South I was stamped as a Northeastern liberal who advocated federal commitment to minorities, civil rights for homosexuals, and equal rights for women. That was a conservative sin. If all these people had had their way, I would not have been on the campaign trail but on my knees in the confessional booth.

Not all of it surprised me. Anyone running for public office, especially those supporting a woman's legal right to abortion, can anticipate opposition. And I was prepared for it. I had been living with antiabortion protestors and hecklers since 1978, at times being physically threatened by them. At a town-hall meeting in my congressional district on Monday night, June 25, 1984, the men in the audience had to stop a demonstrator who was coming toward me at the front of the room. I also expected the members of the far right to come at me politically. I had been fighting their narrow-minded and mean-spirited policies in Congress for years.

But what I wasn't prepared for was the depth of the fury, the bigotry, and the sexism my candidacy would unleash. I didn't expect the antiabortion protests to be so vicious, to be politically orchestrated and funded on the national level. I didn't expect the majority of the Italian-American community in my own home state, who should have been proud of their first member on a national ticket, to abandon me by their silence instead. And I certainly did not anticipate that the Archbishop of New York would step out of his spiritual pulpit into the partisan political ring. I was running not only against Reagan, but, as many tried to insinuate, against my own Church as well.

In the South, members of the ultraconservative far right pulled out all the stops. Spending an enormous amount of money, they ran a heavy media campaign against me on their whole agenda; antiwelfare, anti–gun control, antiabortion, anti–gay rights, anti–day-care, antiwoman.

The conservatives didn't seem to care who spoke for their cause. In Washington, Anne Gorsuch Burford, the Environmental Protection Agency administrator who had herself been forced to resign after charges of mismanagement from Congress—I was one of the members to vote to cite her for contempt—formed a "Ferraro Truth Squad" and vowed to dog my campaign trail to discredit me. And money was no object. The National Conservative Political Action Committee alone pledged twelve million dollars to support Reagan-Bush—and another two million against me.

Publicly the Reagan White House tried to distance itself from the all-out attack the far right was launching. When Burford announced her crusade, Larry Speakes, Reagan's press spokesman, quickly told the press: "The campaign protested and urged her not to do this. It's not the way we want to run the campaign." But of course it was. They just didn't want it to show. When I got the nomination the Republicans were in shock, as was I. They did not know how to go after me. Here I was, the first woman vice-presidential candidate. How to discredit my candidacy without hitting me directly so that the bruises showed?

By looking at my voting record. By getting the far right to go after it in the South, where all the resistance toward my candidacy was naturally going to fly—and all the while disavowing any White House involvement.

Reading my voting record without knowing the background did make me look far more liberal than I actually was. I had voted for the Black Caucus budget, for example, which went way too far in calling for the elimination of many defense programs in favor of programs for minorities. Why did I vote for it? Because I wanted to make a statement about the President's priorities. I had been speaking out for years on the Reagan Administration's damaging and unfair economic policies. My vote on the Black Caucus budget expressed my principles—that funds for nutrition for kids, for education, and for jobs programs were just as important as funds for defense. I submitted a statement in the *Congressional Record,* explaining why I voted as I did. But still, there was my vote, plain to see. In the heat of the conservative attacks, I should have remembered what someone had said to me early in my congressional career: "If you have to explain your vote, you're in trouble."

My support of gay rights was just as inflammatory to the conservatives. And again, my view was a statement of principle. I believe strongly in equal opportunity for everybody. I don't like discrimination against any group. I'd rather that we all compete on an equal level, without anyone being held back. And I wasn't going to back away from my principles just because my stand might be politically offensive and cost me support. In July I had agreed to speak at a meeting of gay activists in my district. After I got the nomination, the reaction was predictable. "Ms. Ferraro could never be accused of being ambiguous about her support of gays," read a full-page ad "proudly" paid for by the Fund for a Conservative Majority in the *Daily News* in August. "Last month, she stated . . . 'A victory for a woman in this election is a victory for lesbians and gay men.' "

A mailing had quickly followed the ad on the letterhead of a conservative group, the Public Affairs Political Action Committee, from the daughter of a neighbor of mine in Queens. This was a young woman for whom I'd gotten a summer job with the National Park Service, even though in my first congressional campaign she had actively worked for my right-wing opponent. She knew me personally, the letter read, knew that I was a "big spender," a supporter of abortion and gay rights. "She is one of us," she quoted a gay activist as saying, implying that I was a lesbian. (Pat Flynn was so appalled that she sent the young woman's mother a copy of the letter.)

I had expected to be hit—and hit hard—by the conservatives. But these blows were coming in well below the belt. And against the vice-presidential nominee. Never have so many people spent so much time and money trying to discredit the second slot on a presidential ticket.

Wherever I went as the vice-presidential candidate, hecklers and single-issue demonstrators were waiting for me. I had sympathy for the antiabortion groups and individuals who constantly challenged my position on choice. That was their conviction—and their right. What I objected to were some of their tactics.

For all that I had been confronted by antiabortion demonstrators since I had been elected to Congress in 1978, I have never gotten over my sensitivity about having my religious faith questioned. I have always accepted the teachings of the Catholic Church. Personally, I have always been against abortion. But my election as a public official who would set policy had forced me to face the issue, to take a stand, one way or the other, on legalized abortion. Could I, in good conscience, make the decision to continue or terminate a pregnancy for somebody else? Coming down on the side of choice, concluding that the decision had to be between a woman and her own conscience, had been very difficult for me.

After all, I was and am a Catholic. I was educated at a convent school, a Catholic college, even a Catholic law school. I take my faith very seriously. I go to mass every week, not because I have to go but because I want to. My husband and I try to live our religion and have brought up our children to do the same. And as a Catholic, I have always accepted the premise that a fertilized ovum is a life, a baby. But others do not always agree. I used to talk about abortion with those of different faiths. Some believed that life began at "quickening," the first time the fetus moved *in utero*. Others believed life began at birth. Why should my Catholic belief override theirs? I felt very strongly that I had been blessed with the gift of faith, but that as an elected official I had no right to impose it on others.

I knew if I were to become pregnant, I would not have an

abortion, because that child would have been conceived in love. But if I were raped and became pregnant, the issue would not be so clear. I had seen too much in 1977 as head of the Special Victim's Bureau in the DA's office. For fourteen months, I had supervised all the prosecutions in Queens County for rape and incest, as well as the child-abuse referrals from family court. And the brutality of those rapes and the humiliation to the women that followed would have been compounded if they had had to bear a child from such violence as well.

While I was weighing my position on abortion, I thought back to the victims I had dealt with in court. I could still hear the voice of a six-year-old girl who had been so brutally raped by a neighbor that she spent two weeks in the hospital for vaginal repair. Later, on the witness stand, she screamed in terror when I asked her to describe to the grand jury what had happened when the rapist took her into the bushes. To comfort her while she continued her testimony, I had to hold her in my arms as she spoke to the jury.

Another victim, a thirteen-year-old girl from an Irish Catholic family, had been dragged up to the roof of her building and raped by a big, heavyset kid. She was totally traumatized. If that young girl had become pregnant, who was I—or the Church—to tell her she had to have that child? I wasn't about to make that decision for her. It should be up to her and her family.

I dealt with many rape victims, from a twenty-one-year-old woman who was almost catatonic from the event and couldn't look at me when we talked about it, to a seventy-eight-year-old woman who, after she was raped, would not leave her apartment because she was too ashamed to be seen on the streets. To a woman, rape is the ultimate violation of self. There is nothing like it, even though people are always comparing it to having a home burglarized. "You don't understand what you're talking about," I would respond to anyone comparing rape to burglary. Yet the church would not allow the exception of abortion for rape.

Twenty-five years ago, even the life of the mother had not been an exception. When John and I were first married, Father Peter Manning, my philosophy teacher at Marymount College and the priest who married us, came to dinner. He had trouble getting into the building because the doorman wasn't there.

"How come your doorman isn't on?" he said when he finally found us.

"His wife is having an abortion, and he's in the hospital with her," I told him.

He was shocked. "What do you mean?" he said.

I explained that his wife had a heart condition and had been told that the strain of a pregnancy would kill her.

"That is no excuse," said Father Manning.

"The woman could die," I replied.

"Abortion is against the church's teaching," Father Manning said.

The conversation ended, and my recognition of the complexity of the issue began.

My position was finally firmed up by the child-abuse cases I had to prosecute. You can force a person to have a child, but you can't make the person love that child. The brutal realities of those kids' lives literally made me sick. I developed a preulcerous condition and had to take medication. I was emotionally drained. There were times when I'd go home and cry and wonder if those kids would have been better off not being born.

One fourteen-month-old boy had had alcohol forced down his throat by his mother's boyfriend, who then beat him to death. Another had survived being burned on his buttocks and feet only to suffocate with his dog a year later in an abandoned refrigerator. I can still see the picture of a four-year-old girl lying on a slab in the morgue with second- and third-degree burns all over her body. The mother's boyfriend claimed the little girl had gotten into a hot bath by herself. Frightened of the truth, the mother had simply put the little girl to bed, where she died two days later with no medical attention. And it went on and on.

I don't know what pain a fetus experiences, but I can well imagine the suffering the four-year-old girl went through being dipped in boiling water until her skin came off and then lying in bed unattended for two days until she died. It is one thing to talk about the rights of the unborn. But the people who object strongly to abortion rarely voice their concerns as strongly for the born. So often in Congress those who would vote against abortion funding for the poor would also be the first to cut back funds for aid to children, nutrition programs, even prenatal programs for poor mothers who want to have healthy children.

Still, my decision to support choice wasn't easy. In 1978, I called Monsignor Bevilacqua (now Bishop Bevilacqua, of Pittsburgh), a canonical lawyer and a civil lawyer as well, who worked in the chancery in New York. "I'm running for Congress and I have a problem," I told him over lunch. "Personally I accept the Church's doctrine that abortion is wrong, but I cannot impose my religious views on others." And I told him why.

But what could he do to help me? "The Church cannot support your position, Gerry," he told me. And I knew that. I knew I would not get the monsignor's blessing, nor that of my Church. But I had to go ahead and make my decision to support freedom of choice because in good conscience I couldn't do anything else.

I thought then, and still do, that my decision was morally right. Who knows better than a woman whether the life she is carrying is truly wanted, whether the child will be loved and protected? A lot of people went on to judge me on that decision during my six years in Congress and especially during the vice-presidential campaign. But I do not accept their judgment. I will be judged by my God when I go to meet Him. And so will all those who disagree with me.

The protestors predictably came with their signs and accusations, claiming I was a "baby killer," a "murderer," even an advocate for experiments on unborn children. It started right away. At a press conference with Fritz in Elmore, Minnesota, the very day after I got the nomination, a sign from an antiabortion protestor in the crowd there—"Ferraro, what kind of Catholic are you?"—led to my first campaign mistake. I resented that sign. The people in my own church parish may have disagreed with some of my political views, but they never questioned my faith. And neither did my parish priest. Yet here in Fritz Mondale's hometown were strangers making a determination of what I was and what I was not without even knowing me.

When a reporter asked me how I would answer that sign, I replied: "Who is anyone to judge whether or not I am a good Catholic? If you take a look at the policies of this Administration when it comes to budget policies and concern and fairness for others, the President walks around calling himself a good Christian. I don't for one minute believe it, because his policies are terribly unfair; they are discriminatory, and they have hurt a lot of people in the country."

What I had wanted to do was to neutralize the question of religion as a campaign issue. If I was going to be challenged as a Catholic supporting choice in abortion, then the present Administration should have to answer for its position on the budget as well. But instead of neutralizing the issue, unwittingly I had inflamed it.

"How'd you think the press conference went?" I said to Maxine Isaacs as I sipped a glass of water afterwards.

"Fine," she said, "except for the Christian comment."

"What was the matter with that? It's true," I persisted. "How Reagan can say he's a good Christian and then walk around with these domestic policies is incredible. At the age of six, I was given the Baltimore catechism to memorize. I can still recite parts of it. 'Who made us?' 'God made us,' it began. But the point of the book was to set out the Judeo-Christian principles we should live by: to care for the sick, feed the hungry, clothe the naked. We were taught to be concerned about someone besides ourselves, to have an obligation toward those less fortunate because we're each made in God's image. And Reagan's doing exactly the opposite."

But Maxine didn't even hear me. She was thinking politics. "The press is really going to do something with that remark," she said, shaking her head. "It's going to be a problem."

Fritz was more comforting. "Don't worry about it. We'll deal with it," he said. I was amazed at their reaction—until the next day.

"Gerry, How Could You?" bannered the headline in the *New York Post,* while newspapers all over the country, such as the *San Jose Mercury News,* headlined: "Ferraro Says Reagan Not a Good Christian.' " As the campaign staff predicted, my remark had backfired. I hadn't *meant* to question Reagan's standing as a Christian but the actions of his Administration. Nevertheless, the furor didn't change my mind.

Still, some of the hecklers who continually tried to interrupt my speeches, to disrupt my rallies, got to me. Usually, their method was just to drown me out altogether. In Texas one group continually booed me while I tried to talk about Reagan's economic policies and the outrageous deficit he was creating. "You're quite right," I finally said to the hecklers. "If my record were as bad as Reagan's, I wouldn't want anybody to hear about it either."

At a rally in Chicago I turned to a particularly vocal group yelling, "What about the unborn?" and said: "OK, ladies, hold it. In addition to teaching me about support for the constitutional right of freedom of speech, my mother also insisted upon teaching me to be polite to other people. I'm sure your mothers did, too."

Of all the campaign issues, abortion was the most deeply emotional to those on both sides. Both sides had a right to be heard. But increasingly during the campaign, the subject was overwhelmed by the vocal protests of the antiabortion demonstrators. They were there not to debate but to disrupt. In Hinsdale, Illinois, two members of the right-to-life group were so abusive the audience couldn't follow a word I was saying. "Do me a favor," I said directly to them. "Let me have my say and I will meet with you as soon as this is over."

The Secret Service had a fit. Here was this huge six-foot-four-inch man, walking toward the podium to meet with me backstage.

"Are you serious about meeting with him?" the Secret Service said.

"Sure," I said. "I said I was going to do it and I'll do it. Bring him back there so he can talk to me, so he can tell me what his problems are."

After my remarks, I followed him backstage. "Where is my guy who was shouting?" I asked. And there he was, all 200-plus pounds of him, waiting for me.

Hastily the Secret Service set up the safest situation they could think of, me sitting in a chair, the protestor sitting on a couch opposite me, with my speech writer Fred Martin sitting between us. It was really very funny, skinny little Fred in his bow tie taking notes furiously to keep himself occupied and this giant next to him. But I had had such confrontations before in my congressional district. I'd invite the extremists into my office, we'd talk one-on-one, and the situation would be defused. It's much better just to listen to them, give them the chance they want to express their point of view, and try to melt the tension that way. And that is precisely what happened in Hinsdale.

"Abortion is murder," my heckler began. "You are condoning the slaughter of millions of unborn human beings."

And I heard him out, every word, listening to his voice

getting less shrill by the moment. "I think it's terrific that you're so involved in the issue, even though I don't share your views," I told him when he was finally finished. "But it's nice we've had a chance to have a discussion."

Then we began to chat. He was a doctor, he told me. Good, I said, because I have a terrible sore throat and a cold. "If I had a tongue depressor with me," he said, "I'd take a look."

The Secret Service agents looked as if they were about to jump out of their skins. They had never handled a situation like this, but there was nothing to handle. My backstage guest was doing a research paper on the abortion issue, he went on to tell me, and I asked him to send me a copy of it when he was finished. (I never got it, by the way.) And that was the end of that. No trouble. No confrontation. No nothing.

"I wonder what the Secret Service expected you to do in there," I asked Fred when it was over.

He looked dazed. "Probably tear off my bow tie and whip him with it if he came at you," he said.

I was also becoming concerned about the increasingly strident voice of Archbishop John O'Connor of New York, now a Cardinal. As a member of the Church hierarchy and the Committee of Pro-Life Activities of the National Conference of Catholic Bishops, he had every right and even the responsibility to speak out on the subject of abortion. But there were other important issues facing the church as well, such as the morality of the nuclear-arms race and world suffering and hunger—the "seamless garment" vision of the world's problems supported by such bishops as Chicago's influential and respected Joseph Cardinal Bernardin.

But during the campaign, Archbishop O'Connor seemed to be a single-issue Bishop. "If the unborn in a mother's womb is unsafe, it becomes ludicrous for the bishops to address the threat of nuclear war or the great problems of the homeless or the suffering of the aged," he had said at an April press conference.

That was not my Church. That was not what I had learned in the beatitudes. The very real suffering of the living was every bit as pressing to me and to many others as the possible suffering of a child not yet born. But the Archbishop was resolute. "No need is more crucial than the protection of the rights of the unborn," he said in an October speech, a speech that one reporter noted contained eighty-seven references to abortion and thirty-two to the unborn.

To Archbishop O'Connor, there was less point to the Church's addressing the "possible" deaths resulting from a nuclear holocaust than the "actual" deaths occurring via abortion right now. "Some, I feel, would be happy to see the abortion issue smothered by the anti-nuclear issue," he stated. "I am personally totally repelled by the possibility of nuclear war; I am even more repelled by the actuality of the war against the unborn." And then in the minds of many he stepped over the line that separates church and state. "I do not see how a Catholic in good conscience can vote for an individual expressing himself or herself as favoring abortion," he said in a televised news conference in June. And the "herself" turned out to be me.

I was a dangerous prochoice spokesperson. I was a Catholic. I was a woman, a mother. It was one thing for Catholic men to speak in the abstract about a woman's right to abortion, as Governor Mario Cuomo would so eloquently in his speech at Notre Dame on September 13. "We know that the price of seeking to force our beliefs on others is that they might someday force theirs on us," he said. It was quite another to have a high-profile Catholic woman support the issue, and so personalize it. Mario Cuomo could talk about abortion. I could actually have one.

That was too much. Getting hold of a letter for Catholics for a Free Choice that I had signed two years previously in Congress, the Archbishop took his case to the press. "I can only say that Geraldine Ferraro has said some things about abortion relevant to Catholic teachings which are not true," he said to a group of reporters on September 8. ". . . As an officially appointed teacher of the Catholic Church, all I can judge is that what has been said is wrong—it's wrong." The gauntlet was down.

The Archbishop, a registered Republican in Pennsylvania who reregistered as an Independent a month before the presidential election in New York, friend of the Reagan White House, whose nephew, according to the *Village Voice,* was employed by the Reagan-Bush reelection campaign, supporter of Reagan's policies in Central America, defender of our role in Vietnam, which he described as "morally and legally correct," had aimed his politically pious sights at me.

So began an unprecedented siege between a partisan archbishop and a vice-presidential candidate, the reverberations of which ran through the Church hierarchy nationally, the political hierarchy in the state of New York, and my ever-present anti-abortion demonstrators.

"Get the Archbishop on the phone," I told my staff in Lexington, Kentucky, where I was campaigning when I heard about his accusations. I didn't know what he was talking about. And I couldn't believe he was coming after me, personally. His singling me out was highly unusual, a contradiction of the longstanding policy of the National Conference of Catholic Bishops, which strongly opposes the targeting of any political candidate by name.

The National Conference of Catholic Bishops has always gone out of its way not to get involved politically at all. In April, I, along with other members of Congress from Queens and Brooklyn had met with the priests and the Bishop from the diocese of Brooklyn to discuss the issues of housing. Bishop Mugavero, the head of the diocese, had invited Bishop Sullivan, the head of Catholic Charities, to join in the discussion. And Bishop Sullivan had been very upset. "Gerry, we've got to do something about housing," he said to me. "You're on the Budget Committee. Can't you do anything?"

"Bishop, I'm going to tell you something," I said. "For four years I have been fighting the Reagan Administration's budget policies. Now you people must put on a little pressure."

But the Bishop was ahead of me. "The Conference has a pastoral letter coming out on housing and other social services," he told me.

"No kidding?" I said. "When?"

"After the election," he replied.

"Why wait till after the election on something so important?" I asked him.

"Because we don't want to be political," he said. And true to the spiritual guidance practiced by most of the Catholic hierarchy, the letter was not issued until the Sunday after the election.

Now Bishop Sullivan's words were ringing in my ears as my staff pressed me to issue a statement answering Archbishop O'Connor's charges. But I couldn't. I honestly didn't know what the Archbishop was talking about. I had never talked about abortion from the Church's point of view. I talked about it from my own, always making it clear that the Church and I did not agree. Yet Archbishop O'Connor was claiming I had misquoted the Church's position. Since I was being asked for a comment by the press, the only solution was to call him up and ask him what he was referring to. My staff couldn't reach him from Kentucky, so we tried again from our next stop that day, in Indianapolis. And though later I told the press our twenty-minute conversation had been cordial, it wasn't.

"This is Geraldine Ferraro," I said. "I have been asked by the press to respond to your statement that I have said the Church is not monolithic in its stand on abortion. I am a little concerned because I don't ever remember making that statement."

"You did make that statement," he charged.

"I don't recall ever having a conversation with you on the subject or using that term in a speech. I'd like to know when and where you think I said it?"

"You said it in a letter sent out for Catholics for a Free Choice," the Archbishop told me.

"I don't recall sending such a letter. Could you tell me the date?"

"Two years ago."

Two years ago? "Who brought it to your attention?"

"Someone gave it to me."

"Who?" I asked.

But he ignored that question.

"I don't remember saying that, but I will check it out," I said. "I do understand the Church's teachings and what they are, and I have always said that the Church and I do not agree on this issue."

Immediately I tracked down the letter the Archbishop was referring to, marveling at the lengths to which the pro-life movement was going to discredit my candidacy. It turned out to be a covering letter I'd signed in 1982 along with two other Catholic members of Congress inviting Catholic members of Congress to a breakfast meeting sponsored by Catholics for a Free Choice. A professor of theology and ethics was coming to speak to us on abortion, along with the Washington correspondent for a Catholic newspaper and a pollster on abortion opinion polling.

"As Catholics we deal each day, both personally and politically, with the wrenching abortion issue, both here in Washington and in our home districts," the letter read. "Some of us have taken strong pro-choice positions. Others are uncertain. But all of us have experienced moral and political doubt and concern. That is what this briefing is all about."

Then came the sentence to which the Archbishop had taken such exception. "It [the briefing] will show us that the Catholic position on abortion is not monolithic and that there can be a range of personal and political responses to the issue."

Did the letter say the Catholic Church's teachings were not monolithic? No. The letter said the Catholic *position* was not monolithic. There are prominent Catholic leaders and theologians who do not agree with the Vatican, along with some nuns, brothers, and priests.

It was these people—and many others who differed with the official Church teaching—who were quickly gathering in my defense now against the Archbishop's attack. More and more signs—"Nuns for Ferraro," "Catholics for Ferraro," "I'm Catholic and I'm Pro-choice"—began to show up at my rallies and speeches, along with increasing numbers of antiabortion signs, such as "Life, Yes—Ferraro, No," "Thou Shalt Not Kill—Abortion Is Murder, Ferraro," and "Mondale-Ferraro for Infant Genocide."

With all the attention being given to the issue, the antiabortion demonstrations started to escalate. The Secret Service was getting increasingly anxious. Four days after Archbishop O'Connor denounced me by name, we were scheduled into the heavily Catholic city of Scranton, Pennsylvania. Four days before my arrival, such local newspapers as the *Scranton Times* and the *Tribune* had published stories with these kinds of headlines: "Pro-Lifers Will Confront Ferraro" and "Anti-Abortion Demonstration Planned During Ferraro Visit."

Scranton had been the scene of a particularly ugly demonstration in 1980 when pro-lifers had mobbed President Carter. My visit was considered even more high risk, fueled by the Archbishop, who had briefly been the Bishop of Scranton before coming to New York, and by the present Bishop, James Timlin, who had scheduled a press conference immediately following my remarks. Five hundred signs and three thousand balloons had been printed with "Mondale-Ferraro Support Abortion," a blimp was to fly over my speech site reading "Unborn Children Are People, Too," banners were to be hung from all of the overpasses between the airport and the city stating "Stop Killing Unborn Children," and a man dressed as a teddy bear, a symbol the right-to-lifers had adopted along with red roses, was due to wander through the crowd carrying a sign: "15,000 Unborn Won't Be Able to Hug This Bear."

When we arrived, twenty-five thousand people were jammed into the block on Wyoming Avenue. John was with me, as was my daughter Donna. (I was tired of the antifamily image the Republicans were foisting off on the Democrats, so I had brought my own family with me.) We'd found out at the last minute about Bishop Timlin's intention to hold a press conference. I quickly wrote an insert about the increasing overlap of church and state into the speech I had been planning to deliver on fairness and opportunity. "I'm going to talk about religion and public policy directly," I told my staff. "This is one place where I am going to deal with this issue once and for all."

We were all very tense as we approached the rally site. Scranton was seen by the campaign as the ultimate showdown between the prolifers and those supporting choice. One of the first signs I saw was "This Is Reagan-O'Connor Country." Driving in from the airport, the Secret Service put my speech writer Fred Martin on the right-hand side of the car, the side I always sat on. The way the barricades were set up, it turned out, the protestors and potential assailants had less access to me on the left. That really made Fred feel terrific.

The local police had done their work well, keeping the thousands of prolife and prochoice demonstrators clearly separated. And the Democratic mayor of Scranton, James Barret McNulty, had already tried to set a more civilized tone to the crowd. "Vice President Bush has admitted he is prochoice, and he is only a heartbeat away from the Presidency," the mayor shouted. "I'm prolife. Geraldine Ferraro is not. But she is our candidate. She has a right to be heard. Let's welcome her."

I wanted the chance to settle the issue of the separation of church and state, to answer the Archbishop in New York, and to defuse whatever the Bishop of Scranton was going to say.

Drawing a deep breath I said firmly to the explosive audience, "I don't want to be misunderstood. Religious leaders and other citizens should speak out forcefully on matters that they feel are important. I respect their point of view. I encourage open debate and I question no person's sincerity. People are doing their duty as citizens and Church officials when they speak out.

"But I also have my duty as a public official. When I take my oath of office, I accept the charge of serving all the people of every faith, not just some of the people of my own faith. I also swear to uphold the Constitution of the United States, which guarantees freedom of religion. These are my public duties. And in carrying them out, I cannot, and I will not, seek to impose my own religious views on others. If ever my conscience or my religious views prevented me from carrying out those duties to the best of my ability, then I would resign my office before I'd betray the public trust."

And the crowd erupted into partisan cheers. For every "Four More Years" from the Republicans, there were equally deafening roars of "Gerry. Gerry. Gerry." The Italians and a lot of the Catholics in Scranton turned out to be just terrific. When I got yelled at from one direction, the others were there saying: You are ours; you are one of us! Despite all the tension, I felt great. It's amazing how a positive audience can carry you, buoy you. After my remarks, I shook hands with as many people in the crowd as I could while the Secret Service stood by anxiously. It was marvelous, even with a lot of people yelling "Reagan, Reagan" right in my face.

Predictably, Bishop Timlin slammed me in his press conference, calling my prochoice position "absurd" and "dangerous." To be acceptable to the Catholic Church, he said, I would have to say that I was "personally against abortion" and would do all I could within the law "to stop the slaughter of innocent human beings." Why was I being singled out in the abortion issue and not George Bush, who supported abortion under certain circumstances? "Because Geraldine Ferraro is a Catholic and is making clear she is a Catholic and Mr. Bush is not," Timlin replied.

Immediately after the press conference, I got a letter from Bishop Timlin in which he asked me to understand that he had nothing against me personally. But later he admitted to the *Village Voice* in New York not only that both he and Archbishop O'Connor had come "dangerously close to telling people how to vote," but that he had no idea what positions the two Republican U.S. senators from his own state of Pennsylvania held on abortion, or even his own governor. Bishop Timlin had lived in Scranton his entire life and had been a priest for thirty-one years, yet he had never bothered to find out the positions of his own national representatives, let alone challenge them. Unbelievable— especially because both senators favored choice.

The crossing of politics and piety was just beginning. In this intense period of the Archbishops versus Ferraro and New York Republicans against Ferraro, I was scheduled to speak on September 14 in New York at the first annual black tie dinner of the Coalition of Italo-American Associations. Who was orchestrating the dinner? Republican Senator Alfonse D'Amato and state Reagan-Bush coordinator Charles Gargano. And who did I end up sharing the dais with? Archbishop O'Connor.

The CIAA had been asking me for a year to attend its meetings, not to speak but just to sit in the audience. I couldn't do that. No elected official has the time to leave Washington to attend a meeting in the middle of the week when the votes are being taken in Congress. And it had not been expected of any of the Italian-American men in Congress. But Judge Louis Fusco, one of the founders of the CIAA, had evidently taken my regrets as disparagement. When I had to turn down his invitation once again during the spring recess to come and listen to Senator D'Amato and Congressman Mario Biaggi speak, he had let his anger at me be very known.

"Why are you badmouthing me?" I asked Judge Fusco over the phone. "Invite me to speak and I'll be there. But don't expect me to be part of an audience for Mario Biaggi and Al D'Amato, any more than I'd expect them to sit in the audience and listen to me."

We set a date for me to speak to the organization in June, when Congress would be out of session, but that turned into a fiasco of its own. By the time my plane finally got into New York at 9:45 p.m., after three hours of sitting on the runway in Washington because of bad weather, the CIAA meeting was over, with their guest speaker a no-show. I called Judge Fusco apologetically. When I was invited to speak to the CIAA again, this time as the vice-presidential candidate, I found myself back in a real bind. I was scheduled to be in upstate New York for a rally in Buffalo and a major speech in nearby Syracuse the next day, and so once again I had to decline the CIAA invitation.

The phone calls to the organization from New York Republicans began. "George Bush is coming to dinner. Is Geraldine Ferraro coming?" The candidate competition intensified. Now the calls coming in from the Republicans suggested that perhaps Ronald Reagan himself would attend.

Eventually the President was out. But Bush, I was told, was still in. Ferraro, unfortunately, was still out. I would be campaigning elsewhere. "See? We told you she wouldn't show up," Senator D'Amato said to one of the organizers. "But George Bush will be there."

Now friends of mine called me up to say that my absence was implying that Bush was more supportive of the Italian-American community than Ferraro was. I was getting annoyed. I had helped form the National Organization of Italian-American Women. Countless times I had been asked by other Italian-American organizations to speak at their fund-raising dinners, go to their fashion shows, address their groups on Italian heritage, Italian education, Italian-American women, white also, speaking out against discrimination and ethnic stereotyping by the media. I was always invited to such functions. And I always went.

As a member of Congress, I had worked with Father Cogo of the American Committee on Italian Immigration and in my district with a group called the Italian Federation. One of my congressional staff worked with both groups to help them process their applications.

I had also fought hard to get Italian-Americans into government positions and onto the judicial bench. One of them, Judge Joseph Golia, who had worked with me in the DA's office and was now a civil-court judge, called me a week before the dinner and said, "You've got to come. D'Amato keeps asking about you."

"Okay, okay," I said. "Tell them I'll be there."

What a setup that dinner proved to be. And I had walked right into it. George Bush, I found out the day before the event, wasn't coming. My Mayor, Ed Koch, was going to be able to stop by only for a minute because he was going to be on MTV, and Governor Mario Cuomo, the Mondale-Ferraro campaign chair for New York State, was returning too late from his speech at Notre Dame to make it down from Albany. In the heat of the abortion furor, I was left on my own with Archbishop O'Connor.

The Archbishop will deliver the invocation, I was told. That was fine with me. That's what Archbishops do. But the ground rules kept changing. Just as I was about to leave to deliver my remarks, a CIAA staffer told me the Archbishop was still in the Chancery across the street from the Waldorf, where the dinner was being held, and was now planning to arrive during my speech and to make his own speech when I was finished.

"What about the invocation?" I asked.

"He didn't give it," I was told.

I was rather surprised. The Archbishop was going to use an old political trick. By arriving during an opponent's speech, the trick goes, the politician stands a good chance of totally disrupting the opponent. Often the orchestrated arrival draws applause from the audience, even brings them to their feet, leaving the speaker looking foolish.

I'd seen enough of that in my first congressional race when my opponent, Al DelliBovi, used to hide until he saw me enter a meeting and then time his disruptive entrance for the middle of my speech to put me off the edge. At the CIAA dinner, I didn't know whether the Archbishop knew this tactic or was simply following the suggestion of his Republican hosts. But I knew I wasn't going to play this game.

"No way," I said to the CIAA staff. "Please ask the Archbishop to come in to the dinner either before I have started speaking or after I have finished—or I won't come down to the dinner at all." My message was delivered. And the Archbishop got it. He agreed to come to the dinner before, not during, my remarks.

But still, the picture being presented by the Republicans was great for them—and bad for me. Whom did it look like I was really running against? The Archbishop of New York, who, in turn, was standing in for George Bush. A vote for Reagan-Bush was a vote for the Archbishop, for the Church.

In my remarks, I tried to appeal to the pride that spread far beyond my candidacy to include all Italian-Americans. "It used to be the only image of Italian women was the one you saw on television leaning out a tenement window yelling, 'Anthony, it's Prince Spaghetti day!' " I said to the subdued audience, who were taking their cue from the dais. In vain I tried to drum up the ethnic pride everyone who was in that ballroom should have felt, but didn't. I tried to call upon the support the Italian-Americans showed me in every other state but New York. "Now, nearly every day, there is an Italian-American woman on television talking about arms control, the federal deficit, and the great issues of our times," I said. But the Republicans had won.

"You did a good job, Chuckie baby," I said to Charles Gargano on the way out, using the name President Reagan had reportedly called him a few days earlier. And on television the next day and on the front pages of all the newspapers were the predictable pictures of me and the Archbishop, seemingly opposing candidates for political office.

So many times during the campaign, and even after, people would ask me if my faith had been shaken by the actions of some of the Church hierarchy. The answer was—and is—no. I managed to dissociate Archbishop O'Connor and the other conservative Bishops from my feelings about my church. One Sunday, in the heat of the Archbishop's attacks, I went to mass in my parish church. At Communion, the priest says, "The Body of Christ," to which the supplicant replies, "Amen." But as I went up to receive that morning, the celebrant added: "Be strong, Gerry. Be strong."

I needed to be. One of the many Columbus Day celebrations I would be invited to in October came from a number of my supporters, including Mayor Wilson Goode, to march in their parade in Philadelphia the day before the one to be held in New York. "There's a big Catholic, Italian-American community here," Mayor Goode urged me. "They are wonderful, they love you, and you'll take this place if you come here. You'll win Philadelphia."

Their enthusiasm was infectious. "I'll do it," I told them, and made backbreaking arrangements to helicopter from a rally in Newark to Philadelphia in time to catch at least some of the parade. The campaign schedulers fought me every step of the way, saying that I had no business making campaign promises and that I needed more time in Newark. But for the thousandth time, I told them I had made a commitment and that I wasn't going to break it.

And I didn't. John Cardinal Krol, the conservative Philadelphia Cardinal who had delivered the invocation the night of Reagan's renomination at the Republican Convention, would break it for me. Two days before the parade, one of the organizers called my congressional colleague in Philadelphia, Tom Foglietta, almost in hysterics. "I can't believe what is happening," she told him in great distress. "Cardinal Krol says that if Geraldine Ferraro comes down he is going to pull out all the Catholic kids from the parade, all the schools that march, all the bands that play."

Why? he asked her.

"Because he's telling everyone that she's a disgrace," she said. "She doesn't represent the Catholic community. She doesn't represent the Italian community."

The poor woman was torn. She didn't know whether she was coming or going with the Cardinal and was afraid of a confrontation with him. So I pulled out. I had no intention of being divisive in a community I cared about. But I was sad that matters had reached that state.

For four months I was the top Italian in the country, and though there were some Italian men who were very proud of my candidacy, a few couldn't stand it. At the nonpartisan Columbus Day parade in New York where I should have been their proudest daughter, they opted for George Bush instead. Where was I positioned to march? In the back with other members of Congress. The march order was set by protocol, the all-male Columbus Club explained lamely to the press. The Vice President would follow Sophia Loren, who was the Grand Marshal, followed by New York State officials, Governor Cuomo and Senators D'Amato and Moynihan. Then came New York City officials Mayor Koch, City Council president Carol Bellamy, and Comptroller Harrison Goldin. A whole band away would be Ferraro.

The Democrats did not stand still for that and moved back to march with me. Fritz decided to march, too, and we all had a terrific time. But you can bet if there had been an Italian male vice-presidential candidate of either political party, the New York Italians would have made a big deal over him. But who was running this nonpartisan Columbus Day parade? Charlie Gargano, Reagan's New York State campaign manager.

More and more Italians in New York were pulling out of my

candidacy. On October 24 a headline in the *New York Post* would read: "Ferraro Linked to Charity with Extensive Mob Ties." I couldn't believe it. The *Post* had picked up on the fact that my name had been listed years before as an "honorary member" on the letterhead of a group called the Angel Guardians for the Elderly, Inc., in New York. It is a group that provides additional income for healthy and still active senior citizens living on Social Security to visit senior citizens who are confined to their homes. It's like a jobs program for seniors to supplement their incomes, and everyone benefits.

In June 1981, Mario Biaggi and I had been asked to present awards at their annual dinner. And both of us had gone. It turned out that the man I presented my award to was alleged by the press to be somehow connected to organized crime. And once again, the slurs would hit the fan.

"For crying out loud, do you know how many times a member of Congress is asked to present awards to people for presumably doing good deeds? How could we run in-depth checks on every one? Most of the time we don't even know who we're giving the awards to until we get to the event," I said to Francis O'Brien, who now had this event to explain. "Tell the press Mario Biaggi is on the same letterhead and attended the dinner as I did."

"I'll have to call him up and find out if we can do that," Francis said.

"Go ahead," I said.

My staff called Mario and reported to me that he had been furious at them for even suggesting that they use his name to take some of the heat off me. Again I was disappointed. I just don't work that way. Had the situation been reversed I would have said: "What's all the fuss about?" I would have minimized it, explaining that this sort of thing happens all the time. Would Mario have been hurt by coming to my defense and saying he, too, had been involved with this group? I don't think so.

But the story was being played up everywhere. Two days later, Aileen Riotto Sirey, president of the National Organization of Italian-American Women, would send telegrams to Cuomo, Biaggi, D'Amato, and seven Italian-American organizations, including the Sons of Italy and the Coalition of Italo-American Associations. "Every Italian-American political leader is vulnera-

ble to the innuendoes related to organized crime," the telegram
read. "We must stop this irresponsible media smear. Will you
join in a nonpartisan press conference to stop the ethnic slander
which at this time is directed at Geraldine Ferraro?" She listed her
phone number on the telegram. And she waited. And she waited.

Out of every leading Italian-American politician and every
major Italian-American organization, only two people would respond, Fred Rotandaro and Bill Armanino. Fred Rotandaro from
the National Italian American Foundation in Washington would
send a mailing to his membership about the anti-Italian campaign, he told Aileen. And he did. Unfortunately the mailing
arrived after the election. It had been sent third class. Bill Armanino
was to organize a press conference of leading Italian-Americans in
Washington before the NIAF dinner in September.

I don't know what happened inside the other organizations,
but members of the CIAA met and decided a press conference
would not be of any benefit before the election, that they wouldn't
be listened to.

Wouldn't be listened to? "Would you keep so quiet if Gerry
were a man?" Aileen asked Richard Grace, secretary-treasurer of
the CIAA. "That has nothing to do with it," he replied.

But that had everything to do with it. Unfortunately, it took
a non-Italian journalist to realize what was going on. " 'If Geraldine Ferraro were a man and we were writing the same stories,
there would be pickets around the building,' " syndicated columnist Richard Reeves wrote, quoting what an editor from the *New
York Times* had told him. " 'For twenty years, whenever we've
used an Italian man's name in the same story with the words
"organized crime," we've been hit by Italian-American organizations. But with Ferraro? Not a peep.' "

"The stoning of Geraldine Ferraro in the public square goes
on and on, and no one steps forward to help or protest—not even
one of her kind. Especially her own kind," Reeves continued.
"The sons of Italy and fathers of the Roman Catholic Church are
silent or are too busy reaching for bigger rocks. Other women
seem awed and intimidated by the charges and innuendo: Heresy!
Mafia! Men are putting women in their place." His conclusion
was even more ominous. "If Geraldine Ferraro is stoned without
defenders, she will be only the first to fall. The stones will always

be there, piled high, ready for the next Italian, the next Catholic, the next woman."

But the stones had already been thrown, even from such respectable newspapers as the *Wall Street Journal*. Joining the media frenzy to find the missing link between the Ferraro-Zaccaro family and organized crime, the *Journal* on September 13 had printed one of the most irresponsible and vicious articles of the campaign. Its "evidence" of our mob connection? The revocation of my father-in-law's pistol license twenty-five years ago. My father-in-law, it turned out, had provided a character reference for the brother of a reputed organized-crime figure, who had applied for a pistol license. I never even knew my father-in-law had a pistol, never knew he'd had a permit to lose. But in the open season declared on my family's Italian-American background, that one incident in 1957, coupled with the charges and innuendo reprinted from other publications, had been enough to warrant a big four-column story in the *Wall Street Journal* titled "Rep. Ferraro and a Painful Legacy."

The *Wall Street Journal* was wrong. It wasn't my legacy that was painful. It was my present. There wasn't even sufficient documentation for the paper to run the piece in the news section of the paper. It was run on the editorial page instead. And other journalists cried foul.

"Short of hard evidence that Ferraro and Zaccaro associated regularly with mobsters—which the press has not come close to finding—was there anything worth printing at all?" Jonathan Alter had written in *Newsweek* magazine on September 24.

The previous day, political columnist Ken Auletta had also taken note of the *Journal*'s insinuations—and of the ongoing silence from the Italian-American community. "Is it because they are for Reagan? Against a woman for VP?" Auletta had written in the *Daily News*. "Where is the voice of the Catholic Church leaders, who denounce Ferraro . . . while the hierarchy permits local priests to accept donations from mobsters and to officiate at their funerals?"

I was out there all alone, unsupported by other Italian-Americans in the barrage of ethnic slurs, unsupported and publicly derided by some of the hierarchy of my Church for my position on legalized abortion. And on the campaign trail, the abortion protestors were getting more and more vocal wherever I went, even menacing. In the Midwest, one sign in the crowd chilled me: "For Gerry's Kids: Rest in Peace," the words read, over a drawing of three tombstones. I was truly frightened. Both of my daughters were with me. After I spoke, the Secret Service rushed us all out of the rally without letting me near the crowds. "Get in the car fast," the Secret Service agents said. "We'll tell you about it later." They shoved Donna and Laura into the car first and then shoved me in. Quickly I realized what a mistake that was.

"Lean back," I said to them, realizing that they, not I, were in the line of fire from the crowd.

We got out of there in a hurry. Three women, I was told later, had been arrested cruising the area in a car with a rifle. And a man in the crowd had been caught carrying a hatchet.

The violence was escalating. And the same signs were popping up at different points all over the country, along with the same hecklers. It was all too organized to be spontaneous. Obviously a national campaign was under way against me, combining ethnic slurs and antiabortion sentiments. Some were organized by the Pro-Life Action League, based in Chicago. But who was doing it in Massachusetts, where a statewide organization gave out my campaign schedule to any prolifer who called? "Gerry Ferraro will be in Boston on Wednesday of next week . . . please keep in touch for more information," the message ran.

Who was funding all these organizations? Who really was organizing them? Jamie Gangel of NBC News traced them back to the Reagan-Bush campaign, something I had suspected all along but couldn't say publicly without sounding paranoid and defensive. After NBC aired its report, however, I could. "If all this stuff is true and they are organizing from the White House, why don't they come out and fight like men?" I said in a press conference in front of my house in Queens on September 22. "We have a lot of issues to discuss."

I could barely conceal my disgust. Recently, I told the press, there had been signs like "Dead Democrats Don't Vote" in Arlington, Texas, as well as the one about my kids with the tombstones. "Those are not people who believe in life," I said.

After the NBC News report and after the press conference at which I acknowledged the fact that I knew there was a national campaign being mounted against me, the Republicans pulled back. The demonstrations toned down, as if someone had simply turned off a faucet. Everyone realized the assault had gone too far, beyond decency.

Finally the backlash began. Letters of support started pouring into the campaign from lay Catholics, nuns, and priests. The nuns were wonderful; I'm still getting letters from them today. And they didn't just write letters. At one rope line holding the crowds back, a nun fought her way through to me to say: "I'm a religious, but keep on fighting. I know you are doing what is right."

NETWORK, a Catholic social-justice lobby in Washington that monitors the votes of legislators, issued a press release citing the biblical criteria Jesus used for judging a true Christian in relation to my voting record in Congress. "For I was hungry and you gave me food, I was thirsty and you gave me drink. I was a stranger and you welcomed me, naked and you clothed me. I was ill and you comforted me, in prison and you came to visit," the press release started, quoting from Matthew 25:35–46. They applied those same criteria to my six-year voting record in Congress: for the food-stamp program, for emergency fuel assistance to low-income families, for support for communities suffering from the recession, for higher salaries for teachers, and for more money for schools, police, and fire protection.

In 1983–84, the press release pointed out, I had supported the first budget resolution, which had put a cap of four percent growth on military spending and restored some money to programs providing emergency health care and nutrition, while also voting for a temporary loan program to help unemployed homeowners make their mortgage payments and for funds for emergency shelters. I had voted with NETWORK on every single issue and had been given an award by them in 1983. "I assure you, as often as you did it for one of these least ones, you did it for me," the press release concluded, again drawing from St. Matthew. It was truly heartwarming. Here was this totally independent group, who had nothing to do with the campaign, putting themselves on the line for me against the negative and single-issue members of the Catholic hierarchy.

Checks, lots of small campaign checks, began arriving unsolicited from other Catholics. They were embarrassed by their church, by the Archbishop, many of the notes accompanying these checks read. They didn't know what else to do but to send me money in support, to apologize however they could for their Church's attacks on me. One retired Catholic laborer from White Plains, New York, sent me a check for a thousand dollars, made up of contributions no larger than twenty-five dollars. He, his family, and friends, he wrote, had felt so upset by what was being done to me that they had gone out on their own to raise whatever money they could for my campaign.

Letters to editors and commentaries, also unsolicited, started showing up in the newspapers, the most moving and heartfelt from Catholic women like myself. "My religion is intensely personal, and I apply my intelligence and sense of integrity to each decision I must make. I do not ask my Church to find answers for me (that's why I pray) as I do not ask my government to make decisions for me (that's why I vote)," wrote Elizabeth Gallo, further identified only as "living in Whitestone," on the op-ed page in *Newsday*. Yet, she continued, "Archbishop O'Connor is threatening me with guilt and eternal condemnation for voting against the beliefs he holds. I have decided, as a good Catholic and a good Christian, that what God tells me in my heart carries more truth than any mortal man's verbal assertions."

The members of Catholics for a Free Choice obviously felt a responsibility for the way the Archbishop had used my letter and ran a full-page ad in the *New York Times* just before the election. About a hundred Catholics supporting my position that the Catholic view on abortion was not monolithic allowed their names to be used in the ad, a group that included Catholic theologians, priests, brothers, and, most important, twenty-four nuns.

The Vatican reacted immediately, though it had no direct control over the lay Catholics, who could sign anything they wanted. The two priests and two brothers immediately backed off, dissociating themselves from the ad, saying they didn't realize what they were signing. But not one of the nuns reversed her position—and not one of their mother houses moved to expel them.

"Do you want to issue a press release thanking the nuns for their support?" my staff asked me.

"No, that would just make it harder for them," I said. "I'll write each one a letter, privately acknowledging my appreciation of her courage." And I did.

For the future, the bigger issue must become the question of what the Church's increasingly conservative and militantly moralistic attitude means for the national political candidates in 1988, 1992, and even 1996. That element of the Church will still be there and will still be very vocal. Will any Catholic woman dare run who does not support the Church's prolife position? Will it be more difficult for any Catholic who does not rate well on the Church's moral checklist to be elected to office? And where does personal morality cross over into public policy?

If every moral command were to be written into law, Ted Kennedy pointed out in a September address, Catholics should seek to make birth control illegal, while Orthodox Jews should try to ban all business on the Sabbath and fundamentalists should fight to forbid the teaching of evolution in public schools. "We cannot let this pluralistic society descend into a collection of competing and embittered groups," Kennedy said. "We cannot be a tolerant country if churches bless some candidates as God's candidates—and brand others as ungodly or immoral."

It was painful for me because this was my Church. The campaign, the Church, and the First Amendment to the Constitution, would have been better served if this controversy had not arisen over my candidacy. I also felt sorry for my ethnic community. Italian-Americans could have attained a new dignity and self-respect if they had come more actively to my defense. We all lost the possibility of constructive dialogue.

Most of these issues had come to a head in the first half of my candidacy. Now I could get back to advancing the other issues of the campaign. I could even debate them. After extraordinary negotiations and petty backing and forthing with the White House, I was on to the next event. And the next event was George Bush.

THE VICE-PRESIDENTIAL DEBATE

*"I almost resent, Vice President Bush, your patronizing attitude
that you have to teach me about foreign policy."*

—*Philadelphia Convention Center,
October 11, 1984.*

NOW THE PRESSURE WAS
really on. It was one thing to take on the Archbishops, the Italians,
and the conservatives. It was quite another to take on the Vice
President of the United States. The Mondale-Ferraro campaign
considered the outcome of the one and only vice-presidential debate on October 11 to be critical to the election.

For the first time since the convention, we were on a roll. In
the previous week Fritz had blitzed Reagan in the first presidential
debate, Reagan appearing old and confused in some of his answers. After the debate the polls had us moving closer—to a
spread of twelve points, from eighteen—and all signs pointed to
our bid for the Presidency turning a corner. The debate would be
a cornerstone of our effort.

There were three considerations. First, there was the Presidency. When Bush and I would stand together on that stage,
most people would be evaluating us to see which one of us could
best assume the Presidency if something happened to our respective running mates. Second, there was the race between the two
vice-presidential candidates for the few people who were going to

vote for the ticket based on the Vice President. And third, there was the uniqueness of my candidacy as a woman. I had to prove for all the women of America that I could stand toe-to-toe with the Vice President of the United States and hold my own. "There's a sense of responsibility that I have to do what I'm doing and not make a mistake," I said to columnist Ellen Goodman the week before the debate. "It's not just for me. It's for every one of us to show that we're as good as . . ."

"As good as men," Ellen finished for me.

The debates would be the perfect forum to present the Democrats' viewpoint on the issues: where we stood on Social Security, what we would do about the deficit, how we would protect the environment without reducing industrial jobs. At the same time, we wanted to draw the contrast between the Democratic and Republican positions: with our call for a mutual verifiable nuclear-arms freeze and by sitting down with the Russians instead of stonewalling them, we would be more likely to keep the world safe; through a negotiated solution in Nicaragua rather than a military confrontation, the conflict in Central America would be settled with no loss of American life; by breathing new life into the Camp David process, we would work to end the senseless killing in the Middle East.

Domestically, fairness would be one of our major themes. Under Mondale-Ferraro, fairness to the poor, the middle class, and minorities would be an achievable goal in our tax and budget proposals and our economic policies. It was blatantly obvious that such fairness had not been a Republican priority or even a concern.

The debate would also allow the American public to see the other side of me, the vice-presidential candidate. The ten-second snippets network television had carried since the beginning of the campaign inevitably showed me tossing off a funny line or bashing Reagan. The "feisty" Ferraro was certainly a part of me. But what the networks left on the cutting-room floor was the rest of my remarks, which were serious.

"Here's your opponent," Scott Miller, my media adviser from D. H. Sawyer Associates, would say to me while we were preparing for the debate. And he ran a two-minute tape of various TV news clips of me being smart-alecky and—feisty. I needed to round out that image during the debate, we all agreed, to show the public the part of me that was a lawyer, a concerned and caring citizen, an experienced elected official, and now a vice-presidential candidate.

The Reagan-Bush campaign wasn't making it easy. We had been after the Republicans from the beginning to schedule as many debates as possible, only to be constantly stonewalled. Their reluctance to go one-on-one with us in public was understandable. An incumbent is always at a disadvantage in an election debate, especially these incumbents. Reagan and Bush had to defend their record of the last four years while we could offer a vision for the future. Allowing a challenger to appear with the President (or the Vice President) is also risky because it elevates the opponent to equal status in the eyes of the public. And there is always the danger that the incumbent will be shown up by his opponent, as Nixon certainly had been by Kennedy in 1960 and as Reagan in his ramblings had just been by Fritz.

But even more damaging for the incumbents would be the avoidance of any debate at all, which would imply a fear on the part of the party in power that their candidates wouldn't measure up. That being the case, the debate pursuit boiled down to logistics. Whatever was decided between the tops of the tickets would dictate the format for the vice-presidential debate. And the bickering began.

Our campaign had called for six presidential debates and three between the vice-presidential candidates. That's how confident we were. But our opponents weren't. Out of the question, the Republican negotiators countered. They wanted only one presidential debate. We wanted the debates to be long, two hours. The Republicans wanted them short, only one hour. We wanted the debates to address as many issues as possible, knowing that Fritz was brilliant at retaining and articulating the most complicated details of any issue. The Republicans wanted each debate to address only a single issue.

The number of debates was finally a compromise—two presidential debates and one between Bush and me. The length of the debates was also a compromise—ninety minutes each. The two presidential debates would be divided between foreign and domestic issues, while our single debate would include both.

Now the negotiations got down to the nitty gritty. The

Republicans wanted the podiums to face each other, knowing that the television cameras would be at right angles to them behind the interviewers. The natural instinct would be for the principals to speak directly over the podiums, leaving them in profile for the television cameras—except for Reagan. A master performer and actor, he alone would turn and play to the camera, upstaging his opponent. Nix from the Democrats.

What about a roundtable format, the Democrats countered, the candidates talking informally with the press. No way, the Republicans said. They wanted their candidate to look ultimately presidential, standing tall over his podium. Then what about a real debate, a one-on-one format with the candidates speaking directly to each other? No again, the Republicans said. They wanted the buffer of the press to handle the questions and the follow-ups in a tightly controlled situation.

Finally, the ground rules were established. The press were to ask us both the same questions, followed by two and a half minutes for the answers, one minute for the follow-ups, and one minute for each opponent to rebut the other. A system of blinking lights would signal when our time was running out on each phase, so that we would be able to pace ourselves. A later agreement with the press was made whereby my opponent would be addressed as "Vice President Bush," which, of course, was proper, and I would be addressed as "Congresswoman Ferraro," which was also correct.

Nothing was overlooked by the two campaigns, down to the tiniest detail. My height compared to Bush's was going to be a disadvantage for me. He's over six feet. I'm five feet four inches. The Democrats didn't want him to be looking down at me or, more important, me looking up at him. Over Republican objections, we had a gently inclining ramp built out of the same material as the floor covering so that as I took my place behind the podium I would be closer to the same height as Bush without having to step up on anything.

While the two campaigns haggled over the details, I tackled the substance. The debate would be a pivotal point in my career—and in the campaign. Here was Bush with his resume, the sitting Vice President, former chief of the U.S. liaison office in Beijing, China, ambassador to the UN as well, former director of the

CIA, and two-term member of Congress. And here was I, a three-term congresswoman from Queens meeting head-on with this paragon of foreign policy—on paper anyway. I was secure on the domestic issues, but foreign affairs, as ever, would be seen as my Achilles heel. We knew Bush would throw around his international credentials as much as he could to highlight my lesser experience. To counter him, I had to become as knowledgeable about the details of foreign policy as he was.

The crunch was on. Robert Barnett, a Washington lawyer who had helped prepare Fritz for his vice-presidential debate against Bob Dole in 1976, was brought on as the coordinator of my debate. My own campaign staff was too busy to take on this project as well, so a whole separate debate staff was assembled. On domestic issues there were Ben W. Heineman, Jr., a Washington lawyer and former assistant secretary for policy and planning at HEW in the Carter-Mondale Administration; Robert Liberatore, staff director of the Senate Policy Committee; Kay Casstevens, on leave of absence from the staff of Congressman John Seiberling of Ohio; and Richard Goodstein, a Washington lawyer. Barry Carter headed up a foreign policy team consisting of Anne Karalekas, on leave from McKinsey and Company; Marcia McGraw Olive, former deputy director of the Arms Control Association; and Richard Betts, on leave from the Brookings Institution.

Together, they and a lot of my colleagues and staff on the Hill, working in their spare time at night, recorded absolutely everything they could dig up about George Bush, from statements he had made during his primary race against Reagan in 1980 for the presidential nomination to those of his tenure in the present Administration.

Everything was used in the research, every existing piece of material, including the Republican party platform itself. Two weeks before the debate Bob Barnett delivered the eight-pound briefing book to me, a three-ring binder that included the material on Bush, an analysis of my voting record and my major speeches, the questions and answers on my finances, which had been developed for my earlier press conference, our campaign's position on foreign policy and domestic issues, the Reagan-Bush position, my own position, just about anything you could think of—and more.

I lugged this incredible tome around with me wherever I

went for the two weeks before the debate, studying it at night in whatever hotel I ended up in on the campaign trail, between stops and on the plane, everywhere. And what a document it was.

There was a section called "General Issues," which included discussion of my qualifications to be President, the nature of the Presidency, the choice in this election, and politics and religion. My suggested "rebuttal" to the question of my qualifications for the presidency began: "My experience is practical and well-suited for making decisions that the next President will face. For all Vice President Bush's qualifications on his resume, it is hard to see where his experiences have availed this Administration anything in the conduct of foreign policy. The fact is that this Administration has not one single foreign policy success to its credit."

And there was a section called simply "George Bush Materials." His career ladder was documented from the two Texas Senate races he had lost, in 1964 to Yarborough and in 1970 to Bentsen, to his criticized appointment to the United Nations in 1971 because of his lack of foreign policy experience! Under "Deplorable House Votes" during Bush's two terms in Congress was one shocker against an open-housing provision banning racial discrimination and another for legislation requiring colleges to withhold financial aid from students who participated in political demonstrations.

The compilation of Bush's statements under a section titled "Inconsistencies and Errors" was equally astonishing. In his 1980 primary race against Reagan for the presidential nomination, Bush had called Reagan's economic plan "voodoo economics." Two years later he had flatly denied saying it at all until NBC played back the tape of his remarks to him. He had done the same thing on abortion, having said in 1980 that he favored federal funding for abortion in cases of rape, incest, or danger to the life of the mother, only to deny it in 1984. "There are an awful lot of things I don't remember," he had said, probably thinking that excused his convenient lapse of political memory.

Bush was phenomenal at avoiding any controversial issue in order to gain votes. In 1980 he had actually said to reporters: "I'll be glad to reply to or dodge your questions, depending on what I think will help our election most." He was no more forthcoming in 1984. When pressed on his stand on abortion, Bush had claimed his "right as an American to remain silent." Maybe I was too forthright about where I stood on virtually everything. But Bush seemed evasive in his nonanswers to the public.

And he had made devastating mistakes, especially in his supposed area of expertise, foreign affairs. As Vice President in 1981, he had toasted Ferdinand Marcos, the president of the Philippines, by saying: "We love your adherence to democratic principles and to the democratic processes." This despite numerous human-rights violations in that country. And it got worse. As Vice President in 1981, he had said that the Salvadoran "government was elected by the people," when a military junta had seized control of the country in a 1979 coup.

You couldn't help but fear the confrontational attitude embodied in his remarks—and his actions. In a nuclear war, he had claimed in 1980, "you can have a winner." Twice in the Senate, Bush, as Vice President, had cast the tiebreaking vote to allow U.S. production of nerve gas. And although he had voted for the Gun Control Act in 1968, now he was participating in the GOP's campaign to repeal it. Were there differences between his policies and mine? You bet there were.

On Friday, October 5, after four full days of campaigning in Ohio, North Carolina, Illinois, Tennessee, Georgia, and Pennsylvania, I started in on preparing for the vice-presidential debate in earnest. It was only six days away and I still had three more campaign swings to make, as well as commitments to march in the Columbus Day parade with Fritz and to speak at a fund-raiser in Maryland.

It was too much, and I put my foot down. "I'm not going to Maryland," I told the scheduler. "I'm going home to prepare for the debate." But Nate Landow, a key Mondale fund-raiser in Maryland, will be very upset, the schedulers argued. "I think Nate is terrific, and I will explain. He's a good friend who wants us to win." We rescheduled the fund-raiser for later that month.

Suite 4901 at the Sheraton Centre in New York became a battle zone for the next three days. We never left it during the day, ordering in lunch and endless cups of coffee. One "expert" after another came in to grill me on the issues, time and tape my responses, and critique my substance and style. On that first Friday morning we started off by watching the tapes Scott Miller had put together of me and those of Bush debating the other Republican candidates in the 1980 primaries.

But Bush's clips were not very helpful. They were very short and only showed him answering questions. We all knew that the Bush of 1980 was not the Bush of 1984. He had four years of national experience under his belt by now and would be thoroughly prepared for our upcoming debate by the top people around. So I didn't pay much attention to the old Bush.

Watching those tapes was the easy part. The inquisition was about to begin. On Friday afternoon we taped our first question-and-answer session, with Bob Barnett acting as the moderator while Ben Heineman questioned me on domestic matters and Madeleine Albright, from my own campaign staff, questioned me on foreign affairs. It was not my finest hour. Once more I had to playact, to rehearse spontaneity, something I've never done well. When I'd had a similar session with political consultant David Sawyer in the spring to help with Platform Committee activities, he had taped the same sort of mock interview. His subsequent critique was not reassuring. I had hurried through my answers and showed little patience toward my questioners.

At the beginning of the preparation for the vice-presidential debate, I felt just as impatient. It seemed like such a waste of my time, and everybody else's as well. I felt embarrassed sitting there, surrounded by three people the first afternoon and many more in subsequent sessions, giving thoughtful answers in such an artificial circumstance. All the candidates were doing it, of course. Mondale. Reagan. Bush. But that's what has always made these debates so phony. You get to say so little, and what you do say is so well rehearsed that I'm not sure the public has any more idea of what the candidates really stand for than it did before the debate. And besides, that's not what a real debate is all about. A real debate involves a direct exchange between the opponents, a point-counterpoint. But the formats for these political debates have dictated that the results are contrived—more like theater than an intellectual contest.

Superficial as the debate might be, however, I soon began to see the value of all this preparation. Looking at the tapes of our first session, I could see the expression on my face was a dead giveaway to what I was feeling. When I was asked what I perceived to be a hostile question, my mouth curved down and I glared at the questioner. That was obviously not a good image to project. I also started to take notes from the beginning, to jot down key points to refer to in my answers. Trial lawyers do that in court while listening to testimony and the arguments of the opposing lawyers, in order to store up points to make in cross-examination or in the summation to the jury.

My taking notes didn't look so hot on these tapes. Don't look down, look at the camera, everyone started saying to me. But I had been a trial lawyer far longer than I'd been the vice-presidential candidate, and I kept reverting to my old habits.

The pace didn't let up for a minute. On Saturday, Madeleine Albright and Fred Martin came out to my house in Queens for four hours to run through more questions and answers on foreign policy. It was crazy. All the kids were home, the dog never stopped barking, and John was in and out all day trying to make order out of the confusion. In the midst of this chaos, we sat in the den while Madeleine and Fred grilled me and then refined my answers. Fred was being particularly brilliant that day. "Why don't we just put you in drag, and you can debate George Bush," I said to him.

Sunday was no easier. I had two parades to do, the Columbus Day parade in Newark, followed by a speech at the North Ward Cultural Center, and then the Pulaski Day parade in New York. I had nothing but words whirling in my head about our policies in South Africa and our trade imbalance with Japan as I marched along the streets of the Northeast. And then it was back to the den. The topic now was domestic policy, the inquisitors Ben Heineman and Steve Engelberg. And another four hours of battering went by.

I felt as if I were on a relentless time clock, ticking its way toward Thursday. All this preparation was essential, but at the same time it magnified the significance of the debate. I'm not one for butterflies in the stomach, but I will not deny that I felt a lot of pressure. On Monday morning I had to march again, this time with Fritz in New York's Columbus Day parade, and then go on to a big rally with him. Fritz was in a great mood after his debate, and I could feel the spirit of optimism in the gigantic crowd at the rally. Now it would be up to me to keep the momentum rolling.

On the way to the parade, one of my Secret Service agents had asked me a favor. "My girlfriend is in the hospital for a cancer operation Wednesday and she's a total wreck about it," he said with obvious anxiety. "I hate to ask you, but could you call her up and wish her luck?"

Sure I could, I told him, taking down her name and number. Cancer. Now that really was a crisis. The debate was just one night out of my life, my healthy life. "How you doing?" I said to her on the phone that afternoon back at the Sheraton Centre for more rehearsing. "Your friend is very worried about you."

"I'm worried, too," she said. "But I think I'll be all right."

"Listen," I said. "I'll make a deal with you. I'll say a prayer for you tomorrow if you'll say a prayer for me on Thursday night."

"You've got a deal," she said.

The pressure was getting to everyone, including Barbara Bush. Her husband had just taken a beating in the press from the White House itself. After a private political-strategy session with Reagan at his ranch in California the week before, Bush had come down the mountain to announce at a press conference that his President had decided tax increases were still an "option," while at the top of the mountain Reagan was announcing he had "ruled out any plans for a tax increase" in 1985. According to one of Reagan's strategists, the *Washington Post* reported, Bush's contradiction at the press conference had been a "disaster," Reagan's confidence in his running mate had been shaken, and the presidential staff was uneasy about Bush's upcoming performance in our debate. Then Mrs. Bush came perilously close to the edge.

On *Air Force Two* en route from Washington to New York to march along with everybody else in the Columbus Day parade, Barbara Bush let her tongue get away from her. She and her husband had no intention of hiding the fact that they were wealthy and enjoying it, she said to two news-agency reporters, "not like that four-million-dollar—I can't say it, but it rhymes with 'rich.' "

I was dumbfounded. The issue of rudeness aside, it was an astonishing thing to say to the press. And, of course, they jumped on it.

Barbara Bush realized what a gaffe she had made, and after the parade she called me at the Sheraton Centre. "I just want to

apologize to you for what I said," she told me over the phone
while I was in the middle of another debate rehearsal. "I certainly
didn't mean anything by it."

"Don't worry about it," I said to her. "We all say things at
times we don't mean. It's all right."

"Oh," she said breathlessly. "You're such a lady."

All I could think of when I hung up was: Thank God for my
convent-school training.

By now there was a podium set up in Suite 4901, the video-
tape was whirring, and more and more people crowded into the
room. Some were there for the substance of my answers—Ben
Heineman, Steve Engelberg, Madeleine Albright, Bob Barnett,
Fred Martin, Anne Wexler, Francis O'Brien, John Sasso, and Barry
Carter. Others were there for the style of my presentation—David
Sawyer and Scott Miller as my political consultants and Dayle
Hardy, my public-speaking coach. After every four questions
we'd stop, watch the tape, and critique it.

"You must stand at the podium with your hands squarely on
it," Dayle told me. "Take the pencil out of your hand."

But instinctively I kept going back to the pencil, taking notes.

"We don't want to keep seeing the top of your head," everybody said. "Look up. Look up."

For a moment I relaxed.

"Stand straight," quickly came the comment.

"Remember what I told you," Dayle said. "Don't lean on
one foot. Don't turn your shoulder in."

And always, always, there was the caution not to speak too
fast, to carefully enunciate everything I said. "Don't garble your
words," they kept saying. "Speak s-l-o-w-l-y."

To drive the point home, Scott Miller gave me a role model
to study: actor Jimmy Stewart. The correlation between Hollywood and politics was getting a bit much, but I dutifully took
home his video cassette of *Mr. Smith Goes to Washington* to watch
how relaxed and laid back Jimmy Stewart appeared delivering his
speeches to a celluloid Congress. Scott was right. Jimmy Stewart
was relaxed and easygoing to a fault. I fell asleep in front of the
VCR and never got to see how it all came out.

I had been hearing about my too-fast Queens talk forever.
But it wasn't until I started reading my remarks in the press

during the campaign that it really struck home. Every story, it seemed, opened with my saying "Lemme tell ya" instead of "Let me tell you." Many New Yorkers slur their words. Still, I tried to correct it. In subsequent speeches I'd start off with "Lemme" and then catch myself and say "L-e-t m-e t-e-l-l y-o-u" in an affected way. The problem has always been that I think faster than I talk, and my mouth is trying to catch up to my mind. For the debate, I tried to get them in sync.

On Tuesday we moved into a rented television studio on East 47th Street for two days of formal rehearsals. Everything in the studio at Modern Telecommunications was a re-creation of what there would be in Philadelphia for the actual debate: the height of the podiums and the distance between them, the position of the television cameras, the lighting, the moderator's desk, the reporters' desks, and the panel of red, green, and orange lights to time the answers, follow-ups, and rebuttals.

Bob Barnett, who was playing Bush now, really started getting into it. He had studied Bush's habits and his speeches and clips so much that he was actually a much more impressive Bush and much harder on me than Bush himself would be. Bob had even drafted what Bush's responses would be to the questions. Now he read them during the rehearsals.

It got to me that he could read the answers while I wasn't even supposed to hold a pencil. "You cheat," I accused him. "No wonder you're able to do so well."

No one knew what tactic Bush was going to adopt in the debate. So Bob had laid out three possibilities: attacking Mondale, attacking me, and not attacking anybody. He played all three attitudes, driving me particularly crazy in his attack mode.

"You lied. You lied. That wasn't true," I muttered under my breath more than once while he breezed through preposterous answers to the questions. This was serious stuff, of course, but we had to have some fun.

An age-old debate strategy is to rattle the opponent, to do something unexpected to set him or her off stride. Fritz had been very successful doing that in his first debate when he had suddenly turned and talked to Reagan directly, obviously startling the President. What could I do?

"Say 'Good luck, Poppy,' to him at the beginning of the

debate," suggested Bob, knowing it was Bush's hated nickname. "He'll get furious."

But I went one better. "What I'm going to do is go up on the stage, shake his hand, grab him, and give him a kiss straight on the lips," I deadpanned.

The debate team bit. "You can't do that," they said in horror.

"Now, do you really think I would?" I chided them.

Bob was also having a lot of fun immersing himself in the world of George Bush, Phillips Academy at Andover, class of '48 from Yale. He took to wearing a striped cloth multicolored watchband from Brooks Brothers, like one of the bands that Bush evidently chooses every day from his large collection. To get me in the mood, Bob gave me one to wear as well. I couldn't wear the watchband without the proper outfit, could I? So one day I pulled an old Madras suit out of the closet and wore it on the set. "Now who's preppy?" I challenged Bob.

I was especially delighted when someone stumped him by asking if he knew the difference between a tax increase and a revenue-enhancement measure. "No," Bob said shortly. "Next question."

At times I, too, drew a total blank on certain answers and more than once stopped my responses midway. "That's not the way to answer that question," I'd say. "Let's start again."

During the two days in the studio, we ran through four full ninety-minute mock debates, divided into foreign and domestic sections as they would be on the night of the debate. Bob, as ever, was Bush, I was Ferraro, and others from the debate team played the moderator and the four questioners. These people were David Aaron, Mondale's chief foreign policy adviser and former deputy assistant for national security affairs in the Carter-Mondale Administration; Gail Harrison, Fritz's former chief domestic policy adviser and now a partner with Anne Wexler in their Washington government relation and public affairs firm; Rob Liberatore; Ben Heineman and John Holum, former assistant secretary of state and a Washington lawyer. Each debate was taped, played back, and discussed for substance with one group and for style with another.

My answers got clearer and more detailed. People remember only those points made in the first two sentences, I had been told.

By Wednesday morning everyone agreed that my replies were sharp and focused, with the key points in the first two sentences.

The questions and the follow-ups in the rehearsals were tough, but I was doing OK. After sitting through two full quizzing sessions on foreign policy, David Aaron said I had made no errors. But still, the pressure mounted as we finished rehearsing on Wednesday afternoon. When Bob Barnett made some accusation about the Democrats wanting to keep God out of the schools, I said, "Well, Vice President Bush, I think you know silent prayer has always been permissible. Indeed, I wouldn't doubt that there's some silent prayer going on on this stage tonight."

Even the studio technicians cheered and whooped at that answer. They were wonderful. After it was all over I had pictures taken with them and signed autographs. I wished they had been able to come with us to Philadelphia.

I was all set. The only matter to be settled, again, was what I was going to wear. Everyone, it seemed, had an opinion. And everyone wanted me to wear something I didn't like. The backdrop on the set, both in New York and in Philadelphia, was blue. My daughter Donna, who has better taste in clothes than anybody I know, had bought two light wool suits for me to choose from, one blue, the other a beige and gray tweed.

But no. "You'll wash out against the backdrop," Anne Wexler warned me, along with Mandy Grunwald, a Sawyer associate, and Eleanor Lewis. "You need to wear something bright to stand out."

"No, I don't," I said. "Just being a woman on that stage in Philadelphia will make me stand out."

But the clothes argument raged on. "You'll perspire under the television lights in those suits," they said.

"I will not," I claimed. "The place has got to be air-conditioned."

They went back to the "washed out" theory, but I wouldn't budge. The suits Donna had selected for the debate were both perfect, making me look businesslike and vice-presidential. And besides, this was a way a mother could say thank you to her daughter.

But my staff was relentless. At one point Eleanor went out to my house in Queens to bring back several different outfits for me to test against the blue backdrop. The clothes debate had been really annoying throughout the campaign. There are certain things

I don't let people dictate to me, and what I wear, how I cut my hair, and whether or not to wear my glasses (they also tried to get me into contact lenses) are just a few of them. When Madeleine Albright told me her view on foreign affairs, I paid attention because she was an expert in that area. But I knew when I felt comfortable in my clothes and what looked right on me. My gut feeling was as good as anybody's. And I was going to wear one of those wool suits.

I didn't try to memorize all the answers we had gone over and refined and gone over again. We didn't know, after all, what questions I would actually be asked. Instead, we had tried to anticipate every possible subject that could come up, gone through a whole array of questions tailored to each, and nailed down as many responses as possible. There was only one line everyone agreed I should use on the subject of national security when Bush would offer the inevitable insinuation that as a man and a former Navy pilot he was better equipped to defend the country than I was. "You don't have to have fought in a war to love peace," I would say back to him. A good line, to be sure. But an irritating subject.

Women were simply not supposed to know as much about foreign policy or be as strong on defense as were men. Somehow, working out the intricacies of trade policies with Japan or the deployment of Marines in Lebanon was seen as built into the male chromosomes and alien to women. We were better suited to working out domestic policies affecting women and children and minorities; when the going got tough, the men, especially those who had served in the armed forces, would handle it.

What a dangerous stereotype. All veterans are not necessarily experts on war. Tactics have changed. Technology has changed. It certainly does not require any strength to launch a nuclear attack. It would probably take more "strength" not to. Yet men are seen as the keepers of the peace—and the custodians of our nuclear arsenal. Apart from everything else, no one seemed to remember that Reagan was not a combat veteran, and had no foreign policy experience when he first ran.

Nowhere was the double standard more apparent than over this issue. On the one hand, the perception was that men could speak with more authority than women on foreign affairs. Yet these same men also felt entitled to speak out just as forcefully on abortion. Though they may have been involved in military combat, they had never been pregnant. But their views on abortion were respected and taken seriously, whereas women's attitudes toward national security were not.

The bias was even played out in my own campaign staff against Madeleine Albright, my foreign policy adviser—a Columbia University Ph.D., National Security Council staff member, and a professor of international relations. One of the questions during my debate preparation was: "Can you push the button to launch a nuclear attack?" Madeleine, who had anticipated that the question would come up, had drafted an answer, but when it was asked, David Aaron interceded. He sounded authoritative. It seemed he was more believable than Madeleine, simply because he was a man.

Maddening as this bias was, it was there. And it raised the ante in my debate with Bush even higher. The Republicans had made "patriotism" one of the most emotional issues of their campaign. Patriotism to the Republicans was America "standing tall," invading the tiny island of Grenada, escalating the tension with the Soviet Union by bluster and bravado, proposing to spend billions on arming space with nuclear missiles, supporting a covert war run by the CIA in Nicaragua. That was not my definition of patriotism, and I intended to say so.

Thursday morning I woke up with a sense of relief. There were no more rehearsals scheduled except for the hour we would spend on the actual set in Philadelphia in the afternoon. Brady Williamson had done the advance for Fritz's first debate, and he would be with me there. I could relax, get my head together, and practice my closing remarks. Both Bush and I had five minutes to wrap up the debate, to present our separate cases to the public. I had gone over my closing again and again, memorizing it, changing it, getting it exactly the way I wanted.

The television audience was estimated to be eighty million. This was my chance to let each one of them know me, see our vision of the future of America, and understand why I sincerely felt Fritz Mondale would be a fairer, more just President than Ronald Reagan. I had decided that patriotism, my definition of real patriotism, would be an important part of my remarks. And

I practiced my closing off and on all day, delivering it to my husband and children at home that morning, three or four times to different people on the plane going down to Philadelphia, and again on the predebate stage at the convention center.

To finally satisfy everyone on the wardrobe debate, I tried on both suit jackets Donna had bought me against the blue back-drop in Philadelphia. They both looked terrific, and I chose the beige and gray tweed. We checked the lights and tested the sound levels from the microphones. John sat in the moderator's seat, while John, Jr., Donna, and Laura took over the reporters' spots.

"Tell me, Congresswoman Ferraro, is it true you favor one of your children over the other?" Laura asked me.

"No," I replied solemnly. "I dislike them all equally."

Laura pressed on. "I have heard, Congresswoman, that after you and Mr. Mondale win the election, you are going to buy presents for all your children," she said.

"Absolutely true," I replied. "I am going to take them all out for Chicken McNuggets."

Back at the hotel, we tried to relax. There was a note waiting for me from Ted Kennedy in Texas wishing me luck. A private phone line had been installed in the room to handle all the calls to and from national headquarters in Washington. Kennedy had asked for the number as had Fritz so that they could call me when the debate was over. An early dinner was sent up to the room, but I wasn't hungry. Several months later Laura commented that she knew I was feeling a bit uptight when she saw me attack the junk food instead.

My staff was trying to protect me, to reduce the number of questions directed at me, even from my family. But of course that didn't work. And why should it? Being ourselves was more relaxing than anything else at this moment.

"Which dress should I wear?" Donna asked, holding up the two she'd brought with her.

"The dark blue one," I suggested.

Laura wandered in. "Should I wear white or beige tights?" she asked.

"Beige," I told her. Finally it was time for me to take a bath and to deliver my closing remarks for the last time, to a wall of white terry-cloth towels.

All the omens were good for the debate, I told myself. While

I stood on that stage in Philadelphia, two women astronauts would be orbiting the earth in space. And, coincidentally this day, October 11, was also Eleanor Roosevelt's one hundredth birthday. We had found a wonderful quote of hers to use in answering the inevitable question about arms control, and I practiced that one, too, in the bathtub. "It is not enough to want peace, you must believe in it," Mrs. Roosevelt had said. "And it is not enough to believe in it. You must work for it."

And then it was time. We got into the car to drive over to the convention center.

"Are you nervous?" John asked me. I thought for a minute.

"No, John," I said. "I feel the same way I did when you were driving me to the hospital to have Donna. I remember thinking to myself then, 'I wonder how I got myself into this situation,' and knowing I had no choice but to go in and deliver." And on we went.

A lot was riding on the debate. In the jargon of political campaigns, my credibility as the vice-presidential candidate was the "spin" of the day. I had to hold my own.

Bush was even more at risk. He had to stand up to me yet not be so aggressive he'd end up looking like a bully. At the same time, he could not be patronizing or condescending, either. He had to defend Ronald Reagan's policies. And he also had to present himself as not only a loyal follower but a potential leader as well. For Bush, the debate was really the kickoff of his campaign for the Republican presidential nomination in 1988. The Republican National Committee would be watching his performance very carefully, just as the conservatives would be weighing his every word on abortion, on civil rights, on aid to Nicaragua. Bush would also be on the political tightrope tonight, not just me.

The pressure showed. Bob Barnett, acting as my representative in a predebate meeting to decide such things, won the coin toss and, at my direction, elected for me to speak last, thereby giving Bush the first question. When that question came, Bush, instead of being poised and consistent, seemed about to jump out of his skin with nerves. He was erratic. He was rushed. And his enthusiasm seemed more appropriate for a cheerleader than a Vice President. In his very first answer to a question about how his policies would differ from Reagan's were he to step into the presidency, Bush said he "believed firmly in his [Reagan's] leadership," that he'd "been with him every step of the way," that of course he supported Reagan's economic program "and I support him in everything else," that he couldn't turn his back on him as Mondale had Carter (which was untrue) because "I have too much trust in him. I have too much real friendship for him."

We were off and running.

And I was taking notes. I couldn't believe what Bush was trying to get away with. In his rebuttal of my criticism of the economy in which I cited the stores I'd seen boarded up in Ohio and the obstacles even high-tech companies in California faced trying to sell their products abroad because of the high value of the dollar, Bush tried to turn the facts around. The liberals in the House, he claimed, had delivered 21.5 percent interest rates, interest rates "that were right off the charts," "take-home pay checks that were shrinking, and we've delivered optimism." Six million people had gone back to work under Reagan, he claimed, and three hundred thousand jobs a month were being created.

"I think what I'm going to have to do is start correcting the Vice President's statistics," I started my one-minute rebuttal. An additional six million people in the work force were expected in a growing economy, I said, but the Carter Administration with all its difficulties had still created ten million jobs. The interest rate for housing in Reagan's Administration was 14.5 percent. Under Carter it had been 10.6 percent. And what about the six million people who had descended below the poverty line under Reagan, and the 500,000 people knocked off disability rolls?

I was into it now, concentrating on the substance of the debate rather than on the blue light on the television camera. Every so often I heard a dim voice in my subconscious say, "Look up—look at the camera—we don't want to see the top of your head." But then Bush would take off again, I'd start scribbling notes, and I'd forget.

"Human-resource spending is way, way up," Bush was claiming. "Aid for Dependent Children spending is up. Immunization programs are up. . . . Spending for food stamps is way, way up under the Reagan Administration." I couldn't believe Bush was professing Republican responsibility for these programs. The truth was that the Reagan budget policies had slashed funds for all of them in 1981, and I had worked hard along with other Democrats to restore some of the funds the following year.

Bush had also conveniently left out one reason spending for the programs had actually increased. We had just been through the biggest recession since the Great Depression. Eight and a half million people were out of work. They had become part of a bigger pool of disadvantaged people than ever—and now they were applying for food stamps and other federal assistance. But Bush had no shame. "Almost every place you can point, contrary to Mr. Mondale's—I gotta be careful—but contrary of how he goes around just saying everything bad. If somebody sees a silver lining, he finds a big black cloud out there. Whine on harvest moon! I mean, there's a lot going on, a lotta opportunity." That's exactly what he said.

The questions, answers, and rebuttals ticked by on the separation of church and state, on our differing views on abortion. I took it a question at a time, thankful when each one passed, bringing us closer to the end. The only question that startled me concerned the House committee investigation into my congressional financial disclosure forms. Under the rules of the debate, that question should not have been there because it couldn't also be asked of George Bush. But I'd already answered that one a million times.

Bush's corresponding question pointed out that he had paid less than thirteen percent of his income in federal taxes in 1983, while the norm for others in his bracket was twenty-eight percent. Was that fair? he was asked. He claimed it was, saying that his actual tax was forty-two percent of his gross income and that only the deduction of his state and local taxes on his federal returns had reduced the amount of payment to thirteen percent. It sounded good, although it wasn't exactly accurate, as we were to point out after the debate.

Then Bush went too far. In response to a question about what I would do to prevent such terrorist attacks as the recent series against our embassy and troops in Lebanon, I had acknowledged that terrorism was a global problem but said that President Carter had brought all fifty-two hostages home safe from Iran, while under Reagan over two hundred and forty young Marines had been blown up in their barracks in Beirut and our embassy had been bombed not once but three times. ". . . The President

said: 'I assume responsibility.' I'd like to know what that means,"
I said. "Are we going to take proper precautions before we put
Americans in situations where they're in danger, or are we just
going to walk away, throwing our arms up in the air?"

And that drew Bush's true chauvinistic colors. ". . . Let me
help you with the difference, Mrs. Ferraro, between Iran and the
embassy in Lebanon," he said, going on to point out that the
hostages were held by a foreign government in Iran while the Marines were in Lebanon by invitation "to give peace a chance."
And I got angry. Not only had Bush persisted in calling me
"Mrs. Ferraro" instead of "Congresswoman Ferraro" throughout
the debate, but now he had insulted me.

"Let me say first of all that I almost resent, Vice President
Bush, your patronizing attitude that you have to teach me about
foreign policy," I said in my rebuttal. "I have been a member of
Congress for six years; I was there [in Congress] when the embassy was held hostage in Iran; and I have been there and I've
seen what has happened in the past several months, seventeen
months, of your Administration. Secondly, please, don't catego-
rize my answers, either. Leave the interpretation of my answers
to the American people who are watching this debate."

I couldn't believe he'd been so foolish to talk down to me
like that, especially since he had already been warned about being
patronizing in his own debate rehearsals. Just as Bob Barnett had
played Bush in my preparation, Illinois Congresswoman Lynn
Martin had stood in for me against Bush. More than once in the
course of their mock debates, Lynn told me later, she had had to
put him down for being patronizing. But the lesson obviously
hadn't taken.

Many people thought my rejoinder to Bush had been rehearsed, but it wasn't. I wish I had not had to say it to him at all.
No one likes to have her intelligence not only questioned but
dismissed, as Bush had done to me. I won't sit still for that under
any circumstances. And I certainly wasn't about to in this critical
debate between the two vice-presidential candidates.

The debate was winding down when, at the end of my response to a question about a nuclear freeze, the moderator, Sander
Vanocur, lost track of the sequence. Instead of calling for my
follow-up question, he skipped it and went directly to Bush's

rebuttal. By the time Bush had finished, Sander had realized his error, but was still a little confused. "I have robbed you of your rebuttal," he said to me. "Therefore you will have two minutes to rebut." But it wasn't my rebuttal I'd been robbed of, but my follow-up, I pointed out to him. He stood corrected, but halfway through my newly reinstated follow-up, the panel of lights started to blink. It was really distracting.

"I don't know what your lights are doing, Sander," I said to the moderator. "You have another minute," he assured me. But still the lights flashed, the technicians behind the scenes getting lost themselves in the sequence change. I kept going and finished my remarks about the Limited Test Ban Treaty successfully negotiated by President Kennedy in 1963.

The format mixup and the blinking lights were the only glitch in the debate, but at least I knew exactly what was going on. How did it come across? In a subsequent letter to the editor in a local newspaper, one viewer protested: "I don't know why everybody was so upset about Ronald Reagan appearing senile during the course of his debate when Geraldine Ferraro couldn't even understand the rules of her debate, time her answers, or understand the system of lights." Oh, well . . .

And then came the final and inevitable question. "Congresswoman Ferraro, you have had little or no experience in military matters and yet you might some day find yourself Commander in Chief of the armed forces. How can you convince the American people and the potential enemy that you would know what to do to protect this nation's security, and do you think in any way that the Soviets might be tempted to try to take advantage of you simply because you are a woman?"

I didn't hesitate. "Are you saying that I would have to have fought in a war in order to love peace?" I shot back, forgetting that I was supposed to have rebutted Bush with that statement, not the reporter.

Nevertheless, it was a terribly important question and I had thought a great deal about how to answer it. Equating military experience with the ability to defend our country, I said, was about "as valid as saying you would have to be black in order to despise racism, that you'd have to be female in order to be terribly offended by sexism. And that's just not so," I said. ". . . Quite frankly, I'm prepared to do whatever is necessary in order to secure this country and make sure that security is maintained." If the Soviet Union were to challenge this country militarily, I went on, and I were in a position of leadership, the Russians "would be assured that they would be met with swift, concise, and certain retaliation."

But the most important issue as a leader, I stressed, was to do everything possible not to get to the point of having to decide whether to use force. Moving toward arms control was imperative, yet over the past four years the Republican Administration had not done that. "I think if you look at the failures of this Administration that would have to be number one," I said, and promised that as a leader I would "move immediately toward arms control negotiations."

But not everyone is ready to believe that a woman is capable of such leadership. And predictably, Bush in his closing statement stressed his experiences in World War II as a qualification for keeping the peace. "Yes, I did serve in combat," he said. "I was shot down when I was a young kid, scared to death. And all that did, saw friends die, but that heightened my convictions about peace." What a pointless resume for leadership, excluding over half the population from the top rungs of government. If you hadn't fought at the halls of Montezuma, ran the argument, you couldn't understand the need for peace on the shores of Tripoli.

It was time for my closing statement. For once I looked straight into the camera. I told the public exactly how I felt, from the heart, about the true meaning of patriotism.

". . . When we find jobs for the eight and a half million people who are unemployed in this country, we'll make our economy stronger and that will be a patriotic act," I said. "When we reduce the deficits and we cut interest rates—I know the President doesn't believe that, but it's so—young people can buy houses; that's profamily and that will be a patriotic act. When we educate our children, they're going to be able to compete in a world economy, and that makes us stronger, and that's a patriotic act. When we stop the arms race, we make this a safer, saner world, and that's a patriotic act. And when we keep the peace, young men don't die, and that's a patriotic act."

The debate was done.

*   *   *

"Congratulations," I said to Bush, shaking his hand in the middle of the stage. "I'm glad that's over."

He must have said something to me, but my mind was so overloaded at that point I've forgotten. There was still a lot of tension. The verdict on who had won was not in yet. And Bush seemed shaken. I thought my closing statement had been good, that I had said it the way I had wanted to say it, that I had reached out to the American people. And Bush must have felt that, too. I'm sure he'd never admit it, but I think at that moment he felt I had won the debate, mostly because of my final statement. Between the jolted expression on his face and the rattled way he shook my hand, he seemed very unsure of how he had done. But the moment quickly passed.

Our respective families were coming to join us, practically racing each other to be the first onstage. Reagan had seemed absolutely dumbfounded when Joan Mondale and the kids had surprised him by joining Fritz on the stage after their first debate, while not one of the Reagan children was present. The Republicans were going to make sure that didn't happen again and had rounded up all the Bush children. There was no big deal about my family appearing. After all, they had been campaigning with me or on their own since the beginning of the campaign.

I had to leave almost immediately for a postdebate rally at the old, historic Bourse, and Fritz was already on the phone in the convention center's holding room to congratulate me on the debate. "Thank you," I said to him. "But I'm not interested in doing this again for four more years." I threw my arms around Bob Barnett. "You were ten times tougher than George Bush," I said, giving him a big hug.

"How'd I sound?" I asked everyone.

"Great," they said. "And you looked terrific."

But I didn't want to hear about how I looked. I wanted to hear how I'd sounded. That was the point. People were always saying things to me like "Gee, you look pretty on TV," but what about my words? My own mother drove me crazy about it. The first time I had been on television as a member of Congress I'd called her up afterwards to ask her how it went.

"It was terrific," she said. "You looked beautiful."

"But how did I sound?" I had pressed her.

"I don't know," she said. "I was so excited when I saw you I went totally deaf." Then I bought her a tape recorder so she could listen to my words after the picture had gone off the screen.

Now in the holding room there were tears and congratulations from my debate team, whose members were both delighted with the debate itself and relieved that it was all over. Everyone, including me, thought I had won, actually won the debate against the sitting Vice President of the United States. I had made few if any errors. The debate staff had been brilliant, anticipating every single question that had been asked, so that every single answer had been considered and refined. There wasn't one thing Bob Barnett and his team had missed.

Nothing about the debate—or its outcome—had been left to chance. We had a computer in the convention center in Philadelphia linked up to our issues staff in headquarters in Washington. Throughout the debate the issues staff had checked everything Bush had cited about the accomplishments of the Reagan Administration against the facts and then wired the discrepancies back to Philadelphia. As soon as the debate ended, the five principals on my campaign staff, Anne Wexler, Francis O'Brien, John Sasso, Madeleine Albright, and Steve Engelberg, my issues director, pointed out the errors to the press. There were quite a few.

Bush's major claim, that the Reagan Administration had actually spent more on domestic programs for the poor, was as false as I had called it. In "constant" dollars (adjusted for inflation), the Reagan Administration had actually spent 300 million dollars *less* in 1984 for the food-stamp program than had been spent in 1980, and 1.6 billion dollars less on welfare. Without our efforts in Congress to reinstate what money we could for these programs, the cuts in welfare would have been twice as large, the reduction in support for food stamps *four* times as great.

Bush didn't get away with his insinuation that he had paid forty-two percent of his income in taxes in 1983, either. That percentage turned out to have been pro-rated over a three-year period. In 1983, a spokesman for his own campaign even admitted, Bush had paid only 12.8 percent on his federal income tax return. His assertion that he had been "quoted wrong, obviously" about a nuclear war being "winnable" was also struck down. There was the quote, in black and white, in a 1980 article in the *Los Angeles Times.*

"Gerr-eee! Gerr-ee!" the overflow crowd chanted at the postdebate rally. The mood at the impromptu after-party in my hotel suite was just as ebullient. Ted Kennedy called in his congratulations as did Michael Berman and my congressional colleagues and friends. Barbara Kennelly, Barbara Mikulski, Frank Guarini, and Tom Foglietta were there as well as my brother, Carl, and his wife and sons. The television set was on to get the reaction to the debate, and in the midst of flipping the channels, someone discovered that it was being rerun.

We all gathered round and I watched it for the first time. I was unhappy about my staring down at my notes, doing the unspeakable and not looking up at the camera. During Bush's closing remarks, I hadn't looked up at all and instead had spent the time jotting down the high points of my final statement. There was no doubt that it looked as if I were reading material I'd brought into the debate with me, which of course I wasn't. But we were beyond critiquing me at this point for style—or substance. There were cheers every time I said something really good, especially my remark about Bush's patronizing me. And when it came time for the rerun of my closing remarks, the whole room fell silent, only to erupt into applause at the end. What a night. There were toasts, champagne, more toasts. The party didn't wind down until two a.m.

Of course we were disappointed by the polls. CBS and NBC both gave Bush an edge, while ABC's viewers went further, giving Bush forty-three percent and me thirty-three percent. Not surprisingly more men thought that Bush had won and more women thought I had won. In a more complete ABC poll over the next four days, however, the differences between us had evened out, with those respondents calling the debate a draw, which was terrific.

But still, I think the polls giving Bush the edge reflected how people felt about the Presidency. They already had their minds set on who they were going to vote for. And no doubt about it, Bush won on style. He had much better eye contact with the camera and with me than I did with him. He never looked down and I did. But in terms of the substance and my handling of the issues, I think I did extremely well. I was constrained and thorough throughout the debate—in fact, too subdued for those who later felt I should have been more the "feisty" Ferraro.

I didn't agree. I was responding to the circumstances, a debate between the two candidates for the Vice Presidency of the United States. What I wanted to do was to show the American people that I was qualified to be Vice President.

From the point of view of the campaign, the debate was a success. My approval ratings shot up in the campaign's own polls, while the negative ratings from all my Reagan bashing went down. My performance had maintained the momentum of the campaign after Fritz's triumph over Reagan in their first debate and, I hoped, would be of help to Fritz in his upcoming second debate, just ten days away. We were still very much in the running. The morning after the debate I called back the Secret Service agent's girlfriend in the hospital after her operation, knowing from him that it had been a success. "How'd you do?" I asked her.

"Great," she said. "And so did you."

"Thanks," I said. "Both of our prayers must have worked."

The Republicans were edgy. And they showed it, sinking to a new low. The day of the debate, Bush's press secretary, Peter Teeley, had been asked by the *Wall Street Journal* to assess me as a candidate. For the second time in a week, the Bush camp put me down. "She's too bitchy," Teeley had said. "She's very arrogant. Humility isn't one of her strong points, and I think that comes through." Not missing a schoolboy beat, the day after the debate George Bush boasted to a group of longshoremen in New Jersey that "we tried to kick a little ass last night." I chose not to react to that remark, either. I had learned from my days as a prosecutor not to give in to provocation, and I certainly wasn't going to rise now to such locker-room bait. "I would not address my opponent in the same way," I said simply, when asked about Bush's remark the next day at a press conference in Chicago.

What counted was that the campaign was on a roll. A rally with Fritz on the steps of the Capitol in Madison, Wisconsin, the day after the vice-presidential debate drew our biggest crowd to date—30,000 plus. The crowd went crazy when Fritz called me "the fighter from Philly." And I tried to keep the momentum going. "I beat George Bush, and George Bush beat Ronald Reagan," I said to a roar. Of all four debaters—Reagan, Bush, Fritz, and me—Reagan had polled the worst after his debate with Fritz. Now our campaign had been revitalized, and the energy from that crowd sent our spirits soaring.

While George Bush was spending a day cracking locker-room jokes with the longshoremen and Ronald Reagan was whistle stopping on Harry Truman's campaign train, shamelessly quoting not only that Democratic President but Franklin Roosevelt as well, I was pressing on. In the next six days, I would go from Madison to Chicago; to Davenport and Des Moines, Iowa; to Allentown, Pennsylvania; to Cleveland, Ohio; to Springfield, Illinois; to Los Angeles and Sacramento, California; to Seattle, Washington; to Jefferson City, Missouri; and finally to Pittsburgh; before returning to New York for one day and then starting out again.

The pace would be brutal. But we were optimistic. With the point spread closing between the tickets and the second presidential debate looming, now more than ever I thought Fritz Mondale had a good chance of becoming the next President of the United States. In the final twenty-four days before Election Day. I would be on the road for twenty-three of them.

A DAY AT A TIME

*"We've chosen the path to equality. Don't let
them turn us around."*

—*Valley College, Van Nuys,
California, November 2, 1984.*

W E PULLED OUT ALL THE
stops now, jetting around the country in seemingly perpetual
motion. As we flew from one time zone into another and then
back again, no one could figure out what time it really was. The
only continuity in my life was the interior of the campaign plane,
the staff, and the traveling press corps, who were starting to fall
apart from fatigue—and food. During one day Gloria Steinem
counted up six different meals she'd been served on the plane—
and had eaten—and she was with us for only a week.

The pace never slackened. Between the beginning of October and Election Day, November 6, I logged over thirty thousand
miles alone. Almost always now, my speeches started: "It's great
to be back in Illinois" or "I've been to Ohio many times since our
convention, and each time I feel more at home" or, on my seventh trip to California, "It's always great to be back in the home
state of the next ex-President of the United States."

Toward the end of the campaign, we flew in and out of as
many as five states a day. On November 1, I started the morning
with a rally in Cincinnati, flew to New York for the traditional
garment-center rally with Frtiz, went on to yet another rally at
the University of Iowa, and landed in Los Angeles at six p.m.

268

New York time. On November 4, I went to Mass in Chicago and then on to rallies in Lansing, Michigan; Warwick, Rhode Island; and Waterbury, Connecticut, landing in Cleveland, Ohio, at two a.m. and getting up what seemed like minutes later for an early-morning rally there—only to fly on to rallies in Pittsburgh, Jersey City, and then to my last night speech, at Marymount College in New York—eight states in two days.

There was so little time. I felt frustrated by the fact that even though the polls consistently found support by the public for the Democratic ticket on the issues, the vote was still going to Reagan. It all came to a head on October 2, when I visited a Chrysler plant in Belvidere, Illinois. These were our people, blue-collar workers, union members who wouldn't have been working at all if the Carter Administration, over Republican objections, had not pushed through the federal guaranteed loans in 1979 to keep Chrysler operating. Yet at our early-morning staff meeting in Belvidere, I'd been told that one in three members of the United Auto Workers was planning to vote for Ronald Reagan. I couldn't believe it.

We had bailed out Chrysler. Fritz Mondale had led the fight from the White House. I had voted for the legislation. This was a Chrysler plant. These were the guys whose jobs we had saved. "Just tour the plant, shake a few hands, and make a few remarks," my staff had advised me at our morning meeting. But there was no way I was simply going to stroll down the production line, kicking the tires and admiring the rivets. I had to find out what was going on with the very constituency that should have been—and always had been—our staunchest supporters.

"What are you going to do?" my staff wanted to know somewhat anxiously.

"I'll think of something," I said.

After I toured the production line, I was asked to say a few words. But a torrent came out. "I don't need to give you a speech," I said. "I need to know something from you. I'm absolutely floored that we are losing one-third of you to the Republicans. Why are you doing this? Tell me why you are voting for Ronald Reagan in the numbers you are?"

At first the workers didn't say anything, shifting from foot to foot in embarrassment. But I had to know. "People have to be talking," I said. "Tell me what they're saying."

And little by little, they began to open up. "America is finally standing tall again," one worker said, parroting the Republican definition of patriotism based on the former hostage crisis in
Iran.

"All fifty-two of those hostages walked off the plane alive.
Do you know what has happened to the Marines in Beirut?"
And I told them.

We were scheduled for twenty minutes, but I stood there for
forty, listening to their grievances about abortion and about the
welfare rolls.

"You Democrats are always giving away my hard-earned
dollars," one worker in overalls said.

"Tell me about that," I urged him.

And he proceeded to talk about a woman he'd seen at his
local post office receiving three different welfare checks.

"No kidding," I said. "How do you know she got three
checks?"

"She showed them to me," he said.

That was interesting enough, since he admitted he did not
know the woman. Nor was he sure where the checks had actually
come from.

"She told me they were from welfare or someplace," he said.

I kind of doubted the story, but he was repeating a popular
myth about welfare cheats—and basing his vote for Reagan on it.

It was enraging. "We were the ones who kept Chrysler alive,"
I pointed out to them. "Is this your way of saying thank you?
You don't turn your back on people who have been good to you
and people who are looking to the future."

But though the atmosphere was getting warmer and warmer,
the Reagan mind-set seemed firmly implanted. "I'm voting for
Mondale and you, OK?" said one of our supporters. "But what
Reagan has done is said the things the workingman believes."

Their applause rang in my ears as I left the plant to go on to
Vanderbilt University, in Nashville, Tennessee. But the problem
was clear. What could I do to get through to the American people, to strike the chord that would make them see Ronald Reagan
and the Republican Administration for what they really were? I
wanted to take an attribute for which Ronald Reagan was so

admired—his leadership—and analyze it, using his own actions and words.

"A new issue has arisen in this campaign—the leadership of Ronald Reagan," I said that same afternoon at Vanderbilt. I proceeded to review several incidents that revealed the problem. In a recent speech, Reagan had proudly told the story of a doctor, the grandson of an Italian immigrant, who had treated the President after he had been shot in Washington, D.C. In that speech Reagan was promoting the idea that with effort we can lift ourselves up by our bootstraps. I have no quarrel with that. It's my own story. But the doctor later told the press that the very programs that were giving other medical students the same training he'd had were ones Reagan had tried to cut.

In similar credibility gaps Reagan had shrugged off the latest U.S. embassy bombing in Beirut. After forty-four months of belligerent blustering about our foreign policies, he had made an eleventh-hour attempt during remarks at the United Nations to sound peace-loving and reasonable. And most recently, he had blamed former Administrations for the tragedy in Beirut.

"These recent statements raise a question about the quality of presidential leadership," I told the audience. "The story about the Italian-American doctor is the product of an anecdotal Presidency, when we need a President who gives us straight talk and strong leadership. The UN speech hails from an eleventh-hour Presidency, when we need a leader pulling for us every day of his term. And the blame he cast on former Presidents comes from a pass-the-buck Presidency, when we demand a leader who admits and learns from his mistakes and does not run from them."

But the question was not only leadership but the public's perception of it. And Fritz, who had an exemplary record as Attorney General of Minnesota, as a Senator, and as Vice President for taking tough positions and fighting for what he believed was right, was perceived as a weak leader, while Ronald Reagan, despite blunder after blunder, was perceived as strong.

Bush's campaign stance exposed the real values behind Republican image making. The day before, in Greensboro, North Carolina, I had quoted from one of Bush's recent speeches in my own remarks. "Do you know what wins elections?" Bush had asked a crowd in Columbus, Ohio. And he'd pulled out his wallet. "It's who puts money into this and who takes money out."

What a cynical statement on the democratic process. "That single gesture of selfishness tells us more about the true character of this Administration than all their apple pie rhetoric," I said to the audience of over five thousand. "There's nothing in George Bush's wallet that says we should care about the disadvantaged. There's nothing in his wallet that tells us to search for peace. There's nothing in his wallet that says in the name of humanity let's stop the arms race."

I couldn't believe the polls, which still saw us twelve points away from Reagan. Why weren't the people seeing through the Reagan image? And if the polls were right, why were the crowds that greeted me everywhere getting bigger and even more enthusiastic? How could the polls be accurate when you couldn't even see where the crowds began and where they ended?

"The pollsters and the pundits say we can't win in November. They've decided the race before the first voting booth opens," I said in Atlanta, Georgia; Nashville, Tennessee; Akron, Ohio; Bethlehem, Pennsylvania—everywhere. "But I want to take my own scientific, objective survey right here. Are we going to win in November?"

"YES!" the crowd would roar.

"Are we going to send Walter Mondale to the White House and Ronald Reagan back to the ranch? You bet we are," I'd say, while the crowd went wild.

No one could believe the size of the crowds. Wherever we went, the local officials said they'd never seen anything like it. The people reached out to touch me, held up their children for me to kiss, waved newspapers or magazine covers bearing my picture to be autographed, tried to give me presents. The Secret Service wouldn't allow me to take anything from the crowd and sometimes had to knock the gifts of packaged flowers or rolled posters out of the donor's hands, fearing they might conceal a weapon.

It was very upsetting. Some of these people had been standing there for hours, waiting for autographs or to give me something. I couldn't let them down, so I told the Secret Service to let Eleanor Lewis work the crowd with me, to collect the presents and the papers to be autographed. "Stay right where you are. You'll get your autograph back when this is over," I'd say to one person after another. And miraculously Eleanor always found them again. One little girl's eyes filled with tears when I told her I couldn't sign her autograph book at that very moment. "I promise I will, honey," I said to her. But the tears spilled over. "Did you get back to that little girl?" I asked Eleanor anxiously. She had. Eleanor was fabulous. I insisted that thank-you notes go to the cops and to everyone who gave us presents, and she always kept track.

But in spite of the overflow crowds and enthusiasm, I was still up against it. Even after the debate with Bush, my competence on foreign policy and defense continued to be questioned, as did my qualifications to be commander in chief.

"Are you strong enough to push the button?" Marvin Kalb asked me on *Meet the Press*, three days after the vice-presidential debate.

"I could do whatever is necessary to protect this country," I had replied to him.

But there was a bigger, underlying issue. If my candidacy as a woman were being judged the same as a man's, would I still have to answer questions like that? "That is the kind of question that we have asked on this program before," Kalb quickly countered. But to whom?

Not to one single vice-presidential candidate. And to only three members of Congress, all of whom were ministers. The issue there was quite different. They hadn't been asked if their gender had the strength of character to push the button, as I had, but whether their religious views would permit it. It was so endlessly annoying to be presumed as weak and indecisive simply because I was a woman. And the question of "button pushing" was such a simplistic one. The discussion was never about whether force should be used only when every other avenue is exhausted, or whether or not I had the knowledge and the intelligence and the fortitude to move toward arms control negotiations so that pushing the nuclear button never would become a necessity. No. My "strength" in ordering the destruction of the world dominated the controversy.

Three days later, on October 17, ABC's Ted Koppel was even more judgmental on *Nightline,* grilling me to the point of rudeness on my position on antisatellite weapons; what would or would not constitute the Democratic stand on no "first use" of nuclear weapons; and how I would verify the number of Russian warheads in a nuclear freeze with the Soviet Union. Citing an editorial in the *Wall Street Journal* as if it were the Bible, Koppel challenged my statement during my debate with Bush that between the Soviet Union and the U.S. we were building six new nuclear warheads a day.

" 'They [the Soviets] are the ones who are building five or six, and we are building none,' " Koppel quoted from the *Wall Street Journal*. "What did you mean?"

"The *Wall Street Journal* is wrong," I told him. "Between us we're building five or six warheads a day. The *Wall Street Journal* makes it look as if we're not building any at all."

Koppel: "That's correct."

Ferraro: "They're wrong."

"No," Koppel persisted. "What they're saying is that for every one that we're building, we have scrapped some others. So that in terms of accretion, we have not been adding to our stockpile of nuclear warheads."

I couldn't believe it. Now we were in a war of semantics. I had never said "adding." I'd said "building."

Ferraro: "We are building."

Koppel: "We are adding?"

Ferraro: "We are building."

And on the sparring went, over such subjects as Reagan's policies in Central America, the accusation that I did not support any covert activity by the CIA, and the differences between the Camp David agreement for the Middle East and the current Reagan plan. There I was, less than three weeks from Election Day, still undergoing a foreign policy exam instead of examining the differences between the two tickets. How counterproductive. And how arrogant of my interrogators.

Ted Koppel, at least, would get his comeuppance after the election. Addressing the School of Foreign Service in December at Georgetown University on the role of the media in foreign policy, he had the great misfortune of having Madeleine Albright, who was teaching there, in the front row. A student asked why the press had not focused more on the issues. Koppel responded defensively that he had invited all four candidates to discuss the issues on *Nightline,* but that only Geraldine Ferraro had accepted.

"That's right, and you did a number on her," Madeleine shot back impulsively. He looked at her quizzically, not recognizing her.

"Well, I have been accused of being professorial, prosecutorial, and pompous during that interview," he said to her.

She readily agreed. "All of the above," she told him while he stared down at her. "Which leads me to the following question: Do you believe that you, as well as other commentators, were harder on Mrs. Ferraro on foreign policy because she was a woman than you might have been on a man?" Madeleine asked.

"Yes, we were," Koppel admitted.

On October 18, we were in the air between Seattle, Washington, where that morning I had given a major speech on foreign policy at the University of Washington, and Jefferson City, Missouri, where I was scheduled to give a rally speech at the airport. I was out of sorts, irritated at the way Koppel had cross-examined me instead of interviewing me the night before on *Nightline,* and a bit put out at the Archbishop of New York, who had refused to let me substitute for Fritz at the annual Alfred E. Smith memorial dinner he was hosting that night in New York. "Massive Snub for Ferraro," the *New York Post* had bannered two days before the dinner: "Rejected as Speaker at Catholic Dinner of Year."

On the plane now, reflecting on all this, I wondered why Francis O'Brien looked so serious as he sat down beside me. "Don't you ever have any good news to tell me?" I teased him. But he didn't smile back. What now, I thought. No one had said anything this morning at our staff meeting in Seattle, the time slot during which we always discussed how to handle the news of the day. I was about to find out why. To delay the damage from this story, my staff had decided among themselves to withhold the news from me until after I had delivered my major speech on foreign policy at the University of Washington. They had even called John in New York to tell him not to mention anything to me if I called home. And they'd been right. The story was devastating.

The *New York Post,* Francis now told me, was already on the stands with a story about my father. The story claimed that in 1944, my father had reportedly been arrested in Newburgh, New York, where we were then living, for possession of numbers slips. On the morning my father was supposed to appear in court, he had suddenly died.

I stared at Francis in disbelief. What was he talking about? I had never heard a word about my father's being arrested.

But there was more. My father's death notice had been altered the next day at the request of the undertaker, the story claimed, leading to what the *New York Post* called a "mystery." The insinuation was that the details of his death, too, had been a mystery. Unfortunately, the doctor who had attended him had died years before, the *Post* story ran, so no one could shed light on exactly how my father had died.

I felt as if I'd been hit in the stomach. My father had been dead for forty years. And my mother would be crushed by this. I wanted to get off that campaign plane immediately and go home to all the people my candidacy had hurt. But of course I could do no such thing.

"We have to talk about what you're going to say to the press in Jefferson City," Francis was saying to me. "The story will be all around by then, and you know they're going to ask you about it."

But I couldn't talk to Francis about a press statement. Not right now. I was too shocked—and worried about my mother. She had stopped buying the *Post,* she was so disgusted with the garbage they were running about us. But would someone call to tell her about this story? Were other members of the press already hounding her? Was she all alone?

"You've got to get me to a phone, Francis," I told him. "I've got to call my mother."

And he did, asking the pilot to land at the nearest possible airport, telling the press on board that we were stopping to refuel the plane. It seemed like hours before we reached Rapid City, South Dakota, where I quickly reached my mother on the airport pay phone. "I love you," I said first. Then I told her the news so that she'd be prepared.

Later everyone wanted to know if I'd cried when I'd heard about the story. The press wanted to know. Phil Donahue wanted to know. Suddenly, the question of whether I had cried at thirty

LEAGUE OF WOMEN VOTERS

Whew, thank God it's over!

My family sharing debate tension on stage, October 11. From left: my sister-in-law, Teresa; brother, Carl; Secret Service, John, and the kids.

Post-debate rally. A typical crowd, as far as the eye can see.

I taught Ronald Reagan everything he knows.

With Congresswoman Barbara Kennelly: my friends were always there when I needed them.

My campaign staff: what a motley crew! Front: Kate Sheaffer (l), Anne Wexler. Center: Ted Myers (l), Eleanor Lewis, Madeline Albright, The Slugger, Francis O'Brien, Steve Engelberg, Mel Schweitzer, Barbara Roberts Mason. Back: Sandy Holt (l), Charles Atkins, Addie Guttag.

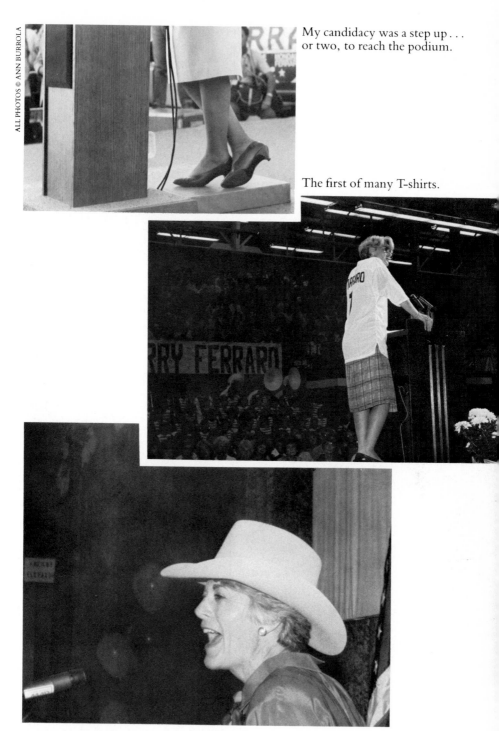

My candidacy was a step up . . .
or two, to reach the podium.

The first of many T-shirts.

If only I had the accent to match.

Messages at every stop.

ALL PHOTOS © ANN BURROLA

The faces of the campaign.

My mom and John, Jr.—
I had to tell them it was all over.
La Guardia Airport. November 1.

Don't let it get you down. Dancing
with John, Jr., at staff and press
party, Chicago. November 3.

Signing last autographs for the staff as the kids look on. November 5.

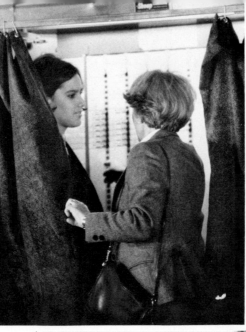
COURTESY OF DAILY NEWS

Laura's first vote—for
her mother as Vice President.
November 6.

© ANN BURROLA

Talking with Fritz and preparing to concede, New York Hilton, with
Congressman Ted Weiss (l), Congressman Charlie Rangel, and John.

© ANN BURROLA

Saying good-bye to my friends
in the House of Representatives.

And impossibly, the crowds were getting even bigger. On the day before Fritz's second debate on October 21, more people turned out for a rally in Amherst, Massachusetts, than at any other point in the campaign. Counting crowds had become a can-you-top-this competition within the campaign, and in Amherst Anne Wexler broke the bank. She and John Sasso, my campaign manager, had a private bet, it turned out, over whose home turf would produce the most supporters. Sasso, right-hand man to Massachusetts Governor Dukakis, had put his money on the crowd of 25,000 I'd pulled in Boston the month before. Anne Wexler was rooting for Amherst, where her husband, Joseph Duffey, was chancellor of the University of Massachusetts. And when more than 30,000 showed up in her New England city, Anne was jubilant.

The futility of our quest for the White House began to dawn on us, however, after the second presidential debate. Once again, Fritz had been brilliant, questioning Reagan's competence in dealing with arms control, quoting his extraordinary misperception that nuclear missiles launched from submarines could be recalled. In our analysis, Reagan hadn't fared much better on his Star Wars proposal, a one-*trillion*-dollar investment in arming the heavens with nuclear weapons, without knowing how any of it would work. How Star Wars would be deployed would be up to the scientists; Reagan had shrugged off the question. "That's what a President is supposed to know," Fritz had snapped, scoring another point.

Terrific. I had watched the debate sitting on my living room floor in Queens with growing optimism. Reagan was certainly more acute during the questioning than he had been in the first debate, but in his closing statement he totally lost it again, rambling on and on about the rhapsodies of driving down the California coast, until the moderator had to cut him off. A clear victory for Fritz, right? Wrong.

I had listened in stunned disbelief as political analyst Ken Auletta gave the edge to Reagan. I had been watching the local news when Tony Guida asked Auletta why he had come to that conclusion. Because the President had finished his sentences and had spoken in complete thoughts, Auletta replied. If that's all it takes, I had thought, we've lost.

As it was, Reagan had succeeded in countering the impression left by the first debate that age was to be an issue in the election. His comment in this debate that he would not take advantage of his opponent's youth and inexperience settled the issue—and the campaign—for good.

On one level, I knew at that moment that it was all over. And the polls supported my instinct, slipping back to an eighteen-point spread. On the Mondale campaign plane, we were hearing, gloom had replaced the optimism that had followed the first presidential debate. The Mondale campaign staff, we were told, was depressed and dispirited. But not us. We still had hope because of the enormous crowds and enthusiasm that followed us everywhere. "Oh, it's so good to see you guys," we heard time and again from the Mondale-Ferraro advance team and local Democratic officials whenever we flew into a city. "You're all so up."

Sure we were up. There was no way we weren't going to be up. I was going to finish out this campaign with style if it killed me. If it fell upon me to take a page from Bush's handbook on preppy enthusiasm, so be it. I started belting out the lead song from the musical *Annie,* loudly singing "The sun'll come out tomorrow" whenever the spirit moved me, cracking jokes with my campaign staff to keep up our energy. In sheer debating skills, everyone, including a panel of debating experts assembled by the Associated Press, agreed that Fritz had won that second debate with Reagan. But Fritz had suffered from a different sort of handicap than I had in facing Bush.

I was an untried woman taking on the Vice President of the United States. Fritz was the challenger in a campaign against an all-time popular incumbent President. Just winning the debate wasn't enough. Fritz had to knock Reagan out of the box.

On we went. "Did Fritz Mondale win that debate last night?" I asked a labor rally in Flushing, New York, on October 22. "Did he show who's really in command? Are we going to win this election? You bet we are."

The polls said otherwise. How could Reagan be getting away with it? I refused to believe the election was going to be won on cosmetics, on superficiality, when there was so much at stake.

"Ronald Reagan can't resist an appeal from defense contractors down on their luck," I went on in my remarks to the union audience in Flushing. "They ask him to spare a dime for a cup of coffee, and he gives them seven thousand dollars for a coffee maker. There wasn't a dry eye in the White House when the forgotten wealthy asked for a handout. So Reagan dug deep into our pockets and came up with seven hundred and fifty billion dollars in tax relief. And he was so moved when they passed the plate for big oil that he kindly donated the whole outer continental shelf."

Back in California three days later, I tried as hard as ever to move the campaign onto the issues. "This election is not a duel between personalities. You can like Ronald Reagan, but you don't have to vote for him," I said to the crowd in Stockton.

I was thankful just to get to Stockton. Earlier in the day in Cupertino, I was almost shot by a maintenance man who had brought a bow and arrow and a handgun to work with him that day. The man, who weighed close to 300 pounds, I read later, evidently did not approve of women candidates and had told a woman supervisor at the company that he might "pretend to be Robin Hood" and shoot me.

She passed on this threat, and the police arrested the maintenance man in the parking lot. In the trunk of his car the police found two bows and a full assortment of razor-tipped arrows, along with a pistol. When he heard the report, John called me, concerned. As for my mother, she was so upset at the news that she called NBC to make sure I was all right. When they said they had no further information, she brought down her wrath on the station. "This is her mother!" she exclaimed indignantly.

Meanwhile, the polls continued to show a widening margin between Mondale and Reagan. In the eyes of the pollsters and, as a result, in the mouths of the newscasters, the election had been called. Our campaign was no longer worth a whole lot of time on the national news.

The television reporters assigned to the campaign were frustrated that they weren't getting as much time on the air as they had at the beginning.

"Come on, Gerry. Do something to get me air time," ABC's Lynn Sherr kept teasing me. The archer in Cupertino had almost provided the solution.

"Hey, Lynn, I really tried for you," I kidded her after the incident. "I tried to get shot."

I couldn't resist needling the Secret Service a little bit, too. The more I thought about it, the more I thought the scare had in fact been a missed opportunity. "If only I could have gotten wounded a little bit, like in the shoulder, maybe I could draw the sympathy vote," I exclaimed in the motorcade just loud enough for the Secret Service agents to hear me. They winced. "Oh, just a scratch," I joked.

With only twelve days to go before Election Day, we tried a strategy change and decided to concentrate on our more natural constituencies, blacks, students, and women. The campaign's internal polls still showed that my candidacy was worth two to three points with the gender-gap vote, and in a close race those points could be a telling factor.

From the beginning there had been a mild division within the campaign about whether to position me as a national candidate with no single-issue platform—or to play up my gender by emphasizing women's issues. The decision for me had been simple. I had decided to run as the vice-presidential candidate of the American people—from Wall Street brokers to apple pickers in the state of Washington. And I had. But at this eleventh hour in the campaign, we were open to suggestions. And the suggestion from the internal memos sent to John Sasso in the last few weeks from Anne Wexler, Pam Fleischaker, Ranny Cooper, and Joan McLean all pointed to going after the women's vote. So I did.

In San Francisco, I challenged Reagan's record on women. "Women are not better off with a President, an Administration, and a party united against the Equal Rights Amendment," I said to growing cheers. "When I take my oath of office for my second term as Vice President, I want to swear to uphold a Constitution that includes the ERA. Name a program that helps women. This Administration has tried to slash it. Name a policy that treats women fairly. This Administration is against it. This Administration is for the gold standard for the economy and the double standard for women."

I tried to recapture the spirit that had swept the Democratic Convention just three months before. Anything had seemed possible then. Anything could be possible again. "If you want to stay on the track we're on, then vote for Ronald Reagan," I said in the same city where it had all begun. "But if you want to treat men and women as equals, if you want to stop the arms race, if you want to be kind to the most vulnerable, if you want to protect this environment, then vote for Walter Mondale."

I was tired, so very very tired. In one day, October 26, we flew on to three different stops in Oregon; to Tacoma, Washington; to Waterloo, Iowa; and then to Detroit, Michigan. I didn't want the campaign to go on another week, another day, another minute. I was sick of pretending that we were going to win, sick of worrying whether or not the district attorney's office was going to press the case against John, sick of worrying whether or not the House Ethics Committee on Standards of Official Conduct was going to come to a decision before the election. I had caught everyone's cold by then, and my throat was killing me during the speeches, rallies, and fund-raisers that were now blurring into each other. But even my cold was misinterpreted. After one speech I gave in that condition, the press reported that I seemed "subdued." The next day I talked my throat raw.

Still there were fires to put out and important issues to put forward. The week before, Reagan had charged in a Long Island synagogue that the Democrats were soft on anti-Semitism, that the Democratic leadership had lacked the "moral courage" to condemn anti-Semitism at the Democratic Convention. Anti-Semitism had been a very touchy point for the Democrats throughout the campaign, provoked by Jesse Jackson's support of pro-Palestinian planks during the primaries and the convention, clouded even further by the racist vitriol of Black Muslim leader Louis Farrakhan. I had denounced Farrakhan. Fritz had denounced Farrakhan. But there had not been a specific plank in the platform denouncing anti-Semitism.

Nevertheless, our party had had a proud history of opposing discrimination against Jews, and we couldn't—and wouldn't—sit still for Reagan's charges. Jewish leaders had been very concerned throughout the campaign about Jackson's influence within the Democratic party, how we would handle Jackson after the election if we won, whether or not he would become an active part of the White House Administration and set policy. After Reagan's speech at the synagogue, we knew we'd have to rebut the President's charges. And it fell to me to do it.

The speech I delivered on October 29 at the Temple Kehilath Jeshurun in New York was one of the most important of the campaign. Not only did I want to state my strong concern for the dangerous ideological course the Republicans had taken in mixing religion and politics, but to answer Reagan's charges as well. "I will not accept the base implication that my party is soft on anti-Semitism. I reject it completely," I told the members of the synagogue. "In an effort to impress his audience, President Reagan insulted it. In an effort to assail us, he debased himself. The President's remark was incorrect, indecent, and he should apologize for making it."

Reagan had also twisted history in his remarks, using the Holocaust as justification for sending our Marines into Lebanon. "He said the Jewish battle cry 'never again' should be, and I quote, 'impressed on those who'd question why we went on a peacekeeping mission to Lebanon,' " I said. "I don't know which is more troubling, the President's ignorance of the facts or his cynical exploitation of the Holocaust."

But most troubling was Reagan's continuing assertion, supported by some fundamentalists, that the world was approaching Armageddon, as if that hypothetical state of affairs justified his lack of progress on arms negotiations and his intention to send weapons into space. "This is a nation that demands much of its leaders. But what it asks for above all is a commander in chief, not a keeper of the faith," I went on. "We need a President who worries about the state of our air and water, and not his own view of our state of grace. We need a President who does everything he can for arms control and does not let the arms race continue merely because of his own belief in the possibility of Armageddon." I got a standing ovation.

But did it really matter? Did I expect the election to turn around on one speech? Of course not. But these issues of war and peace, leadership, and religious influences on public policy were above campaign rhetoric. At that temple, I was speaking from the heart. "Individual freedom and the unfettered expression of religious belief are being questioned in this campaign for the first time in years," I said, warning that the erosion of these liberties should be particularly troubling to "those of us who are Catholic or Jewish or members of any religious or racial minority. When freedom is questioned, the rights of minorities are the first to be cut back." There were few things I felt more strongly about. "Government can be moral—and it must be moral—without adopting a religion," I concluded. "Leaders can be moral—and they should be moral—without imposing their morality on others."

As we headed into the last week, the polls were abysmal, with Reagan now leading by eighteen points. A classic landslide was now being anticipated, and the campaign of 1984 was already being compared to Nixon's blitzing of McGovern in 1972 by more than twenty-three points and Johnson's twenty-three–point victory over Barry Goldwater in 1964. The point spread between Mondale and Reagan still seemed too wide to me. If we were about to be swept away in a Republican landslide, why did these huge crowds keep turning out wherever the campaign went?

A victory for the highly popular Reagan was one thing. But would the Reaganmania sweeping the country also sweep all the Republican candidates running for national, state, and local offices with it? In the last two weeks of the campaign, both Fritz and I now expended our energies to campaign for Democrats in states where our presidential ticket didn't stand a chance. If we weren't going to win ourselves, at least we could throw our weight behind other Democrats.

"When you elect Paul Simon to the Senate it will mean a lot to everyone in Illinois," I said to a rally in West Frankfort, Illinois, on October 30. In Upper Darby, Pennsylvania, later that day, the candidate would be my congressional colleague Bob Edgar. "Are we going to win in November? Are we going to reelect Bob Edgar? Are we going to send Walter Mondale to the White House and Ronald Reagan back to the ranch? You bet we are."

The words were getting a bit too familiar to me. And I almost blew it in Upper Darby. The hecklers there kept interrupting me, jumping in on my sentences, and I got not only distracted but rushed. A vote for Reagan, I was saying, was a vote for extending the arms race into space and a retreat from human rights, while a vote for Walter Mondale was a vote to stop the arms race, preserve the environment, protect Social Security, reduce the deficits, and promote human rights. But instead of saying "If you support all these things, then vote for Walter Mondale," I messed up and said "then vote for Ronald

Rea . . ." before catching myself. I almost died. "My God, how could I do that?" I exclaimed, turning away from the microphone. "Well, at least you know I'm human," I said back to the crowd, who by now were roaring with laughter.

In a last-minute appeal for the women's vote, we decided to say yes to the invitation Phil Donahue had extended to all four candidates to appear on his show. Again, I was the only one to accept, indeed the only vice-presidential or presidential candidate ever to accept—and not without some resistance from my campaign staff. The show was unstructured, they warned, a potential liability to any candidate. And Donahue's style was often more provocatively personal than substantive. Some of my staff argued that Donahue's talk show was pure puffery and would not show me as being properly vice-presidential. Others argued that his viewing audience—seven million traditional women—was exactly the constituency my candidacy had originally been designed to capture. The latter won. And I was anxious to do whatever might help at this late date.

But instead of discussing the issues or even the significance of my candidacy to women, Donahue spent at least half the show on my finances, my family background, and John's finances. I was getting increasingly disappointed at the turn the show was taking. When Donahue quoted the *Wall Street Journal* as saying John had received "a fee" as the result of the Port Authority Credit Union loan, I misheard him instead as having called John "a thief."

"They did not say that my husband was a thief," I snapped at Donahue, turning to the audience for clarification when he denied saying it.

But I had been wrong. And I apologized. It had been an unnecessary moment. I was getting too tired. I was making mistakes, and there was still half an hour of the program to go.

The inevitable "crying" question came up. Why was it so important to Phil Donahue, to everyone, to know whether a vice-presidential candidate could be forced to tears? "Does it make any difference to anyone whether or not I cried?" I responded. "There are certain things, Phil, which are personal."

Finally, it took a question from the audience to get the show on a more substantive track. Weren't the Democrats trying "a desperation tactic," a man asked, when we said Ronald Reagan was leading the country ever closer to nuclear war?"

"I didn't say Ronald Reagan was going to plunge us into a nuclear war," I quickly corrected him. The issue was our sitting down and talking to the Soviet Union before it was too late. "Did you think Richard Nixon was weak? General Eisenhower was weak?"

"No," the man replied. "They made an effort."

"That is precisely the point," I said to him. "They made an effort and this Administration has not."

In the last days of the campaign, the historical significance of my candidacy became more important to me. Whether we won or lost, I would still go down on the books as the first woman vice-presidential candidate of a major party, an extraordinary fact that I often overlooked in the heat of the campaign. And four days before the election, I started recording my thoughts. "Today is November 2, and I'm finally picking up on this thing," the first transcript begins. "I should have done this all along."

My recollections began with the speech I had made at the temple in New York on October 29 and went right through the final eight days of the campaign, all of which were spent on the road. But my recording kept getting interrupted. "This plane is getting to be like a zoo," I said in the air en route to California again. "One of the television crew guys has just 'skysurfed' by me in the aisle. What they do is they take the emergency cards out of the seat pocket, and while the plane climbs, they slide down the aisle like they're on a surfboard."

Half an hour later I was interrupted again. "Laura Zaccaro has just brought the entire press corps dancing up the aisle in a conga line with Robert Kur from NBC right behind her. Incredible. All the national press, all kinds of people including the staff, dancing up and down the aisles. They want me to get up, too, but I want to tell you something. Nothing is left off the record, so they're going to have to have their good time without me."

Joyce Allen, a dynamite camerawoman for ABC, agreed with me. "You're right about not getting out there with them, because one of them is liable to write about it. And who knows what could happen to affect the election in the next four days?" she said.

I taped my recollections of the rally we'd had in Erie, Pennsylvania, right after the Temple Kehilath Jeshurun speech, the rally we'd gone on to in Baltimore at the Head Start day-care center in the Union Baptist Church, and then the fund-raiser that evening with Barbara Mikulski and Maryland Senator Paul Sarbanes. I had been on stage at the day-care center with the most gorgeous little kids, only three or four years old. They had behaved themselves throughout, even after having waited an hour for the event to begin. When I left, the organizers gave me a big scroll with all the kids' little handprints on it, reminding me of a handprint I still have of John, Jr.'s, from kindergarten. "I read my son's fortune from his handprint when he was five," I told the kids, "and I'll read yours, too. You will have lives of opportunity and peace, and that's what I want for you."

The whole evening in Baltimore had been one of excitement and enthusiasm. I was the first national politician ever to come to this black community, the organizers kept telling me. I was very glad I had gone. We had been a little concerned about our black constituency after Jesse Jackson had lost in the primaries, worried that support for the Democratic ticket might have dimmed. But I was wrong. Donna Brazile, the former Jackson coordinator who was working with us, was most helpful in organizing this event.

"Our future depends on how we vote next week," I told them. "We aren't voting for just the next four weeks or the next four months or even the next four years. We are voting for the rest of this century." But they were way ahead of me; they had been registering new voters and working incredibly hard.

Back in Pennsylvania the next day, on my eighth campaign visit, Congressman Bob Borski met me at the airport and asked if I would go into his district just as I was doing for others.

"What do you want me to do?" I asked him.

"A subway stop," he said.

Subway stop? I thought when I finished running for Congress that I was never going to have to stand at another subway stop. As a national candidate I had graduated at least to airports. But at seven-fifteen a.m., there I was working the subways again, shaking hands, feeling amazed as always that people on their way to work stop to say hello, wish you luck, give you a kiss. Congresswoman Barbara Kennelly was traveling with us on this campaign swing, and she, too, showed up at the subway stop, where people were lined up for a block.

"Just like your wedding, huh?" she yelled at me.

"No, Barbara," I said to her gravely. "There are no envelopes."

At an Italian market later in the day, my spirits were buoyed again. The people there were just so excited and enthusiastic. I was one of theirs, coming home. And so was the congressman I was stumping for, Tom Foglietta, as well as the entire upcoming Democratic slate. *"Noi poniamo i nostri sogni nei figli—e con fede in dio, lavoriamo affinche questi sogni si realizzino"*—we place our dreams in our children, and with faith in God we work toward the realization of those dreams—I said to the crowd.

There were so many things that struck me in these last days, so many images that stood out. At an indoor meeting with unemployed families in Racine, Wisconsin, I talked about the deficits, the Pentagon budget, and our trade imbalance. But understandably, the people were caught up in their own problems. If you're unemployed, you worry about unemployment. If you're hungry, you worry about eating. And if you're sick, you worry about medical bills.

On the way out, a woman came up to me with two beautiful little girls, around eight and ten. "My daughter is a diabetic, the medication costs a hundred and forty dollars, and my husband is out of work," she said to me. "I can't get the money from the government because of the budget cuts. It's a matter of life and death for her." And the poor woman started to cry.

"Why didn't you tell your story during the course of the meeting?" I asked her.

"I couldn't in front of the television cameras," she said. "I can't talk in public. But please, please, can you help me?"

That's what I was getting throughout the country, people hanging on to me, saying, "You've got to help." I had helped them as a member of Congress by voting against the Reagan budget proposals, but only if we won the election would I be able to help them again. I felt so frustrated—and sad.

It was Halloween and on the way from Racine to Kenosha with Wisconsin Governor Tony Earl for a UAW rally, we stopped the motorcade to pass out candy to the kids all done up for trick-or-treating. The picture brought back floods of memories of my own children going off as Raggedy Ann and Andy. Later, in Evanston, Illinois, after an overflow rally at Northwestern University, a group of Democratic volunteers decided that the plane needed some ghouling up. One of the volunteers, Joan Rapp, bought balloons and witches and paper pumpkins for us. She also bought a special mask for me to wear as a joke—Ronald Reagan. Now wouldn't that have made quite a picture . . . ?

In Cincinnati, I got up at six-fifteen to go to Mass, since it was a Holy Day of Obligation. The church was absolutely beautiful, and when I went up to receive Communion, the priest said, "Peace be with you and good luck, Mrs. Ferraro."

After mass, Dick Celeste commented about the vote. "It doesn't look good," he said. "The polls were moving up and now they're moving back."

But I shrugged it off. "I am not going to get discouraged," I told him. I still wasn't convinced there weren't votes out there that we hadn't counted, that the pollsters hadn't counted; we were going to get them.

Yet everybody wanted to talk about losing. In an interview later, a reporter spoke of nothing else. "What are you going to do if you lose?" she said.

"We don't intend to lose," I replied.

"But what happens to you if you do lose?" she persisted.

I couldn't believe it. "I haven't thought about it," I said.

"What do you mean you haven't thought about it?" she said quite rudely. "You mean you haven't thought about running against Al D'Amato for the Senate?"

"I don't know if I can impress upon you sufficiently that I'm not interested in anything else right now except winning this election," I said in a steely voice. "We are talking about the future of this country, my children's future, my grandchildren's future." Why should I concede the election four days before the election? There was always a chance, however slim.

I felt that way right through the rally Fritz and I had on Thursday, November 1, in the garment district in New York, when close to 200,000 people turned out, including Theodore Bikel, actress Joanne Woodward, and her husband, Paul Newman, who was sitting next to my mother.

"Thank you for all the wonderful work you've done on the nuclear freeze. You're terrific," I said to Joanne, who is an activist on the issue. I sneaked a look at her husband. And it was true. Paul Newman did have the most gorgeous blue eyes you'd ever want to see.

I had ridden to the rally with Fritz, the last time I would see him before the election. He, too, was having trouble believing the polls as we exchanged impressions of the crowds we'd been seeing, the enthusiasm we'd been feeling. "Fritz really thinks we can win," my notes read, "though I don't know if he's as convinced as I am." We talked a little bit about what we'd do on election day—just a hundred and twenty hours away.

"What do you want me to do on Wednesday?" I asked him.

"If we win, you'll come out to North Oaks and we'll have a joint press conference," he told me. "If we lose, we'll be on our own."

But of course we both knew. We just weren't ready to admit it to each other—or to ourselves. At the rally in New York, the campaign good-byes were starting. John Reilly gave me a kiss. "You've been absolutely fabulous," he told me. "Everything you've done has been great." It was classy. I was aware of how difficult my personal problems had been for the Mondale people. Less than four months ago, Reilly had flown to San Francisco on the eve of the Democratic Convention to give me the final vice-presidential checkout. It seemed like five years.

I also had to start to prepare my mother to say good-bye to a Democratic victory and to her dream of her daughter, the Vice President. "There's a real possibility that we might lose the election," I said to her in the car after the rally.

She was shocked. "What makes you say that?" she said in dismay.

"The polls are not good," I told her. "But don't worry. We're not going to get discouraged. We're going to keep on doing the things we have to because we believe in them. But if it does happen—if we lose—don't be upset. We'll just go on to the next thing the way we always have."

She refused to believe it. "I'm praying for you," she said. "You'll see."

I took her out to the airport with me so she could at least see what the plane we had used as a flying office for three months was like. If only she hadn't been so afraid of flying. I would have loved to have taken her with me those last few days of the campaign.

And on November 1, back we went to California. En route I worked on a very important speech for women I was going to deliver the next morning in Van Nuys, and refined my Christmas card list, adding the people who had helped so much on this campaign. For the picture, I chose a wonderful one of the whole family at the Convention the night I accepted the nomination. Laura was not too nuts about the way she looked, but it was the best photo we had. It broke my heart every time I looked at the picture of John. He had been so happy at that convention, so filled with enthusiasm for the future. It was unbelievable what my candidacy had cost my family.

Thinking back now, it is amazing how up I was feeling, what little triumphs and fun I was still discovering at this eleventh hour, as we headed west for the second time in a week. At a rally in the pouring rain in San Francisco the next day, Congress-woman Barbara Boxer put a raincoat on me, and speaker of the California House Willie Brown held an umbrella over my head while I spoke—but what I really needed was windshield wipers for my glasses. " 'Duster' [my Secret Service code name] will need a hair dryer for her 'do,' " I overheard the advance man saying into his walkie-talkie.

I had to laugh. " 'Duster' will not need a hair dryer because her 'do' does it all on its own," I told him.

The crowd in San Francisco on November 2 was unbeliev-able, over twenty thousand people, some of them hanging out of windows. It was very, very exciting, with people screaming, "We're with you—we're going to win!" I spoke on civil rights, human rights, and the tragedy going on in Ethiopia. Never has a crowd been more responsive.

When the rally was over, Barbara Roberts Mason brought a man in a wheelchair over to me. He had been injured in an industrial accident and was a paraplegic, she told me, but he believed so much in my candidacy that he'd spent almost all his money on advertising for our campaign. I was always amazed at the number of handicapped people who came to our rallies, and I tried in each instance to stop and talk to them, as I did now with this man.

"Thank you so much for all your help," I said to him as he reached out to touch me.

"Thank *you*," he said. "I never thought I would get to meet you."

We all have our heroines, and one of mine was and is Sally Ride, one of the astronauts who had been orbiting the earth while I had been debating George Bush. Now the first woman in space was not only back on the ground but in San Francisco, where we met for a private lunch. An employee of NASA, Sally couldn't be seen as endorsing a candidate of either party—literally couldn't be seen with me at all, even down to riding in my car. I was delighted that Laura and John, Jr., who were with me, would have an opportunity to meet this historic first. We talked about a recent poll that had found me to be the number-one role model for women in the country, just ahead of her.

"Hey, Sally, not bad being first and second," I said to her.

She laughed. "I don't mind being second to you," she said, giving me a campaign bumper sticker she'd autographed for me that read: "Mondale/Ferraro—Second Giant Step for Mankind."

Women had been very much on my mind all day. Earlier that morning I had delivered what was probably the most emotional speech of the campaign at Valley College, in Van Nuys. I'd wanted to speak to women about women, explore what my candidacy had meant to all of us and what it meant for the future. Laura had been asked to introduce me, and she had written her remarks on the plane coming out. John, Jr., was a little upset that she had been asked, not he, but this was a women's event. Donna probably would have introduced me if she'd been with us, but she was campaigning on her own in Arkansas. "We have a chance of winning there," she'd told me. "If we lose the state and I hadn't gone, I'd feel terrible."

When Laura introduced me to the audience in Van Nuys, my heart swelled for this eighteen-year-old who just five months ago couldn't bring herself to speak in front of the assembly at her school. "One thing that remains implanted in my memory about growing up in the Zaccaro household," Laura said, "is the unparalleled importance placed upon eating a solid breakfast," Laura said, "Throughout my childhood, my mom would wake up half an hour early to make our family breakfast.

"As I got older, I began to cherish my sleep more. Consequently, I could no longer motivate myself to get out of bed to make it to the breakfast table. But that didn't stop my mom from fighting for the cause of my breakfast. As I would say goodbye to go to school, she would place in my hand an aluminum foil package and a thermos. The package was a toasted English muffin; the thermos was filled with juice.

"Even last Monday on the campaign trail, she held up the motorcade so that I could have time to eat. While I was finishing a roll, I heard her aides saying the equivalent of 'Gerry, you're crazy. We have the Phil Donahue show to make. Forget the food.'

"As I look back on that event, I realize that it is exactly that 'craziness' that has kept our family sane. One thing I must commend my mom for, aside from her professional career, is her ability not to get wrapped up in this whole campaign and forget about my dad, my brother, my sister, and me. My mom has juggled career and family and has not compromised the latter one bit.

"Please welcome the Queen of Breakfast, my mom, Geraldine Ferraro."

Then it was my turn on a more sober note. "When we go to the polls next Tuesday, remember that Eleanor Roosevelt was thirty-six before she was allowed to cast her first vote. What a waste," I told the audience in Van Nuys. "She should never have been barred from choosing public officials. She should have been one." As I spoke on, I realized half the audience seemed to be on the verge of tears. "From Abigail Adams to the women of Seneca Falls, this moment is a triumph for all those who stood for the cause of equality through the years," I said, watching a middle-aged man nod "yes" until actual tears began to stream down his face. "From Harriet Tubman and the abolitionists of the underground railroad to the suffragists, this campaign proves what Susan B. Anthony always knew: Because our cause is just, we cannot fail."

This was my chance to explain what my candidacy had been all about, that options had been opened to women that had never existed before. We no longer lived in either-or situations. We could be whatever we chose to be. "We can win Olympic gold medals *and* coach our daughters' soccer teams. We can walk in space *and* help our children take their first steps. We can negotiate trade agreements *and* manage family budgets," I said. "We can be corporate executives and also wives and mothers. We can be doctors and also bake cookies with our six-year-old future scientists. The choices are unlimited. We can be all these things. But we don't have to be any of them."

I looked over to see my own staff, female and male, now crying. One of my speech writers, Richard Medley, had been standing near me on the stage, but he, too, had been so caught up in the emotion of the moment that he had moved behind me, where his tears would not be as public.

"My candidacy is not just for me, it's for everyone," I concluded. "It's not just a symbol. It's a breakthrough. It's not just a statement. It's a bond between women all over America." I wished that someone in that auditorium was not crying. I was beginning to get a lump in my throat myself. "My candidacy says America believes in equality," I managed to finish firmly. "And the time for that equality is now."

There were only three days left to go. My whole family was traveling with me now, which was great. But time became a blur. "Gerry, you look tired," my husband said to me as we walked into the holding room before my speech in Dayton.

"Oh, John, you know how it is at the end of the day," I told him.

Laura looked shocked. "Mom, it's only nine-thirty in the morning," she pointed out. And on we went to Green Bay.

By the time we got to Chicago, I was completely worn out, as was everyone else on the plane. So what do you do when you're exhausted? Give a party, of course. I invited the members of the traveling press for cocktails, along with the off-duty Secret Service agents and my campaign staff. It was the reporters' turn then, and downstairs I went to their disco party in the hotel. I took pictures of them. They took pictures of me. Finally we could unwind.

It was two a.m. by the time I got to bed, seven-thirty when I got up the next morning to go to Mass. And for once, except for one local reporter, the traveling press decided to sleep. The only reason they followed me to church, anyway, was to be sure to get the story if I were shot. But they had finally dropped in their tracks.

"She's not going to get shot at that hour," I overheard one say to another. "I'm staying in bed."

And off I went to church, where, to my dismay, a photographer from the *Chicago Tribune* clicked picture after picture of my family and of the priest when he came up to deliver the homily.

My religion is very personal to me, and I did not want it flaunted during the campaign. I had laid down the rule at the beginning that no one was to take pictures of me or my family in church—and no one was going to start now. I wanted to concentrate on the mass, and I did not want to distract other people who were there to pray. "Get him out of here," I finally muttered to the Secret Service, and out the photographer went, still clicking.

In Illinois a Gallup poll now had us down only two points. And Reagan had finally given us a real opening. The Republicans had been beating up on us from the beginning when Fritz had said up front at the convention that he was going to have to raise taxes—and so would Ronald Reagan. For three months Reagan had walked around saying he was absolutely not going to raise taxes—until a leak from the Treasury Department four days before the election suggested otherwise.

"Yesterday we found out the truth," I told a labor rally in Joliet, Illinois, on November 3. "It turns out the President wants to eliminate your deduction for state and local taxes—including income taxes as well as real-estate taxes. That means under Ronald Reagan's plan you'll be taxed twice on what you earn. And just think what that would mean for average Americans who wants to buy a home." As usual, Reagan's attitude was to take from the poor to give to the rich. Under this outrageous new plan, I went on, unemployment and workers' compensation benefits would be taxed as well. "That's hitting below the belt," I said to the increasingly outraged audience. "I say it's unfair to increase the burden on those who are already hurt or jobless."

But the clock was running out. Even when Reagan had been confronted with the tax-plan leak from his own Treasury Department, he had begged off responding to it, saying, "I'm not going to comment until I have the report." And when was the report due? In December. A month after the election.

But still, the predicted Reagan landslide seemed unbelievable to me, even forty-eight hours before the election. On November

4, the crowds in Michigan, in Rhode Island, in Connecticut, and in Ohio seemed more enthusiastic than ever. Connecticut was hopeless for us. We knew that. But we went in anyway for Bill Ratchford, who was in trouble in his congressional race, just as we had that same day in Michigan for incumbent Senator Carl Levin and in Rhode Island for Senator Claiborne Pell. In spite of the polls, the whole day was a triumph. In Connecticut, the Mayor of Waterbury wanted me to speak in a Knights of Columbus hall that seated six hundred people. Give us a gymnasium, we said. We'll fill it. You'll never get three thousand people out, he told us. We did.

Again I voiced my support for Fritz, citing his twenty-year record of public service, which included his authorship of the Fair Housing Act of 1968, the landmark Child Care Act in the early 1970s, his stand for migrant workers even though they were hardly a large Minnesota constituency, his lifelong fight for arms control. "He's a lawyer, not an actor," I said to every crowd that day. "He levels with the American people and deals in fact, not fiction. He lives in the real world, not on Fantasy Island. He's a good man. He's a courageous man. And when he asked me to be his running mate, he did more for equal opportunity in one day than Ronald Reagan has done in four long years."

I had done everything I could to get Fritz Mondale elected. But the Republicans still weren't through with him. Maintaining his record of bad taste, George Bush had now turned his sights on Fritz.

"Yesterday, George Bush said, 'I'd hate to be on a ticket with Walter Mondale this year,'" I said incredulously to the crowds two days before the election. "Well, George, let me put your mind at ease. We wouldn't have you."

On the night of the fourth Fritz called me in Cleveland. I was always glad to talk to him. But my notes on that conversation reveal that I saw the writing on the wall. "We talked about what was left of the campaign," I had taped. "I was in Cleveland again, and I don't even know where he was. Maybe the two of us were just trying to kid each other, but our chances, we knew, were extremely slim. What we were trying to do was at least come out with a respectable showing."

For a moment the next morning, my hopes skyrocketed. A Harris poll released Monday, November 5, started: "In a dramatic eleventh-hour turn, the race for the presidency is narrowing." Reagan's lead had dropped in the last few days from nineteen points to twelve. When measured on the basis of the negative vote—the people who were voting against, rather than for the candidate—Reagan's edge had dropped even further, to seven points.

Democrats were leading in the races for the House, the survey went on, and in a last-minute reversal, for the Senate as well. The gender-gap spread was widening. Men were still going for Reagan over Mondale by a twenty-four–point margin, but the margin of women for Reagan had dropped from an eleven-point lead only the week before to a "razor-thin" margin now of just one point. That shift, coupled with Harris's assertion that the likelihood of both women and blacks voting was increasing, while that of men and young people was not, threw new doubt on the outcome of the election.

All day long I was on a seesaw of expectation. At an eight-thirty a.m. rally with senior citizens in Cleveland, the crowds for the first time were smaller, and I felt it was all over. If the voters had really thought I was going to be the next Vice President, they would have been there. As we left Cleveland, we began to focus on the fact that the election the next day was hopeless. Until we got to Pittsburgh. The crowds there at noon were huge and wildly enthusiastic. We were convinced that we would at least win Pennsylvania. Between the farmers and the steelworkers, who were really suffering, there was no way the state could go for the Republicans.

But what about the rest of the country? The final polls seemed conclusive. We weren't going to make it. In Pittsburgh after the rally I met with the women strategists of my campaign to discuss damage control. We didn't want women to be blamed for the loss, which we knew by this time was going to be a big one. Our internal polls showed a gender-gap vote of eight points, which in a close race could have made a difference. But with an overall twelve points between Reagan and Mondale on the presidential level, this was hardly a close race.

That day we concentrated on the positives, many of which I learned about for the first time. We had raised a record amount of money. We had drawn twenty-six thousand new contributors to the Democratic party, who had not existed before. We'd made women more politically aware and truly, I think, opened the doors of opportunity. "Next time it might be a woman running for President, though not this woman," my notes from that meeting read. "But there will probably be a woman running for the presidency in 1988."

My staff was as strung out by now as I was. To relax during the long months of the campaign, Francis O'Brien had taken to ironing. Making rough places smooth soothed him, and now he started on John Sasso's shirts, even packing them for him so they wouldn't come out rewrinkled, as they had here in Pittsburgh only a day after Francis had first ironed them. I had had to rely on Francis's skill as a valet myself, when my skirt looked as if I'd slept in it. Francis had come to the rescue and quickly run his iron over it, so I could arrive at the rally neatly dressed. If we had to lose the election, at least it wouldn't be because we looked rumpled.

And on to our last rally, in Jersey City, where again I did not sense the energy from the crowds that had followed us right up to this last day. The support flowing from my colleagues Senator Bill Bradley, Senator Frank Lautenberg, and Congressman Frank Guarini, however, was absolutely wonderful.

"You've done the best you could," Frank Lautenberg said to me. "No matter what happens, you come out OK."

I left for my final speech in New York, feeling totally heartened by my colleagues. Every state I had gone into—and back to—during the campaign, the Democratic members of Congress had been there for me. What a difference it had made.

In the car going into New York, I made it very clear to the kids that in spite of everything I'd done, and every thing they'd done, we were going to lose the election. Of the three, I was the most concerned about John, Jr.; he had been the one who was optimistic to the end. Like my mother, John, Jr., refused to accept the polls. With the typical ghoulish humor of the young, he had called me at one point in the campaign when an NBC poll had us behind by thirty-two points, Harris by eighteen points, and Gallup by some other incomprehensible number, to announce that if the trend continued, we should be behind by one hundred points on Election Day. He kept reminding us about the Truman-Dewey presidential race, which had been called wrong up to the famous headline in the newspaper. And he had talked to me about his working with the transition team. But it was time to face reality.

I felt very subdued when I arrived at Marymount College on election eve. I had deliberately chosen to do a small event that night. I didn't want a big impersonal crowd. I wanted my family around me, my old classmates, and the college teachers who had meant so much to me. I especially wanted to honor my mother, who had been so bounced around by my candidacy. It was important to me to acknowledge publicly the fact that I never would have become the first woman vice-presidential candidate or a congresswoman or even a lawyer had it not been for the sacrifices she had made for me. Now she had been the one sacrificed during the campaign, and I wanted to make it up to her.

The campaign was finally over, and I could say what I really wanted to say to my family. I had reviewed the speech perhaps forty times the night before, knowing it now almost by heart. I didn't want to cry in public. But I also knew how I'd feel when I spoke what was on the paper—and in my heart.

From the beginning, there were tears in the audience. "Tonight we come to the end of a journey without precedent in our nation's history," I said. "Tomorrow the nation votes. This is the clearest choice in fifty years."

My education had been invaluable in making possible the choices I'd had in my life, I went on to say, as had the tradition of my parents, who believed they should give their children a better chance than they had of achieving the American dream, regardless of the cost. And then I spoke about my mother.

"Because of her sacrifice, I had the privilege to attend this college," I said. "Because of that dedication, I am what I am today. And tonight, I would like to say to her from the bottom of my heart: Thank you for everything." I turned to face her then. And the practice hadn't helped. "I hope you are proud of me," I said, my voice breaking for the first time in the campaign. "I will always be proud of you."

I had to look away from her to regain control. Taking a steadying breath, I continued to speak, pointing out the changes that had taken place in my life—and my classmates' lives. "Ours was perhaps the first generation of American women free to choose our own careers," I said. "Against that background of achievement and progress, every woman of my generation has felt discrimination. All of us know women our age who were denied opportunities they had earned. And despite the progress we've seen in our lifetime, we want for our daughters more freedom to develop their talents than we had.

"Let's be clear about this," I said. "Sexism has no place in American life. Racism has no right to a home in our land. Ageism has no role in our values. And if there's one thing my candidacy stands for, it is that Americans should be able to reach as far as our dreams will take us."

And I spoke about my own family. "The voters decide in a few hours," I said. "But yesterday, today, and tomorrow, my concern is also for my family." I turned to face them. "In the last three months, my children and my husband were my mainstays, just as they have been for the last twenty-four years." Donna and Laura were in tears, and John and Johnny were close to it. Again I had to look away. "They have encouraged me, comforted me, loved me, and backed me all the way. I couldn't have done this without them," I said.

"It hasn't always been easy," I admitted, "but it's been worth it for all of us. Even if this moment were frozen in time, this campaign would still have made a difference. My candidacy has said to women, the doors of opportunity are opening. And for me, life can never be the same, because I have been touched by the support, the love, and the goodwill of men and women all over America."

But the business at hand was the election of the next President of the United States. And again, I reached deep inside me for the words. "No election in recent memory has mattered more to our country than the one we hold tomorrow," I said. "We're choosing between peace and the rising risk of war, between freedom and intrusion into our personal lives, between fairness and growing inequity. These are the choices we face. And here at Marymount Manhattan, where I first learned to make serious choices, I ask you to pull the lever for peace, raise your voices for jobs, vote for fairness, and pick a President who will fight for the American people. His name is Walter Mondale."

*　　*　　*

There was nothing more to do, except to accept a terrific poster signed by the students reading "Some Women Are Born Leaders" and to hear that the senior class of 1985 was dedicating its yearbook to me. I was pleased and honored and worn to the bone. Finally I could go home to sleep, knowing, as I had pledged from day one, that I had done everything I possibly could against Reagan, for Fritz. The 1984 presidential campaign was over, with all its briefing books and position papers, press conferences and interviews, hecklers and supporters, issues and innuendo. The choice, just a few hours away now, was up to the American people.

the office to receive the Medal of Honor. Their loss really put my anticipated loss in perspective.

You must record your emotions on the day of the election, Bob Barnett had told me, thinking of history. "Are you sorry it is going to end?" he'd asked me. No, I was glad it was over. I wouldn't have to wake up dreading the morning headlines. The campaign had exacted a cruel personal toll that would take months to clear up. We had paid dearly for my candidacy. And at that point we still didn't know how high the price was going to be.

I had one more campaign stop to make before it was all over, but this time it was as much for Tom Manton as it was for me. I had always spent Election Day with my senior citizens, and I wanted this Election Day to be no different. I also wanted to introduce Tom to the senior citizens at the Ridgewood-Bushwick senior center. He would represent them now. Off we went to our meeting, which went on and on while the seniors heaped all kinds of gifts on me, including the biggest cannoli possible, with about fifty little cannoli inside it, cookies, and an honorary membership at the center. By the time we got to the honorary membership I felt old enough to take advantage of it. I was really tired. It had been a long four months.

But it was time to get ready to go now to the New York Hilton to await the election result. After returning briefly to my office to sign some letters and autographs, I went home. I gave my hair my last vice-presidential shampoo, got dressed, and gathered up John, the kids, my mother, and my mother-in-law. At six p.m. we set out for the hotel.

It was like the last day of summer camp, with everyone wanting pictures of everybody else, mostly me, the head camper. I was so grateful to the people who had worked on my advance teams throughout the country. They had been totally dedicated. Many of them had flown in to New York for election night, and now in the Hilton I gladly had my picture taken with them. They had been fantastic, each one of them, and I thanked them all individually.

By election night we only hoped to pick up a few states— Minnesota, Massachusetts, New York, Pennsylvania, possibly Illinois, and maybe even Iowa. But who knew how it would all turn out? We might just as well have fun while we waited. So my staff came into the suite we'd taken for the night, ironically called the presidential suite, along with my family, friends, my congressional staff, New York elected officials, my congressional colleagues—everybody—while Francis O'Brien tried to organize what quickly turned into a mob scene. My Secret Service detail was there, too, and I posed for pictures with each agent, then in groups, and with the different shifts.

"No matter what happens, you're a winner," one of the agents said to me. But dinner wasn't. The election results coming in now on television were just slightly worse than the prime ribs we had ordered.

One after another, states were going for Reagan. One network map of the United States was entirely blue for the Republicans. On another network the color motif was a blanket of red. It was unbelievable. I watched John, Jr., munch his way nervously through the hors d'oeuvres. As every state in which he'd campaigned—New York, Massachusetts, West Virginia, North Carolina, Delaware—fell, he'd groan and take another fistful of food. And we still hadn't heard from the West Coast.

It was ridiculous. We couldn't just sit there like corpses watching the Democratic ticket being slaughtered on television. Impulsively I sat on Johnny's lap to cheer him up, whereupon Laura got on my lap and Donna on hers. *Life* magazine snapped a photo of this family pile, John laughing on the couch beside us, my mother and mother-in-law looking on with big grins. The picture looks as if we had all just come home happily exhausted from a family wedding. Which is exactly what we felt like. Except that on election night it was more like a wake.

One by one, the elected Democratic officials stopped by to pay their condolences—Mario Cuomo, Ed Koch, Pat Moynihan, Charlie Rangel, Ted Weiss, Gary Ackerman, and Jim Scheuer. The women came too—Carol Bellamy, Bella Abzug, Gloria Steinem. All night long, people were filing in and out. Each of them was supposed to have five minutes with us in the suite and then go on to the ballroom, where I was scheduled later to make either my victory speech or my concession.

Talk about a wake. All these officials felt as obligated to murmur their sympathies to me as I felt obligated to receive them. This is craziness, I thought. But just as there had been a rhythm, a sort of prescribed dance of celebration at the convention four months before, now we were locked into a rhythm of loss. The convention and election night were bookends framing the most extraordinary four months of my life.

Fritz called twice from North Oaks. "I think we've got something going—a trend," he joked during the first call. "Minnesota just fell into line."

I was relieved to be able to banter back to him. "Next time I see you, I'm going to give you a kiss and I don't care who's watching," I told him.

We talked about our concession statements. I'd been working on mine that afternoon, I said. I wanted it to be very up. This was a time for healing.

When Fritz called again later, he told me he was about to call Ronald Reagan to concede and suggested I call Bush. In the age-old political custom of courtesy, I got the Vice President on the line to congratulate him. But he sounded absolutely strange; he seemed not to know what to say. "We'll have to have lunch when you're in Washington," he said, as if we were old school chums with a lot of news to catch up on. And then, saying, "Barbara wants to speak to you," he handed the phone to his wife. "You're a very fine lady," she said to me.

It was time then for me to go into the ballroom to make my concession remarks. For the last time in the campaign I heard the familiar litany of "Gerr-eee! Gerr-eee!" swelling from the crowd. It felt good. But in the days ahead I wouldn't miss it. I just wanted to go home, to relax with my family. There was only one more public appearance for this vice-presidential candidate to make. Around eleven-thirty p.m. I delivered my final remarks.

"Tonight the campaign ends. The race is over. This is not a moment for partisan statements," I said. "It is a moment to celebrate our democracy and to think of our country. The American people have put their trust in President Reagan. And in the interests of the nation, with hope for the future, I ask all Americans to join together, work together, and pledge our support for our President in the search for a more just society, a strong America, and a world at peace."

I thanked Fritz Mondale not only for the public service he had performed for the good of the country for the last twenty-five years, but for the battle he had waged for equal opportunity in 1984. "For two centuries, candidates have run for President," I went on. "Not one from a major party ever asked a woman to be his running mate—until Walter Mondale. Campaigns, even if you lose them, do serve a purpose. My candidacy has said the days of discrimination are numbered. American women will never be second-class citizens again."

The campaign had tried to focus the country's attention on critical matters—the danger of the nuclear arms race, the needs of our changing economy, the millions of Americans unemployed— and overlooked. It had not been in vain. "I think America can be the vanguard of change," I said firmly. "I have faith in the American people and I believe in this country. Our society is the fairest on earth, but can work even harder for fairness. Our nation is at peace, but we can do more to reduce the risk of war. America is a great nation, but if there's one thing our campaign has stood for, it is that our country can be even greater. That cause—our country's cause—is never finished. And I, for one, will continue to work for it."

I didn't want to risk a tear on election night, so I didn't single out my family again. This was the moment to go forward. "All of us can go to bed tonight confident that we did everything we could to win this election," I concluded. "So let me say to our supporters and my staff, my family and my friends: We fought hard. We did what was right. And we made a difference. Be proud of what we have done. Thank you from the bottom of my heart. Thank you very much."

Of course there were tears from the volunteers and staff members and supporters crowded now on the ballroom floor. But not from me. We had done everything we could.

Historically, I had no regrets. As Geraldine Ferraro, I had received the highest honor to date bestowed on a woman by her party and had tried to carry it with pride. Personally, though, I wasn't so sure. As the mother of Laura and Donna Zaccaro, my candidacy had been well worth it, expanding their life options a thousandfold. As the mother of John Zaccaro, Jr., my candidacy as the first Italian-American on a presidential ticket had given him new pride in his heritage. But as Mrs. John Zaccaro, I had my doubts.

I was torn about John. But my debate within myself lasted only until John and I appeared at a political fund-raiser several months later. I began to answer the inevitable question about the toll my candidacy had taken on my family. But when I started to express my doubts about whether it had been worth it as Mrs. John Zaccaro, my husband interrupted me. "We have no regrets," John said firmly. That sums it up.

REFLECTIONS

"There are thousands of talented women who should be in politics but are not. And it's our job to bring them in."

—Hubert Humphrey Institute of Public Affairs,
University of Minnesota, March 14, 1985.

A T FIRST READING, THE election results were grim. As predicted, Reagan won by an eighteen-point margin. In overlapping categories he won the vote of the majority of Catholics, who make up twenty-five percent of the electorate; of Yuppies (younger people—under forty—with college degrees), representing twenty-three percent of all voters; of moderates, who make up forty percent of the vote; of independents, who each account for twenty percent of the voting public; and of women. The only blocs to vote solidly Mondale-Ferraro were nonwhites in general and blacks in particular, who voted eighty-seven percent and ninety-two percent respectively for the Democratic presidential ticket; Jewish voters; and all those earning under ten thousand dollars a year. Union members supported us by a narrow margin.

There were disappointments but no surprises in the regional breakdown of the vote as well. In the East we lost by eight points, in the Midwest by sixteen, in the South by twenty-six, and in the West by twenty points. Reagan carried the suburbs, which are home to fifty-one percent of all Republicans, while Fritz and I took many of the cities. Reagan's hometown of Los Angeles voted for us, as did the voters in Chicago, Cleveland,

Seattle, Denver, New Orleans, Milwaukee, Detroit, New York, Baltimore, Philadelphia, and Washington, D.C. All in all, over thirty-six million people pulled the lever for Mondale-Ferraro, forty-one percent of all voting Americans. But over fifty-two million people voted for Reagan-Bush.

I was disappointed and surprised by the sluggish voter turnout. Both the Democrats and the Republicans had predicted that a greater number of people would vote in the election in 1984 than had in 1980, a year that had seen the lowest turnout in twenty years. But even with the addition of new voters, the total count in 1984 remained about the same. In fact, it took only about thirty percent of all eligible voters to reelect Ronald Reagan.

But was I devastated? No. No incumbent President has ever been turned out of office in a year of economic growth. The country was not presently at war. Reagan's image as the "great communicator" had remained intact, as one blunder after another just slid off him. Short of a major disaster that he couldn't grin away or shrug off helplessly, Reagan was virtually unbeatable. We had been up against one of the great "image" Presidents, whose style had been more appealing to the voters than his substance.

"The election was dominated, first to last, by four P's," George Church wrote in *Time* magazine's election issue: "Prosperity, Peace, Patriotism and Personality."

Reagan had drawn the vote. But his policies hadn't. A Gallup poll two weeks after the election found that public opinion was still heavily in favor of a mutual verifiable nuclear freeze, increased spending for social programs, the Equal Rights Amendment, and the enforcement of pollution controls—all campaign issues Reagan had come out against. During the campaign, one of the most difficult things to accept was the fact that the voters were with us on the issues but were still planning to vote for Reagan. It was just as difficult after the election. His politics of optimism, of never being the bearer of bad news, had catapulted him into popularity—and victory. Our more realistic politics had addressed the pain of a large segment of the population and the price we would all have to pay for Reagan's economic policies. But no one likes to hear bad news.

Most devastating of all, many of the voters had associated us with the Carter years of high inflation and unemployment due to the escalation in oil prices, as well as with the hostage crisis in Iran.

In this election, even college students voted against the recent past ("It was our Depression," they would explain) and for the alternative, although they agreed with Reagan on virtually nothing.

Reagan captured the presidency, but the Republican sweep stopped well short of Capitol Hill. In the 1984 election, the Republicans picked up only fourteen congressional seats, half the number the Democrats had gained in 1982—and they *lost* two Senate seats. After the 1984 elections, thirty-four of our fifty governors would be Democrats, as would two-thirds of the state legislatures. And who had voted Democrat at these levels? Every single one of the same "swing" voting blocs that had gone for Reagan—white Catholics, Yuppies, moderates, independents—and women. As more than one columnist pointed out, the American public hadn't voted in a President. They had voted in a king.

But what about the women's vote? What had happened to the gender gap? The answer was simply—nothing. The gender gap was still there. Though more women voted for Reagan than voted for us, women were still less supportive of Reagan than were men. Sixty-four percent of the male vote went to Reagan, while only fifty-five percent of women voted for him, leaving that critical gap of nine percent, which might have made a substantial difference if the total women's vote had been larger. Regionally, women in the Northeast and West voted far more for Mondale-Ferraro than did women in the South. Among specific groups, young women, working women, and black women voted heavily for us. Older women did not.

As in prior elections, the gender-gap vote was most influential in closer races on the state level. The women's vote helped reelect Senator Carl Levin in Michigan and elected Paul Simon to the Senate in Illinois, John Kerry in Massachusetts, Tom Harkin in Iowa, and a woman, Madeleine Kunin, to the governorship in Vermont. Though there has been some conjecture that the gender-gap vote died in the 1984 elections, that is not so. It is a sorry fact in this country that the defeat of one woman is often read as a judgment on all women.

But why didn't the gender gap work solidly for us? Did our defeat mean my candidacy had been denounced by women? Of course not. It demeans women to think that they would vote in a mindless bloc just because of their gender—or a candidate's gender. Women had benefited less from the improving economy than had men, but, like men, many based their vote for Reagan on what improvements there had been. Women are advocates of peace, and, like men, they voted on the fact that we were not now at war, even though Reagan's policies were seen as risking the possibility of future war. Women, too, were disarmed by Reagan's charm and, like men, they voted for his popular image. But women are no fools. Fewer of them bought the Reagan vision of America, because they understood they were not equal to men within it.

The Monday morning quarterbacking began immediately. What effect had my candidacy had, if any, on the election? While I started to unwind in St. Croix with my family, the pundits and pollsters were trying to find out whether I had been an asset, a negative, or a factor at all in the race. But no one could really tell. That I had not drawn enough of the women's vote was obvious. But then few, very few, people vote for a President based on who his Vice President will be. So that was discounted. That I had not carried my own district in Queens seemed a sensational revelation, but that also was irrelevant. In 1972 my constituents had voted for Nixon by seventy-three percent to McGovern's twenty-seven percent, a percentage they were still bragging about. In 1980 they had voted for Ronald Reagan for President by over fifty-three percent to Carter's forty percent. This election was no different. Reagan got 56.7 percent to Mondale's 43.3 percent. My constituents were voting as they always had, *for* the Republican presidential candidate, not against the Democratic vice-presidential candidate.

So what did the postelection polls reveal? Little about the past, but a lot about the future. For women, it was all positive. In a survey of five congressional districts in Utah, Kansas, Missouri, New Hampshire, and Florida, commissioned by the National Women's Political Caucus, twenty-seven percent of the respondents said they would be more likely to vote for a woman than before the 1984 election; seven percent said they would be less likely; while by far the largest percentage, sixty-four percent, said it would make no difference. And that is the most significant

for reopening the case. So where could they go? My record as a prosecutor? They tried it, only to have the *American Lawyer* print a very flattering article about my career. So they went back even further—to my years as a teacher. They actually went to the school and talked to my old neighbors. They tried everything they could to find something, but they couldn't. So what did they do? They went after my family.

Many among the press were willing accomplices in playing the Republicans' game. It is one thing to legitimately report the news, but it is quite another to knowingly print errors that support the slant of a particular story.

Three months after the election I went back to Newburgh for the first time in forty years to talk to the same people the *New York Post* had. The *Post* had reported that my father's time of death in the death notice in the newspaper had been altered at the request of the undertaker, leading to a "mystery." It was the *date of burial* that had been changed, the undertaker now told me, because my father had died on a holiday and the cemetery could not have prepared the grave in time. Big mystery!

In addition, the *Post* had insinuated that the details of my father's death from a heart condition were also suspect, implying that there might have been a cover-up. Unfortunately, the doctor who had treated him had died years before, the newspaper claimed, so no one could shed any light on the subject.

"Isn't it a shame that the doctor who attended my father died so long ago," I now said to the undertaker. He looked surprised.

"Doctor Steinthal died only two weeks ago," he said. "And I'm sure he talked to the newspapers."

I went over to the doctor's house to see his housekeeper. The newspapers had been there to interview the doctor, she confirmed. He had told them that my father had had a heart condition and that the doctor had treated him for it the night my father died; Doctor Erich Steinthal had himself signed the death certificate. There was no cover-up because there was nothing to cover up, he had told the press. (On August 7, 1985, Guy Hawtin, the *Post* investigative reporter, would admit in a radio program on WOR in New York that he had, in fact, interviewed the doctor.)

Even after the·election, the *New York Post* continued its campaign against me, an effort still riddled with errors. My family and I had gone to St. Croix two days after the election to relax, only to find a *New York Post* photographer waiting for us. Could he take pictures of us, he asked. No, I said. The election was over and we were there to unwind. The *Post* ran pictures of us anyway, taken with a telephoto lens. But the story they ran six days later was reprehensible.

"No Candidate Is An Island When You're Ferraro," blared the new headline, on November 12. During Mass at the local church in Christiansted, the article claimed, the Reverend Paul Oslovich spotted me in the pews and called abortion the sin of murder, while the church pastor, John Furey, was quoted as saying that I would have been a better Catholic if I had listened to the Pope. Moreover, the article also quoted the Bishop of the area, Edward J. Harper, as saying during a sermon the previous day that I had fallen under the spell of sin.

None of it was true. None of it. John and I had slipped into the back of the church on Sunday, not wanting to disrupt the service. Reverend Oslovich didn't even know we had been there until after the service, when he saw my family leave. His homily had not been on abortion but on confession, one of a four-part series on the subject the priest was stressing because so few Catholics were going to confession. There had not been one word on abortion. And Bishop Harper hadn't even been on the island.

The *New York Daily News* sprang to our defense three days later in a story titled: "Roast POST Over Gerry." Both priests in St. Croix and Bishop Harper denied their quotes in the POST. Calling the piece "a total lie," the Reverend Oslovich readily admitted that he had no idea we had been at his service and denied he had made any mention of abortion during his sermon. Calling his quotes a "complete fabrication, a falsehood," Pastor John Furey said the POST reporter had twisted his words "all out of whack." And Bishop Harper, who had been conducting a private Mass in Brooklyn, not St. Croix, before traveling on to Washington to attend the U.S. Catholic Bishops' Conference called the story "a piece of nonsense."

"You never accuse anyone of a personal sin," Bishop Harper told the *Daily News*. "Only God can do that."

And still it goes on. Right after the election, the *Philadelphia Inquirer* assigned a reporter to do an extensive series of pieces on me and to hash over my family background once more. He's been working full time for over six months. I asked him why he was doing it.

"Because the public has a right to know everything there is to know about an historic figure," he said, as he tried to rehash the allegations, going back to the early twenties, that had been raised and addressed over and over again. You had to wonder.

Yes, the 1984 campaign was dirty. Yes, the Republicans beat us. But was my run for the Vice Presidency worth it? Sure was. Regardless of what it cost us personally, the benefits of my candidacy to women, all women, eased the pain. From the moment of my nomination in San Francisco, my candidacy touched a nerve in the country.

Thousands of supportive and enthusiastic letters poured into my offices in Queens and Washington, and to campaign headquarters as well. Almost all of them started off with the admission: "I have never written to a public official before, but I cannot let this moment pass without . . ." Many were prompted by a sense of history. One woman, the mother of twins, wrote me the night I was nominated: "I ran into the bedroom to see if the twins were still awake so I could tell them. They are four years old and took the news casually since they don't know yet this is an historic first. It means more to me than I can ever express that the childhood lessons they learn will include your name."

An associate professor of history at St. Mary's College of Maryland was just as moved by my nomination. Her letter cited Mistress Margaret Brent, who had requested the right to vote in the Maryland assembly in 1648 and was turned down; the first women's-rights convention in Seneca Falls in 1848, which also had called for women's right to vote; and the final victory in 1920. "May the dream of a woman Vice President and the reality of one be not years but a short four months," she wrote. "You speak not only for millions of your contemporaries, but for the millions of our foremothers who dared not even dream this dream. You go forth with their and our hopes and blessings."

I heard from many Republican women, one from Oak Brook, Illinois, on July 18. "I'm sitting here this morning with my coffee and this week's *Time* with you on the cover," she wrote me. "As I begin to read, I find myself in tears. Tears of joy, of relief, of saying at last, at last, I don't have to feel second class anymore.

I'm thirty-six years old. I'm a Republican. For years something's burned inside me. Resentment about the way women are perceived in the world. Shame in halfway believing it. And now you've come along to say—never again do I have to feel this way. I am free. Thank you for my liberation. You have changed my life—maybe even my vote! Good luck."

Other Republicans actually did change their party affiliations. "This Republican from Riverside, California, wants you to know that your nomination for Vice-President of the United States has been one of the proudest moments of my life," wrote a convert. ". . . We have been a country without heroes for almost a quarter century. This week that fact was reversed. Today the first thing on my agenda is to re-register. I plan to work for the Mondale-Ferraro ticket with every fiber of my being—and WE WILL WIN IN NOVEMBER."

When I was getting hit from all sides in the worst moments of the campaign, the supportive mail increased. "You have been superb through such a campaign of harassment," wrote a woman from Berkeley, California. "It seemed clear to me, at least, that they (media, Republicans, etc., etc.) are after you because you have dared to invade a male territory. Please keep on being superb, and keep your cool. Whether you and Walter Mondale win or lose, you and American women will have won because of what you are living through. Thank you for all of us."

Even after the vote was tallied, the mail continued to pour in. "The psychological impact of your candidacy and the manner in which you conducted your campaign have meant more to women of my generation and in my situation, have given us more self-esteem and courage, than it is possible for me to convey in words alone," wrote a thirty-nine-year-old single woman. "We have a voice now in the affairs of this country greater than we have previously had. I no longer fear that that voice can be silenced. . . . Thank you for the courage to be the first and for the gift you gave all us women by being strong, rational, well spoken, but always concerned and compassionate."

I can't tell you how these letters warmed me. I especially loved the letters that referred to kids. One woman wrote me about a scene she'd witnessed on a New York bus between a three-year-old girl and her mother.

"Knock-knock," the mother said.

"Who's there?" the daughter replied.

"Jennifer," said the mother.

"Don't be Jennifer," the little girl protested.

"Who do you want me to be?" the mother asked.

"Geraldine Ferraro."

Some political analysts feel I was sacrificed by the campaign—that the Democrats knew they were going to lose from the beginning and used my candidacy as a wild card that would either work magic or give themselves someone on whom to blame the loss. I think that's way too cynical. In July I truly believed a Mondale-Ferraro victory was possible. The people were with us on the issues. Fritz Mondale was an experienced and articulate leader. And I thought the American people would finally see through Reagan's carefully orchestrated image. No, I don't believe I was a sacrificial lamb. I thought we were going to win.

The crowds themselves seemed to mock the polls. Every morning I got up into an incredible world, introduced as the next Vice President of the United States to tens of thousands of people applauding and cheering, saying we care about you, you are doing something for us. Did I believe that we would actually do it? Absolutely, almost to the end.

There were many personal satisfactions along the way. I was honored to have been chosen as a standard-bearer for the Democratic Party. I was grateful to have had the highly visible opportunity to speak out on the issues—and to know that people were listening. There was the undeniable pride in making history. And there was the legacy I could leave to other women with leadership aspirations.

We know now that women can run for high political office. We have proved we have the stamina to get through a campaign, to stand up for our beliefs in a national televised debate, to articulate the issues. And we have certainly proved that women are able to stand up under pressure. I don't think the press will be looking to see if the next female candidate will burst out crying every time she has a press conference. Perhaps the style of her campaign will be less important and the substance of her campaign will get the attention it deserves.

Not the least, the impact of my candidacy made people more aware of their attitudes, if not their discrimination, toward women.

Will the Secret Service now make sure there are more women agents in the force? I'm sure they will. Will other male-dominated groups sit back and take stock? The Chula Vista Police Department certainly will. When I paid a campaign visit to them in California, I looked around at the twelve cops on duty that morning and said, "Wow! Half your police force is female." They laughed, although with more embarrassment than jocularity. "Actually, these are all the female cops we have," they admitted a little sheepishly. They had brought in *all* the women on the force so I would see them. But did they realize at that moment that the numbers simply weren't there? I certainly think so.

The new awareness of women brought people up short in many professions. Most of the media wanted women to cover my campaign, for example, but when they looked at their assignment sheets, again the numbers weren't there. Still they managed to find some real talent, such as reporters Jackie Adams of CBS and Lynn Sherr of ABC, and Susan LaSalla, a producer at NBC. In print there were Ann Blackman, then of the Associated Press and now a deputy bureau chief at *Time* magazine; Maureen Dowd of the *New York Times;* and Pat O'Brien of Knight-Ridder. There was also a wonderful *New York Times* photographer, Sara Krulwich.

Nevertheless, newspaper editors and television news producers were quickly aware that the majority of their women reporters were still automatically hired in "light" news areas and allowed to have no political experience. I'm sure that won't happen again so easily. Covering gardening and cooking, and documenting new forms of "relationships," may be interesting for both male and female reporters. But a national political campaign is vital to all of us—men and women, reporters, viewers, and readers.

The fallout from my candidacy gave new strength and a sense of purpose to women no matter what situations they were in. I got letters from secretaries who had finally summoned the courage to ask their bosses for raises, from women who for years had meant to go back to school and now were enrolling, several from women athletes who had been intimidated by the thought of high-stakes competition but had now decided to go for it. A kind of "woman fever" spread in the most unlikely places. A week after the election, Anne Wexler got calls from two of her top corporate clients asking her specifically to recommend women, not men, for jobs as senior lobbyists. That's just two people, two jobs, two small events in Washington. But the same sort of thing was happening everywhere.

It was like a giant light bulb going on. A lot of the general public and a lot of women as well had not been aware that they were missing out on something. For two hundred years very few women had been encouraged to think: "I really wish I could be a national candidate." With my nomination, they were suddenly turning around and saying: "Why haven't I been allowed to participate?" A new political consciousness was born that no longer asked "why" a woman candidate, but "why not?" Consider the former U.S. ambassador to the United Nations, Jeane Kirkpatrick, or Elizabeth Dole, the secretary of transportation, both of whom are now being discussed as potential Republican vice-presidential nominees or even presidential candidates in 1988. Would their names have been mentioned so casually or automatically before my candidacy? Absolutely not.

The real test of my candidacy will come when the next woman runs for national office. Only then will we know if she, too, is going to be judged by a standard different from that used for her male opponents; if she, too, is going to have to be better in order to be judged equal. It will be interesting to see what the press will do to her on foreign policy. Was my siege peculiar to me because I was a three-term member of Congress—or because I was a woman? It will also be interesting to see how the spouse of the next female candidate will be treated. Will any successful man sit still for the kind of inquisition John had to go through? Or was it more intense because we were the first?

But someone had to be first. And I was the one. There are those who say that the timing wasn't right for a woman, that the conservative mood of the country wasn't ready to accept the idea of a woman at the top. Well, I don't agree. If it had been fifty years from now, there still would have been the same reaction to the first woman. The country is never going to be ready for anything new until people are put in the position of experiencing it. And it naturally follows that the first woman out was going to draw unprecedented attention, no matter who or what or when.

If the timing had indeed been perfect for a woman, then we

would have voted in the Equal Rights Amendment, women would no longer be stuck in pink-collar jobs, people wouldn't still be looking down their noses at single heads of households. Should we have waited for another ten or fifteen years hoping that things would be better for women? No. The barrier had to be broken.

It is now more important than ever for more and more young women to enter politics and make politics a career. For all that we make up fifty-two percent of the population, women are sorely underrepresented in the policy-making bodies of this country. There are still only twenty-three congresswomen out of 435 members of the House, two senators out of one hundred, two governors of fifty states. An important voice—springing from the knowledge of women, their bond to living things—is not being heard.

What has happened to this country's priorities? What has happened to compassion? Almost half the children in New York City now are poor. Malnutrition and hunger are on the rise in the richest nation on earth. The United States ranks sixteenth in infant mortality—*sixteenth*—worse than Sweden, Australia, and Singapore. Perhaps Reagan should spend more time reading the words of a former Republican President, Dwight D. Eisenhower, whenever he ups the defense budget. "Every gun that is made, every warship launched, every rocket fired, signifies, in the final sense, a theft from those who hunger and are not fed, those who are cold and are not clothed," Eisenhower said to the American Society of Newspaper Editors in 1953. "This world in arms is not spending money alone. It is spending the sweat of its laborers, the genius of its scientists, the hopes of its children. . . . This is not a way of life at all in any true sense. . . . It is humanity hanging from a cross of iron."

Democratic Party members may have their work cut out for them after the 1984 election, luring back those who defected. If only the voters would look at the facts and not be swayed by slogans. For example, the Republicans love to say that the Democratic Party is ruled by "special interests." But when pressed to name these "special interests," the usual reply is women, blacks, teachers, and unions. Those are "special interests" to be proud of—because together they comprise the majority of Americans. What about the "special interests" that dominate the Republican

Party—the oil companies, the banks, the gun lobby, and the apostles of religious intolerance?

The move among some Democratic officials is to trade in our constituencies for more powerful and wealthy ones. What a soulless solution to a party's problems. Imitating the adversary is not the path to victory. And I won't go along.

The history of the Democratic Party is the story of men and women standing for principles and ideals. When the Democratic Party wrote the rights of labor into law, when we passed the landmark civil-rights acts, when President Truman recognized the state of Israel only minutes after it was founded, when we wrote the Equal Rights Amendment into our platform, when we created programs to help family farmers, the elderly, and the poor—we didn't do these things in order to capture new constituencies. Each time, our Party acted to help someone in need and to do what we believed was right for the whole country. Turning our back on our past is not the solution. The last thing our country needs is two Republican parties.

Sure we have work to do to rejuvenate the Democratic Party. But energy, innovativeness, initiative, conviction—these are the traits that have fueled this country's two-party system since the beginning. And though we may have lost the election, we didn't lose the battle. The Democratic Party, in the person of one courageous man, Walter Mondale, gave fairness and equal opportunity for women a new definition. And for all the trials my candidacy cost my family, not one of them, including John, wishes the nomination had gone to someone else. "We're no quitters," John said, even in our darkest moments. "We're in it to stay and we're going to win."

When I think back over the four months of the campaign now, I think of people like my tiny "body person," Eleanor Lewis, loaded down like a pack mule with my briefing books and the many mementos people handed me—because she didn't dare entrust them to anyone else. I think of my press secretary, Francis O'Brien, ironing everyone's shirts in the middle of the night to relax, of the grueling hours my campaign manager John Sasso put in. I think of Bob Barnett driving me crazy playing George Bush and of our lunch with the Vice President after the election, at which Bush ripped off his watchband of the day to give Bob as a souvenir.

I think of my children exhibiting a poise and presence they didn't know they had—and that I didn't know they had either. I think of my mother sending prayer cards to my supporters, not believing it was possible for me to lose until the vote was finally in. I think of the new strengths everybody found in themselves, right down to the cops of the 112th police precinct in Forest Hills, who had never had a national candidate in the neighborhood and who spent so much time patrolling our road, making sure we were OK.

What it all boiled down to was choices. Choices between two political parties, two very different philosophies, two very different pairs of candidates. But more enduring in the campaign of 1984 were the new choices opened up to women, choices which will be passed on down for generations. Everything is more possible for women now. And the hundreds of thousands of women who turned out everywhere to urge me on knew it. I've never felt such excitement, such emotion, such pride and downright joy, from the masses of women who seemed to cheer with one voice from one coast to the other. Any one of a number of women could have done what I did. It was my good fortune to have had the opportunity to stand in for them.

A few months after the election, Bella Abzug, Carol Bellamy, and Donna Shalala, president of Hunter College, hosted a reception for me at Eleanor Roosevelt's former home in New York. Hundreds of women who had been involved in the campaign—and in my nomination—came, including the heads of the National Organization for Women, the American Nurses Association, the National Abortion Rights Action League, the National Women's Political Caucus, the Women's Campaign Fund, the treasurer of the Democratic National Committee, and the head of the bipartisan Voter Education Project.

It was more like a reunion than a reception. Dotted among the crowd I spotted all the members of my Team A. It had been nearly a year and a half since they had sprung that fortune cookie on me that read "You will win big in '84," eighteen months since I'd first heard their dream of getting a woman on the ticket. That seemingly impossible dream had passed into history. Now it was time for the next one. In the corner, Joan McLean was listening intently to a young woman I didn't recognize.

"I want to run for President in '96," the young woman, a student at Sarah Lawrence College, was saying. "What do I have to do to get ready?"

Joan didn't blink an eye. "Give me your name and number and we'll be in touch," she answered, taking out her notebook.

I smiled. That moment said it all. My candidacy had been worth it. Absolutely.

EPILOGUE

Many people have been asking me about my plans. I tell them I'm looking forward to the future. I'm not one for sitting around and hashing over the past. No way. We made mistakes, we learned from them, and we've moved on. And the pace I'm keeping now is almost as grueling as that of the campaign. The fact that we lost the election does not mean I believe any the less in the principles on which we ran. It does not mean I'm going to retire from politics. Far from it. Reagan's reelection has spurred me on with ever-greater urgency to speak out against the Republican policies that continue to discriminate against women, the elderly, and the poor; the Star Wars proposals that make arms-control agreements more difficult while adding to the already enormous deficit; the increasing threat of our military involvement in Nicaragua; and the tax-reform plan that once more shifts the burden to the middle class to benefit the rich.

Once you've been involved in the inner workings of government, in the legislative bodies that set policy, in the debates that involve the future of this country, you don't just walk away. You can't. Or at least I can't. How could I just empty my mind of all I learned in Congress, the issues involved in the 1984 campaign—

and work on my tennis game instead? There is no way I'm not going to be involved in trying to serve the public interest.

The campaign of 1984 interrupted the lives of my family, but they are all back on track. After spending six months studying in Italy, John, Jr., returned to Middlebury College in the fall of 1985. He is the only one of the children who has been bitten by the political bug and is considering going into politics himself. Laura, who always wanted to be an actress, worked at the Astoria Motion Picture Studio as a production assistant on *Death of a Salesman* after the election and is now at Brown University—a year late. After two years at Salomon Brothers on Wall Street, Donna decided to get an advanced degree, and is now at Harvard Business School, earning an MBA. And John is back to running his business.

We've both become very careful. I was unsure this year whether I had to file my congressional disclosure statement for my last year in Congress.

"You don't," my lawyers told me. But I no longer take anybody's word completely.

"Get me a ruling from the ethics committee in writing," I asked them.

One change in our life has been for the better. This year we're not going to pay extra taxes by filing separate tax returns. As I'm not presently an elected official, there is no point in continuing to pay the IRS more just to keep my finances separate. For the first time in six years, we can be just like any old married couple and file jointly.

On February 10, 1985, we renewed our wedding vows in our parish church. Throughout the campaign I had been constantly amazed by all the rumors about our impending divorce, rumors that continued to circulate after the election. I never understood how people could even think that. Why should I divorce the man who has stood by me and supported me since the moment I met him? It never crossed my mind to leave him (though I do wonder if it ever crossed his mind to leave me!). The vice-presidential campaign lasted four months, and if anything, those months strengthened our marriage.

We couldn't celebrate a Democratic victory at the presidential polls in 1984. But we could celebrate our twenty-fifth wedding anniversary. And all of us—John, Jr., Laura, Donna, John, and I—took a family honeymoon to China and Japan in the summer of 1985. We were a close family before my vice-presidential candidacy began, and now we're even closer. We have our health. We have our happiness. We have our self-respect. And for all of us, I believe, the future is whatever we want it to be.

INDEX